QUALITY IN LIBERAL LEARNING

Curricular Innovations in Higher Education

A Report
of
Project Quill

Katharine S. Guroff, Editor
Margaret C. Boeker, Editorial Assistant

aac Association of American Colleges

Project QUILL was supported by a grant
from The Ford Foundation.

Quality in Liberal Learning

Curricular Innovations
in Higher Education

Published by the
Association of American Colleges
1818 R Street NW,
Washington, DC 20009.
ISBN 0-911696-09-1
© Copyright 1981

TABLE OF CONTENTS

108756

iv

Part II: Projects Which Improve Continuing Education

Part III: Projects Which Combine Career Education and Liberal Learning

Appendix I

Innovation—How to Create New Programs in Liberal Learning
QUILL Panel: Association of American Colleges Annual Meeting
Phoenix, Arizona, January 11, 1980

Appendix II

FOREWORD

I count it a privilege to commend this report on the program "Quality in Liberal Learning" (QUILL) to the attention of faculty and administrators in all colleges and universities. When I assumed the presidency of the Association of American Colleges, this program was both funded (through the generous support of The Ford Foundation) and well established. What it has accomplished is, therefore, both a testimonial to the vision of my predecessor, Frederic W. Ness, the commitment of Fred Crossland of The Ford Foundation, and evidence of the enthusiasm and good judgment of its director, George W. Hazzard, and his staff, advisors and panelists. Of course, their vision and efforts would have been in vain without the imagination and commitment to liberal learning with which faculty and administrators in member colleges and universities responded to the invitation to have a part in the action.

Clark Kerr has remarked that colleges and universities have a constant need for effective ways to share results of innovative programs and experiments and thus to learn from one another. I hope that this publication will in some measure meet such a need. Although conditions and circumstances vary from campus to campus, I am confident that there is something helpful in this report for every college or university.

> Mark H. Curtis
> President
> Association of American Colleges

Introduction

Quality in Liberal Learning

Quality in Liberal Learning, a program of direct grants to encourage institutional renewal and creativity, has been a resounding success. It has succeeded because so many faculty around the country have been examining liberal learning through the eyes of constructive critics. They have demonstrated that all disciplines and all educational processes can provide liberal learning as part of education for living, for working, for growing.

How did this experiment in changing higher education come about? How was it managed? What were its results?

In early 1978, the Association of American Colleges launched a direct grants program to provide incentive awards of less than $10,000 to faculty members of AAC member institutions. During the next two years, AAC offered six rounds of competition and received more than 550 applications. Each proposal was considered by a panel of three peer reviewers selected from a national pool of several hundred educational leaders in all disciplines and from all types of institutions related to higher education. By the spring of 1980, 62 grants had been made averaging $5,000 in three general areas:

(a) Helping cross boundaries between or among the humanities, social sciences and natural sciences.
(b) Strengthening the liberal learning component of continuing education.
(c) Helping integrate liberal learning with career and professional education.

Summary reports of these grants comprise the major portion of this compendium. Nearly all reports summarize the QUILL-sponsored activities, although a few projects are just now nearing completion so their reports are more preliminary. In every case we have asked the program director to give us the bad news as well as the good, hoping that all who read these pages will learn what works and what does not as they try innovative liberal learning approaches on their own campus settings.

In addition to the project summaries, we have included papers that were delivered by QUILL project directors at the 1980 AAC Annual

Meeting, as well as a large representation of remarks prepared for a two-day QUILL assessment conference in March 1981.

The projects are so varied that a general summary is difficult to produce. However, a few things can be said in general about the awards that epitomize the thrust of all the applications from which they were selected. First, liberal learning is important in every kind of higher education institution. Proposals with creative ideas come from faculty, not only at liberal arts colleges, but at technical schools, community colleges, and large universities. The projects they outline reach eighteen-year old freshmen, mature women returning to college, students in technical training programs, and adults looking toward retirement. These proposals have generated new ways to link disciplines and professions in creating truly educated individuals.

Second, QUILL is a faculty program—by faculty and for faculty committed to student learning. Most of the project directors are classroom teachers and most of the QUILL funds supported release time for planning and teaching. The record of QUILL demonstrates that neither age nor tenure status defines the creative teacher; fresh approaches to the timeless concerns of liberal learning appear from many sources. Creativity in teaching seems to be everywhere.

Third, it does not take much money to release that creativity. To change a whole institution may take millions, but to test an innovative idea in liberal learning seems to require only a few thousand dollars. In many cases, the dollar amount of a QUILL grant is insignificant in comparison to the national recognition it has brought to faculty and student participants. While some QUILL projects are one-time efforts, others are the first step in the development of future programs. Often these proposals are on such a small scale that development offices are not interested in promoting them. The benefit/cost ratio for these small grants is enormous. I urge all foundations, corporate, private or governmental, to take notice of that fact. The right program can spend a lot of money but it need not be in large grants.

Fourth, QUILL reaffirms the importance of liberal education. There may not be very much new under the sun in higher education, but there is a strongly renewed or reasserted interest in the very basic values of that education. A recognition through faculty action that liberal learning is demonstrably relevant to life in modern society dovetails neatly with a recognition that responding to student interest in careers need not lead to the atrophy of ethical and intellectual concerns. Liberal learning *does* meet the challenges of contemporary education needs.

The projects described herein represent a selection that probably could have been extended to an equal number more had funds been available. As it is, the reader can choose among all kinds of approaches to liberal learning innovations in all kinds of institutions—large or small, public or private, two-year or four-year, college or university, religious or non-sectarian, single sex or coeducational. One cannot but be impressed once again by the strength that comes from the diversity in American higher education.

The entire concept of QUILL owes its very existence to the foresight of Dr. Frederic W. Ness, president emeritus of AAC, and Mr. Fred Crossland, program officer in the Division of Higher Education and Research of the Ford Foundation, who in 1977 saw a need for the creation of an incentive program to improve and make real all aspects of liberal learning. Their creative ideas have given new life to the continuation of all aspects of liberal learning.

Throughout the early stages of the QUILL program, I received invaluable assistance from a special Advisory Board composed of Sister Joel Read, president of Alverno College; Dr. Lois B. Moreland of Spelman College; Dr. Robert W. Rogers, dean emeritus of liberal arts and sciences, University of Illinois; Dr. David Sweet, president of Rhode Island College; and Dr. James C. Gollattscheck, president of Valencia Community College. I am very grateful to this distinguished group of educators for their timely advice.

I would also like to express my thanks to the many reviewers whose insights helped us in selecting winners and in advising many more toward successful reapplication. These reviewers made fair and objective appraisal a reality. At the same time, no words can convey my appreciation of the dedication and creativity through all the years of the QUILL program that has been provided by my associate director, Katharine Guroff. Her day-to-day efforts made anything possible. As a result we can all respond with pride to the results achieved from the project conceived by Fred Crossland and Fred Ness.

George W. Hazzard
Director
Quality in Liberal Learning

Part I

Projects Which Cross Disciplinary Boundaries

Austin College

Art as Participation: The Use of an Aesthetic
Model as an Interdisciplinary Teaching
Method

(August 1979 - January 1980)

In an attempt to heighten student appreciation for the intellectual and experiential comprehension of both aesthetic and artistic elements of the performing arts, a new interdisciplinary team-taught course was created at Austin College. Combining the expertise of a philosophy professor concentrating on aesthetic inquiry and a theatre professor concentrating upon theatre theory, a class of 27 undergraduates prepared for and subsequently produced a full-length untried play.

Through a well-planned integration of "learning" and "doing" in a distinctly interdisciplinary approach to the teaching of philosophy of art, this experimental course provided a carefully selected and monitored pilot group of students with not only the theoretical (symbolic) expression of the art experience, but also the occasion for participating directly in its distinctive (felt) character.

Each student was required to evaluate all phases of the experiment through a sequential, detailed student questionnaire which rated and ranked each segment of the experiment, as well as through anonymous reflective journals maintained throughout the course. In addition, two faculty monitors from Austin College assessed student understandings of the two disciplines in question.

The initial six weeks of the course concentrated on the study of several traditional schools of thought in aesthetics and on introductory accounts of the multiple nature of the artistry of theatre. Following contextual lectures and discussions of philosophers such as Aristotle, Schopenhauer, and Collingwood, the focus shifted to an analytical model of process and structure applicable to current philosophical and theatrical judgments on the art experience. At the end of this section, students viewed a Japanese Noh play and Alfred Hitchcock's *Psycho*, examining both aesthetic sensitivity in a non-western setting and dramatic and aesthetic dimensions of the motion picture.

Following an examination in which the students demonstrated that they had integrated the theory and could illustrate it textually, the focus of the course shifted to the production of the play, *Feast of Ashes*. All students were either involved in the cast or crew so the remainder of the class periods were devoted to preparation for the production.

Feast of Ashes was carefully selected by the two instructors for many reasons. First, since it was an untried drama, it fit well the experimental motif of the pilot venture. Secondly, the play had a very straight-forward plot and was peopled by very basic characters. Thirdly, this play had frequent confrontations of personality and opinion, two very theatrical scenes, and a highly dramatic climax.

Although the performance of the play itself was not given a great deal of publicity, its reception on the campus was far above expectation. Both project directors agreed that the students were solely responsible for the spirit engendered and enthusiastic reception given to the production by most all who saw it. Although the play was never given any media attention, except for reference to its "learning-doing" purpose in the pilot course, it played to overflow audiences on three nights and nearly a "half-house" of would-be audience was turned away at the final performance.

A number of students undertook "projects within the project" for the performance. One student videotaped a performance which resulted in an eighty-minute tape complete with titles, credits, carefully focused scenes, and enhanced audio. Another created an artistic thematic motif for the programs and posters, as well as a photo essay of significant moments throughout rehearsals. As a result of this project, the photographic glimpse at the "process" behind the performance amplified the several inter-connections within a performing art on which so much of the QUILL model/method was based.

Hope for a third "subproject" to elicit testimony from a select portion of the audience remained unfulfilled. Although eighteen questionnaires were distributed well in advance of the performance to faculty, students and community members, only five were returned, all with uninstructive responses.

Additional outside evaluation was provided by representatives from two regional departments of philosophy and theatre, the Council for the Advancement of Experiential Learning (CAEL), and two outside critics who witnessed a performance and then met with the students in a stimulating discussion focusing again on the aesthetics and theatrical focus of the experiment.

The major shortcoming of this experiment lay in the fact that students were unable to accurately perceive how the first and second halves of the course were integrated. In order to compensate for this lack of clarity in the future, the professors hope to find an historical context to join this model/method, keeping the materials studied more closely related to the textbooks assigned and taught in a more integrated manner. In addition, class "team reporting" would be curtailed in favor of individual written assignments, and serious consideration would be given to limiting the class to advanced students in both disciplines with a smaller enrollment.

In conclusion, the project directors believed that the model/method approach used retained some real advantages over the best of separate treatments, because it captured (for a performing art at least) the essence of both the participatory and reflective sides of what "creativity" is all about—whether one chose to accent its intellectual or technical aspects in accord with a particular disciplinary perspective.

Contact: G. H. Hinkle   W. D. Narramore
          Professor of Philosophy   Associate Professor of Theatre
          Austin College   Austin College
          Sherman, TX 75090   Sherman, TX 75090
          (214) 892-9101, ext. 245   (214) 892-9101, ext. 283

Bard College

General Education: Languages of the Humanities

(September 1978 - September 1979)

Following widespread faculty debate, Bard College embarked upon a major new general education curriculum in 1978 aimed at preparing students to be responsible, thinking citizens. The over-all goals of this program were: (1) to teach both the fact and value of tradition; (2) to combat the fragmentation and isolation of early specialization and intense private study through a common intellectual experience; (3) to prepare students for the life-long task of informed active citizenship; and (4) to make students more accurate writers, readers and speakers of English—and in the process, organized and productive thinkers capable of ranging confidently over the outstanding intellectual and artistic accomplishments of man. These goals were to be accomplished through modifications in the curricular structure and a broadening of general education opportunities for freshmen prior to specialization.

Project QUILL participated in this curricular modification through the support of two components of the Freshman Seminar Program—"common" and "individual" meetings. Under this overall program, each freshman was assigned to one of ten independent interdisciplinary seminars which focused upon a particular "language" of the humanities. Every two weeks, the entire freshman class joined together in the common meeting to participate in lectures, concerts, films and panel discussions related to topics covered in these seminars. The individual meeting level of the program provided the students with an opportunity to meet regularly with an advisor to share ideas stimulated by the seminars and common meetings, thereby helping the student understand the purpose of general education and providing a focus for future academic plans.

Originally, this program was created out of a sense of failure of the then current system for advising freshmen. In order to "put teeth into freshman advising," the Faculty Senate decided to provide one academic credit for the freshman advising component in combination with actual academic work. Since common meetings of the entire freshman class were planned to enable students to hear lectures or other presentations relating to the interdisciplinary freshman seminars, it was logical for freshmen to meet in groups with their advisors after the common meetings to discuss their significance.

4

Although this plan seemed feasible on paper, the administration had difficulty recruiting sufficient faculty to staff this plan. Due to all the other demands upon its faculty, Bard offered the professors a choice between teaching a freshman seminar *or* advising fifteen freshmen. Unfortunately, by the end of the summer of 1978 a sufficient number of faculty members could not be found for the fifteen-advisees plan. Therefore, a compromise was reached—advising four freshmen would be considered part of the general faculty duties now expanded to include leading discussions after the bi-weekly common meetings. There would be no remission of other teaching responsibilities for these faculty members.

By the end of the 1978-79 academic year it was clear that the advising component of this new program was not working well. Both faculty and students were dissatisfied. The basic problem was that faculty not teaching in the program did not have the background necessary for conducting the discussions after the common meetings. Therefore, for 1979-80, freshman advising was detached from the freshman seminar program. The freshman seminars continued to have common meetings based on texts common to all seminars, and discussions took place in the individual seminars on the next meeting day. The revised seminars were taught from a joint syllabus on the theme "Utopia and Its Critics," using as texts *Genesis, The Republic* (Plato), *Utopia* (More), and *First and Second Discourses* (Rousseau).

Clearly, in this case, the QUILL grant allowed an institution to experiment with a system and then revise it based on inherent weaknesses. Since Bard's educational philosophy stresses the responsibility of each student for his or her education, and since intellectual autonomy is not the goal of American secondary education, the freshman year at Bard is a crucible for students entering an atmosphere in which they are given a great amount of responsibility for their education. Although a perfect system for advising freshmen may never be found, it is clear that Bard is continuing to seek to promote in its freshmen a strong bonding with the institution.

Contact: Stuart Levine
            Dean of the College
            Bard College
            Annandale-on-Hudson,
            NY 12504
            (914) 758-6822, ext. 120

Bowling Green State University

Approaches to Value in a Technological Culture:
An Interdisciplinary Program in the
Humanities

(June 1979 - June 1980)

In an attempt to revitalize and renew a formerly successful Humanities Cluster College and to attract vocationally oriented students from all schools and colleges of the University, a new interdisciplinary program model was introduced to focus on values in a technological culture.

Originally the Humanities Cluster College was established as a residence-hall based program bringing together faculty from four to six departments to plan a curriculum that centered on a particular problem in values. Rather than offer conventional courses, faculty integrated their teaching activities to allow students to work both in formal classes and informal settings (trips, campus events, visitor seminars) in order to study values from a wide range of different points of view. The Cluster College emphasized performance (painting, acting, composing, creative writing) as well as formal reflection (through oral reports and research papers).

Recently Cluster enrollments had declined due to the shift away from the humanities into careers in health, business, technology and community service. This QUILL-funded project was based on the theory that the Cluster themes needed to extend the purview of the humanities to include science and technology, and thereby attract a wider range of students. Since students were reluctant to commit a full fifteen hours to Cluster programs and faculty were having an increasingly difficult time getting released time from their departments, this new course carried only ten hours of credit. Since Bowling Green was reevaluating its liberal education departments, the University Division of General Studies was especially anxious to develop a new interdisciplinary program model.

During the winter quarter of 1980, 23 students (mostly freshmen) enrolled in the course, "Approaches to Value in a Technological Culture," which met in a spacious dormitory lounge. Basically, the course attempted to focus upon the central dilemma posed by technology's effect upon the human condition: had the benefits to human culture outweighed the costs? Technology was studied both as progress and as regression for human well-being. Course methodology relied

6

upon both traditionally reflective studies (papers, reports, lectures, readings) and hands-on experiences (trips to Henry Ford Museum and a GM foundry, simulation games, improvisations).

During the first two weeks of the course, a series of skills were taught explicitly so that the subsequent course materials and concepts would not be beyond the grasp of the students. These included knowing and using the stages of problem solving; recognizing assumptions and frames of reference in problems; generalizing from specific findings to a higher order of knowledge; and organizing several orders of conceptualizations. These skills were applied to a dialectical framework concerning positive and negative attitudes toward technology, so that students could see the wide spectrum of attitudes possible toward technology. The heart of the course focused upon a thesis that "Technology was the key to the material and moral progress of the human condition," and an anti-thesis that "Technology was a material and moral threat to the human condition." The course concluded with a synthesis of interdisciplinary attempts to resolve the above conflict and with presentations by students of their attempts to utilize the concepts about technology within their own lives.

There were no tests in the Cluster College. Instead, students wrote three "summiques," combination summary-critiques of what happened in the course during a three- or four-week period. Because there was such a variety of events (readings, discussion, trips, guest lectures, small group projects, individual research and interviews, films, slide lectures, etc.) each student was encouraged to take a creative approach in examining the work accomplished in each section of the course. Each student also chose a single technology (e.g. the pill, TV, the laser, the computer, the assembly line, etc.) and worked during a six-week period in a small group investigating its ethical implications. Most groups created improvisations to enact before the class as part of their finished research, and all had to write up their results formally.

By the end of the course, students were expected to understand the skills and strategies of the disciplines of literature, the fine arts, philosophy, and popular culture and their use in approaching similar problems and concepts. In addition, they were helped to understand how these disciplines answered such questions as What is culture? What forces shape a culture? What is technology? and How does a developing technology affect a culture?

Regular classroom evaluation techniques were supplemented in this case by the "Science and Technology" and "Arts" Measurement Batteries newly developed through the College Outcome Measures Project (COMP) of the American College Testing Program (ACT). The faculty was pleased with the results of these tests, and even more encouraged by

7

the revitalization of the Cluster College and enthusiasm for inter-disciplinary teaching among BGSU faculty, especially those who served as guest speakers and participants during this course.

Contact:

Michael Moore
Department of History
Bowling Green State
   University
Bowling Green, Ohio 43403
(419) 372-0202

John Nachbar
Department of Popular
   Culture
Bowling Green State
   University
Bowling Green, Ohio 43403
(419) 372-2531

Thomas Klein
Department of English
Bowling Green State
   University
Bowling Green, Ohio 43403
(419) 372-2531

Bucknell University

Understandings of Social Theory and Human
  Action: New Focus for Faculty Development
  and Curricular Concentration among Social
  Sciences and Humanities

(June 1979 - January 1980)

During the last five years, an informal study group at Bucknell has been examining the relationships between social theory and human action. Composed of several faculty members from the departments of psychology, political science, sociology, religion, philosophy and history, this group has engaged in a weekly study of the works of Bernstein, Habermas, Tilly, Wallerstein, Anderson, Foucault, Sartre, and Whitehead. Following discussions among these faculty in which they expressed concern for the quality of undergraduate education, an enlarged plan emerged for a formal program in Social Theory and Human Action. The two components of this plan were (1) faculty development through continuation of the study group, and (2) curricular design to introduce a set of four interrelated courses in the curriculum of the University. Project QUILL funded the preparation and initiation of one of these courses—"The Social Matrix of Modernity."

Ultimately, it is hoped that all faculty members who participate in the Social Theory/Human Action Program will have the opportunity to participate in each of the four courses in order to enable both faculty and students from humanities and social sciences to deal in a coordinated way with critical issues in the analysis, interpretation, and evaluation of the social and cultural order. For students, the ultimate aim is to understand the concrete historical, social and theoretical matrix of their existence and to discern that what and how they think and act will condition future forms of the social process and their own existence.

The initial course, "The Social Matrix of Modernity" focused on both the historical context and structural dynamics of contemporary patterns of social behavior. This course was based on the belief that contemporary society must be understood dynamically, in terms of structural relations between groups, between institutions, between values and norms, and among all of these. But since each of these elements also had its own history, the course could not ignore contemporary behavior within an historical context.

Three themes were selected for organizing the course: family, work, and the state. These foci, in their intersection and interdependence, have been central to human existence in the modern period (since the late eighteenth century). They both shape and restrict human experience. Any dominant "social problem" of the modern period bears on these three areas of existence both as concrete segments of life and as traditions and conceptual inheritances through which concrete lives are made meaningful. Each of these three areas is a focus of contemporary crisis— a crisis that is or soon will be experienced directly by students as part of their own lives.

Set around these areas, the objectives of the course were: (1) to make the three foci salient for students with reference to how they have lived and how they intend to live; (2) to see how various trends, events, and contingencies of the modern period have shaped current practices and ideas; (3) to create a consciousness of possibilities, past and future, for how one lives in each and to clarify what is at stake in considering alternative possibilities; and (4) to discern the meaningfulness of any historical event in its shaping of current practice and thought in these areas and in their reciprocity.

The scope of the course was limited spatially and temporally. It focused upon England and France (because these are the main soil out of which America grew and the seats of the major changes in the Western world) during the seventeenth through nineteenth centuries (with special attention to the crucial events at the end of the eighteenth century: industrialization and the French Revolution).

The course was divided into three large sections of four weeks each. The introductory section, "The Texture of Life in Early Modern Europe," dealt with everyday life of the fifteenth through eighteenth centuries, with a focus on the seventeenth century. Part Two, "The Transformation of Everyday Life," examined a variety of explanations of the change from early modern (pre-capitalist) to modern society. Part Three concerned "The Matrix of Modernity" as it was shaped in the nineteenth century, following the revolutions of the late eighteenth century. England and France were still focal in this part, but there was now a United States, so its parallel, but in some ways unique, development was examined as well.

Overall the course was termed a success by faculty, students, and outside evaluators. All concerned were excited about the subject matter, and the process in which it was investigated. There were no examinations in

10

the course. The instructors were not concerned with cranking facts into the heads of the students, but rather with getting them to think about the social matrix of modernity.

Contact: J. Ernest Keen
Professor of Psychology
Bucknell University
Lewisburg, PA 17837
(717) 524-1200

College of the Holy Cross

An Interdisciplinary Study of the Impact of
  Gender Differentiation

(June 1980 - May 1981)

In order to overcome the fragmentation which can result from department-
mental structures, especially in a curriculum which has no distribution
requirements, Holy Cross has been offering for the past five years an extensive interdisciplinary Humanities Program with units of "sequences."
This program provides students with the opportunity to elect a carefully
structured cluster of related courses which foster academic coherence and
breadth.

Because relatively few of the fifteen sequences involve faculty from the
social sciences or natural sciences, Holy Cross requested a QUILL grant
to develop a new sequence, "The Impact of Gender Differentiation,"
designed primarily by the psychology and sociology departments, bringing five more faculty members into the program. Although these faculty
members had primary responsibility for the individual courses, a larger
team of men and women representing disciplines from the life sciences,
the social and behavioral sciences and the humanities also were available
as resource personnel and lecturers on their special areas.

A two-week workshop in course development was held in the summer
of 1980 for the entire Gender Resource Team. The faculty read the
material in their colleagues' courses, and shared ideas about unifying
themes which enabled them to understand better the ways their various
disciplines interact. By the end of the workshop, the faculty had drawn
up syllabi which emphasized the relationship among the three courses to
be taught sequentially during the next three semesters, determined the
lectures to be given, and prepared a prospectus for the students explaining the unifying concepts of the sequence. They also arranged such
details as field trips, guest lecturers, films, and other special events. Individual students were not required to register for all three courses,
though it was highly desirable.

Accepting the premise that the assignment of status and role on the
basis of sex is a universal characteristic of social organization, and that
all societies from the most homogeneous and undifferentiated to the
highly complex and stratified use gender as a basic criterion for task

assignment and the distribution of rewards, the sequence sought to study the nature, history and impact of gender differentiation.

Holy Cross College has long believed that liberal learning is inherently associated with an investigation of the values that lie at the heart of human society. At a time of profound social change, it is particularly important to provide the student with the opportunity to examine and reassess the cultural values which have had a formative impact on his personal life. By drawing from history, literature, and the arts, as well as the social and life sciences, Holy Cross is attempting through this sequence to bring together a pool of information within which students might reevaluate the most fundamental assumptions of their own lives in light of the institutionalized values in this and other cultures.

The first course of the sequence, "The Psychology and Biology of Gender," was offered in the Psychology Department in the fall of 1980 for 26 students. The behaviors which differentiate the sexes were examined, using three major models of gender differentiation: the physiological approach, socialization theory, and theories of cognitive development. The second course, "Man, Woman and the Machine," offered for 24 students through the Department of History in the spring of 1981, examined the impact of gender on social and economic organization. The third course, "Images of Masculinity and Femininity in Literature," sponsored by the Department of English, will be offered in the spring of 1982, and will examine the images of gender which have come down to the modern Western world in its mythic and literary traditions. It will differ from the previous courses, which approached the topic from the viewpoints of social and behavioral sciences, by applying the tools of literary criticism to examine these images as imaginative grasps of one's role in the world. Thirty-five students have pre-registered for this course.

The Gender Resource Team of five professors has met periodically throughout the year to discuss the problem of integration of courses and lack of continuity across semesters due to the high turnover of students. In light of this problem, beginning with the 1982-83 academic year, two of the three courses in the sequence will be offered within a single semester, with students required to register for both.

The Gender Resource Team will also attempt to add a new team member from the theatre or fine arts department in order to add breadth and increase the course offerings to four. Hopefully, this will be finalized in time for the fall 1982 semester.

Holy Cross is committed to continuing the sequence as part of the Interdisciplinary Studies Program, and plans to refine the concept of the resource team as a pedagogical tool in the coming years.

Contact: Victoria L. Swigert
College of the Holy Cross
Worcester, MA 01610
(617) 793-2288

Davidson College

The Individual and Society in the Era of Emerging
  Professions: An Interdisciplinary Study of the
  Rise of Professions for College Undergraduates

(August 1980 - March 1981)

In an attempt to help its students better understand the nature of academic and other professional disciplines, Davidson College sought support from the QUILL project to develop a course on the rise of modern professions as discrete fields during the generations before World War I. The intention of this effort was to avoid the narrow-mindedness which limits many professionals and makes interdisciplinary cross-fertilization difficult. A secondary benefit of the program was to encourage collegiality among faculty members of different disciplines, to enrich their thinking, invigorate their teaching, and to let their work together serve as a model of interdisciplinary discourse for students.

The course which was developed, "Emergence of the Professions in America," was team-taught by three faculty members from the departments of biology, psychology, and English. Although the instructors had hoped to attract primarily sophomores to the course before they decided upon a major field of study, the final course enrollment included six seniors, four juniors, and three sophomores.

Following an introduction to the aims and methods of the course, each instructor was responsible for a third of the course in which to present his area. The biologist presented a survey of the rise of biology, emphasizing the nineteenth and early twentieth centuries and the history of Darwin-Wallacism. The psychologist surveyed the rise of psychology as a science of mind and behavior. Finally, the English professor presented a survey of the rise of graduate education (with an emphasis on the Johns Hopkins University) and professionalism (including the founding of professional societies and journals) in the United States. As the course progressed, more and more time was devoted to discussion and less to straight lecturing.

Each student was expected to take a one-hour mid-term and a final three-hour written examination. In addition each kept a journal of notes on parallel reading in the library, presented a report on the founding and early years of a professional journal, and wrote a research paper. All of the work was read by each of the three instructors and graded independently.

Student reaction to the course was excellent and the instructors benefited greatly from the interdisciplinary collegiality. The course will be offered again during the winter term of 1981 with modification. The psychology instructor will not participate; his block of the course will be spread more evenly over all of the social sciences, and one or two guest lecturers from the social sciences will be invited to make presentations. The attention given last year to the current crisis in the professions (for example, the place of ethics in medicine and journalism) will be broadened; next year the students will be led to current readings in the newspapers and journals on the problems of professions today. Although a larger enrollment is expected, the same format of lecture-discussion-student report will be kept.

One other development resulting from the QUILL project has been the institution of a new course in the history of biology in society, which was first offered in the spring of 1981. Plans for the publication of a workbook on the emergence of professions in the United States are underway.

> Contact: J. Gill Holland
> Professor of English
> Davidson College
> Davidson, NC 28036
> (704) 892-2000

Dickinson College

Science as a Human Enterprise

(June 1979 - August 1980)

As part of a total examination of Dickinson's approach to freshman education, the concept of Freshman Seminars was introduced to acquaint students with a topic that provided general access to liberal education, not only through subject matter and methods one encounters in the undergraduate years but also through an understanding of the values and commitments appropriate to an educated citizenry.

The QUILL grant permitted the deliberate choice of a specific subject to test the underlying interdisciplinary seminar concept, focusing upon history and philosophy of science since the study of science is a complex social, cultural and intellectual enterprise. This concentration brought together in a unified and conceptually coherent way concerns involving science (and its underlying structure), society (including value systems), the scientific establishment as a dynamic entity, and the individual.

Initially, a specially selected group of faculty members met during the summer of 1979 in a seminar of their own to explore general issues within the area of history and philosophy of science, and subsequently prepared a pilot seminar on the eighteenth century scientific establishment and the threat to it posed by outside forces.

The interdisciplinary summer seminar was composed of eight faculty members representing the departments of history, literature, sociology, physics, and history/philosophy of science. Although at times the discussions were frustrating since differences in philosophical interests were not easily reconcilable, the most rewarding aspect of the faculty seminar was the "meeting of the minds" and the thrashing out of alternative and in some cases radically different perspectives.

Following this faculty planning seminar three freshman seminars were offered on the topic of "Society, Science, and Self." This particular topic was selected to explore a number of basic questions about the nature of science: Is science something established which solves problems, yet creates adverse situations with which society has to cope? Does science experience revolutionary change through time as political systems do? Can science be conceived legitimately as truth? Is science good or evil? Or perhaps is science value-free until society uses it for some end?

This seminar set out to examine science not only as a rational/empirical activity, but also as a humane enterprise. Based on the assumption that an understanding of science and scientific change requires not only an investigation of the cultural and socioeconomic background of the period, these seminars offered an interdisciplinary approach through a careful examination of the ideas at issue. Only a knowledge of all these components could provide adequate understanding of the course of science and a clear perspective of the complex relation of science to society. Materials centered around the history of science in cultural context can bring together in a unified and conceptually coherent way concerns involving science, society, the scientific community as a dynamic entity, and the individual.

Each of the three groups used the common syllabi developed during the summer faculty seminar, but each concentrated upon small seminar discussions and, at regular intervals, participated in plenary sessions involving all three groups. Ten carefully selected source readings formed the core of the seminar discussions and the source material for two interpretive essays. Journals were also kept by each student in order to encourage a silent, more sustained dialogue with each instructor, who would read the journals on a regular basis and comment on the questions raised therein. Library projects were also assigned not only to introduce the student to local resources, but also further reenforce the seminar discussions.

Evaluations of both the faculty seminar and freshman seminar were extremely positive. The team teaching of the freshman courses allowed for pedagogical flexibility within the broader dimensions of an interdisciplinary approach while at the same time allowing outside speakers to provide different perspectives from those of Dickinson faculty members.

Although these particular seminars were not repeated during the following fall semester, two of the instructors were responsible for planning and teaching another set of three freshman seminars entitled "Culture, Science, and Values." During the fall of 1981 similar seminars were again offered by various members of this teaching group. In fact the initial seminars have helped provide the College with much needed experience in its drive to institute a required freshman seminar experience of all freshmen beginning in the fall of 1981.

Contact: George Allan   E. Robert Paul
                  Dean of the College and   Assistant Professor of
                      Professor of Philosophy   History of Science
                  Dickinson College   Dickinson College
                  Carlisle, PA 17013   Carlisle, PA 17013
                  (717) 245-1321   (717) 245-1545

Douglass College

Pilot Interdisciplinary Course:
Science and Society

(September 1979 - June 1981)

During a recent period of curriculum review at Douglass College, the faculty expressed a general desire to address the need of integrating knowledge across disciplines and invited a team of three faculty members to design a model interdisciplinary cluster of courses capped by an integrative seminar, "Science and Society." Three chief premises lay behind this conception, two of which concerned the students who would take the course and one of which concerned the nature of interdisciplinary inquiry itself. This last premise was that interdisciplinary inquiry is best pursued by teams of specialists who bring to bear on given problems their own training and expertise while simultaneously attempting to create a mutual pattern of communication and understanding with the specialists from other disciplines. With this premise established, the other two followed naturally: that students who would take the course must have completed their distribution or general education requirements, thus having had at least an introduction to the individual methods and fields of study of the three main divisions of the liberal arts; and that these students would also, through their major programs of study, have a more advanced understanding of the methods and bodies of knowledge in various particular disciplines within the natural sciences, the social sciences, and the humanities.

The "Science and Society" seminar funded by Project QUILL constituted an exploration into the possibility of designing a range of "capstone" courses for students nearing graduation. This seminar was experimental and a "pilot" in at least two senses: (1) it was an attempt to test on undergraduates a model of interdisciplinary inquiry generally employed at a more sophisticated level of understanding; and (2) it was an effort to discover how best other upper-level integrative seminars might be conceived and launched, so as to offer a range of such courses, designed to integrate various aspects of the liberal arts, for students in their senior year.

The seminar itself was preceded by a well-defined cluster of courses representing the approaches to the disciplines and introducing students to subject areas addressed in the seminar. It was planned and taught by a

19

biologist, a sociologist, and a religious ethicist who attempted to consider the problem of relationships between the natural sciences and the other fields as paradigmatic for that between science and society. All three faculty participated continuously in the seminar, drawing upon lecturers from other disciplines as the need arose.

The seminar focused upon the subject of human life to demonstrate the differences and similarities among the approaches of natural science, social science and the humanities. The biologist discussed how human life is defined and analyzed from the strictly natural science point of view, as well as the current frontier issues for research and application.

The social scientist focused upon the socio-cultural nature of human life and the attendant problems summarized by Ralph Linton in the aphorism that human beings are essentially anthropoids trying to live like termites. He discussed the socio-cultural sources of the natural science agenda and how the political, economic, and social demands on society implied by such an agenda would be analyzed.

From the humanistic perspective, the moral aspects of defining and analyzing human life were emphasized. Three different moral perspectives were developed and discussed: (1) moral principles viewing human life *per se* as an absolute good; (2) moral principles asserting certain goods as of higher value than life itself; and (3) selected moral systems which try to balance the inherent tensions between the first two views.

Preparation for this seminar was undertaken through the fall semester of 1979 and the course was scheduled for the spring of 1980. However, an unusually low enrollment forced postponement of the course until the spring of 1981, following a more sustained effort to publicize the course. As actually taught, the course was open to both juniors and seniors and fourteen students enrolled.

The course was evaluated by a pair of questionnaires distributed to all students in the course and periodic reflective brainstorming by the three faculty participants. In addition, a final meeting of the course was given over to a frank informal discussion of the strengths and weaknesses of the course as taught this first time and what might be done in the future.

A major positive outcome of this course was the gradual development of mutual understanding among the faculty which was also shared by a significant number of students. Cooperative planning of a course of this nature by faculty members from different disciplines is one matter; genuinely cooperative teaching is much harder and needs to be developed continuously.

On the negative side, it was necessary for the faculty to learn that even advanced undergraduates are not graduate students or professionals, and much of the course clearly overshot the abilities of certain students, especially the juniors. Specifically, the faculty members are now convinced that such a course should offer conscious models for interdisciplinary integration, rather than relying on students to intuit such models on their own. At the same time, as a result of clear and positive student statements, it was clear that a teaching mode relying on directed dialogue is the proper one for such courses.

In the short run, a revised version of "Science and Society" will be offered again in the spring semester of 1982, taught by the same three faculty members and supported from Douglass College funds. In preparation for that, a book of readings with interpretative analyses is being prepared and will serve as the textbook. Over the longer term, the faculty will continue to examine the idea of a "capstone" course either as a senior integrative seminar for the Douglass Scholars Program or as interdisciplinary seminars for all students in their junior or senior year.

Contact: James T. Johnson
              Associate Professor &
                 Chairperson
              Department of Religion
              Douglass College
              New Brunswick, NJ 08903
              (201) 932-9331

Georgetown University

Undergraduate Living/Learning Residence Hall

(June 1980 - June 1981)

For the past four years there has been widespread discussion among the faculty, students and administrators at Georgetown University about ways to integrate better the academic and residential experiences of their students. The particular problems they sought to address were twofold: (1) an increasing separation between classroom and residence hall experiences born of many factors, among them academic pressure and the resulting tendency on students' part to compartmentalize their lives on campus; and (2) the tendency among the undergraduates to group themselves according to which of the five undergraduate schools they attend.

In attempting to address these problems, a project was designed to involve a group of undergraduates which could occupy one complete floor of a residence hall. Recruiting efforts were undertaken for 20 upperclass students and 30 incoming freshmen from all five undergraduate schools. All upperclass students were expected to pursue regular curricular programs of their respective schools and in addition participate in a yearlong interdisciplinary seminar taught by a team of faculty members from several departments. The freshmen students were to be placed in the same sections of the introductory courses in English, philosophy, and theology—all of which were required as part of their general education requirements.

The initial phase of implementing the program was faculty recruitment. Since the effectiveness of the program would depend upon the quality and dedication of the faculty, the grant was sought primarily for faculty stipends to allow the faculty to meet during the summer to plan the upperclass seminar and to discuss ways of coordinating work between the various sections of the freshman courses. This recruitment effort was not difficult. For the seminar, a group of faculty was sought which could offer a topic about which they already had a mutual interest. A group of five faculty members, from the departments of English, economics (The Kennedy Institute of Ethics), philosophy, psychology and theology proposed a seminar on "The Family." Faculty for the freshman courses were recommended by the chairmen of the English, philosophy and theology departments.

Students for the upperclass component were recruited from all those students entering the annual lottery for on-campus housing and those gaining admission to the program contracted to participate fully in the program in exchange for preferential guarantee of on-campus housing. Although only 25 students applied for the 20 available spaces, the relatively small size of this pool was made up by the enthusiasm and quality of the applicants, most of whom cited their desire for academic and residential integration as the principal attraction of the project. Students were attracted from four out of the five undergraduate schools.

Recruitment of the freshmen students was more difficult. Most incoming students were very reluctant to take risks, perhaps because they seemed so career oriented and came to the university with pre-defined agendas about what was important and "useful." By late July only sixteen freshmen had been assigned to the corridor and the remaining fourteen places had to be assigned randomly to other freshmen.

Academic planning for this experiment went more smoothly. The faculty for the seminar on "The Family" began meeting in July to discuss the format of the course which was to be approached from the five separate departmental perspectives. Each professor agreed to develop one perspective through assigned readings and discussions. During the fall semester, the seminar met for an hour and a half one evening a week in the student lounge on the residence hall corridor. Readings and discussions focused upon the nature of the family, personal and cultural images of the family, personal experiences within the family, and conflict between careers and families. The second semester of the seminar was devoted to more in-depth studies of family groups, based upon a case study approach which allowed the students to use many of the strategies developed in the fall semester.

Faculty assessment of the upperclass seminar was generally positive, although they were unprepared for the intellectual conservatism of the students. Students complained at the beginning of the course that they perceived a "lack of structure" in the course and it was difficult to tell whether the strategy of breaking down disciplinary narrowness and overspecialization was in fact too random or the strategy was colliding with the students' expectations about courses which were shaped by their experiences in traditional disciplinary courses. This problem could also have been a byproduct of the topic itself which necessarily involved the participants more personally, and did not lend itself to the safety of "objective" analysis. For the second semester the students suggested that the group subdivide for the latter part of the course in order to get to know the professors better and work on some smaller aspect of the general topic, but unfortunately time ran out before this request could be fulfilled.

The program was far less successful at the freshman level. Since the initial pool of students was so small, there was no option to select participants. As a result, more than half of the sixteen freshmen involved had scheduling conflicts with language or science courses. In addition, exclusive use of one section of the freshman English and philosophy courses was impossible because of the small enrollment, so the impact of the program was diluted from the start. Both professors involved in these courses, however, generously compensated for this problem by organizing additional meetings for the project students as well as participating in residence hall activities. Nonetheless, momentum was compromised from the beginning and fewer students were willing to continue in the theology and English courses during the second semester. The final problem encountered at this level was the lack of a unifying project like the upperclass seminar. Each week they saw their neighbors gather for something which was their own and had special significance.

In spite of these problems, this program will continue into the future. With the exception of the seniors who have graduated, most of the upperclassmen will return, and will be joined by a number of the freshmen. The proportion of upperclassmen to freshmen will be reversed, making it more likely to attract a larger pool of freshman applicants. The freshman component will also be simplified to include enrollment in only one special course each semester which will meet in the residence hall (English and philosophy). Finally, the upperclass seminar for next year will examine "The Idea of a University" which will continue to provide a cross-disciplinary mix without requiring additional faculty stipends for planning purposes.

Contact:

Hubert J. Cloke
Assistant Dean
College of Arts and
   Sciences
Georgetown University
Washington, D.C. 20057
(202) 625-4042

William Stott
Dean of Student Affairs
Georgetown University
Washington, D.C. 20057
(202) 625-4243

Hobart and William Smith Colleges

American Indian Studies: Creating an Interdisciplinary Program and Introductory Course

(June 1980 - February 1981)

In 1979 Project QUILL awarded a grant to Hobart and William Smith
Colleges to initiate an American Indian Studies program through the creation of an introductory, two-term course, "American Indian Texts and
Testimonies." The course was designed to meet the growing interest
among students and faculty at the colleges in diverse American Indian
topics.

The course is a bidisciplinary offering which seeks to introduce
students to the wealth and diversity of American Indian "productions"
from both North and Central America, past and present. Two
professors—one an historian-religionist and the other a folklorist-
anthropologist—designed and taught the course in the spring of 1981.

In order to introduce students to American Indians, the instructors
chose to use almost exclusively texts which were the products of Indian
making. Since the course was designed to "touch base" with the sundry
offerings on native Americans at the colleges, it was necessary to choose
a wide diversity of texts, and the following types were selected: myths
and other forms of oral narratives, films, autobiographies, tribal
histories, grammars, oratory, pictographs, calendars, village plans,
music, ceremonial librettos, various arts (including masks, cloths and
sandpaintings), visionary episodes, poetry and novels.

The planners became immediately aware that the two major difficulties in designing such a course were: (1) how to select a suitable
number of texts from the seemingly infinite possibilities, and (2) how to
organize the texts so that the course would be more than a "show and
tell" assortment of amusements. The first problem was solved by deciding to focus on three major culture areas within North and Central
America (Northeast, Southwest, and Mexico) and on two major Indian
groups within each culture area (respectively, the Ojibiwa and Iroquois,
the Navajo and Pueblos, the Maya and Aztec.) The second difficulty was
solved partially by choosing one non-Indian book, Harold Driver's
Indians of North America, as a reference aid. The encyclopaedic quality
of the book helped students who wished to consult it regarding most of
the topics which arose during the term.

The more serious problem of overall organization was not easily solved. Four main organizational frameworks presented themselves: (1) to unite the varied texts around some theme(s) which either the instructors or Indians consider to be "Indian"; (2) to present the texts each as a genre, with discussions of the formal qualities of each genre in culture and history; (3) to gather the texts from each culture area in order to show holistically the interrelations between texts in the formation of culture, and (4) to treat the texts historically, moving chronologically from ancient to modern. The result was to combine all four approaches in a ten-week, one-term course with nineteen class meetings. The same course will be offered again in the fall of 1981, with different faculty and texts.

While the course format centered around individual or combined lectures and discussions, slide and film shows on Indian ceremonies and customs were also used. A field trip to New York City museums containing excellent collections of Indian art provided the setting for a lecture on the historical and cultural dimensions of Indian life. A guest speaker, a Mohawk-Delaware Indian, who spoke on "Iroquoian Women, Past and Present," helped students contrast the various lifeways that Iroquois women have chosen for themselves today, and helped them to understand the traditional and contemporary positions of status and power that women have held in Iroquois society. Two Mayan weavers from Guatemala, together with their translator, demonstrated their weaving techniques, and conducted two five-hour workshops for students in the use of backstrap looms.

The last class consisted of a talk by Chief Corbet Sundown (Seneca) who, in combining seriousness and humor, encouraged the class to "understand" his people. He spoke eloquently of land claims, language, ecology and ceremony, the need for community and the need for cross-cultural empathy. Mostly he spoke in stories, and he urged students to "remember, remember everything." His talk was a fitting close to the term.

Student enrollment in Indian Studies program is exceptionally high for such a small institution. In the 1980-1981 academic year, approximately one quarter of the student body was enrolled in at least one course on American Indian subject matter. Part of the reason for this intense interest is the colleges' proximity to approximately 10,000 Reservation Indians. In addition, a recent Cayuga land settlement will shortly bring Indians within a few miles of the campus.

The Project QUILL grant funded not only an introductory course, but also the purchase of materials for the colleges' libraries. With QUILL money, the instructors purchased approximately 1,700 art, history and culture slides, 100 books either by or about American Indians, 20 tapes and records of Indian music, and began subscriptions to three periodicals regarding Indian topics. The result is what the school's head librarian called "as fine an Indian library collection as can be imagined in an undergraduate school of this size."

Contact: Christopher Vecsey
Assistant Professor of History
Hobart and William Smith
  Colleges
Geneva, NY 14456
(315) 789-5500 ext. 533

Illinois Wesleyan University

American Agriculture in the Liberal Arts Setting:
An Interdisciplinary Approach

(September 1978 - May 1980)

As a direct outgrowth of a previous world hunger workshop, Illinois Wesleyan University undertook two major projects to further capitalize upon its location in a rich farming area. Under the auspices of Project QUILL, Illinois Wesleyan held an agricultural institute and introduced an interdisciplinary course into the curriculum on aspects of American agriculture.

The first part of the project to be completed was the Agricultural Institute, the aims of which were to sensitize the campus community to some major concerns of farmers and farm organizations and to foster greater understanding of the legislative process in the agricultural area, all within a liberal arts setting. More than 65 persons registered for the Institute including area farmers, college faculty (from both IWU and Illinois State University), agricultural professionals, students, and representatives from area media.

A morning panel emphasized prospects in 1979 for the marketing of agricultural products within a global perspective, touching upon possible grain purchases by China and the Soviet Union as well as the impact of the Brazilian soybean crop. The basic outlook was favorable for the producer, but emphasis was also placed on the importance of vigilance for unforeseen developments in marketing programs.

The luncheon session featured a dialogue on "The Task of Making Agricultural Policy," between the local congressman and a Legislative Assistant in the U.S. Department of Agriculture. Although they were at times combative, the two presenters offered quite different perspectives on the proper role of the USDA in shaping agricultural policy.

The concluding panel in the afternoon presented a philosophical and historical perspective on government-agricultural relations within the topic "Government in the Farmer's Market—Blessing or Burden?" The tone of this final event was more philosophical than the earlier sessions, emphasizing an historical perspective of government-agricultural relations, the preference of many young farmers to keep government out of the marketplace, and the suggestion by some older farmers that government can also provide security in bad times.

At all three sessions the audience was very responsive and eagerly questioned the presenters as well as one another. Evaluations from the participants were generally favorable and one of the greatest gratifications came from the sense that Illinois Wesleyan could play a constructive role in discussions on agricultural policy. In addition, the Institute taught the university some important lessons to apply to future efforts in this area. These lessons included the importance of targeting publicity and reaching a wider geographical area; the importance of making special arrangements to encourage student participation; the importance of maintaining a tight program schedule; the importance of timing the Institute to accommodate the needs of the local community; and the importance of released time for those responsible for planning such an event.

In the final analysis, IWU concluded that the Agricultural Institute was a great success for an initial program in this area, and although it was not repeated in 1980, the university hopes to obtain outside funding to make possible a second Institute in 1981 or 1982.

The second part of the QUILL project at IWU took the form of an interdisciplinary course offered during the Spring semester 1980. "American Food—Problems and Policies" was described in the University *Bulletin* as "an interdisciplinary course emphasizing the nutritional requirements of humans, analysis of production, processing and distribution of food, and the major policy issues concerning America's responsibilities to its farmers, consumers and the hungry world." Taught by a team of professors from the economics, history, and biology departments, the course enrolled 50 students, some of whom took the course to satisfy general education requirements in the social sciences.

The course developed from a troublesome paradox which had been addressed on the IWU campus in two earlier January-term interdisciplinary courses—namely that American plenty exists in a world of undernutrition and even starvation. The faculty involved in this undertaking clearly felt that such a dilemma should be confronted in a liberal arts setting in which special knowledge is combined with a discussion of policy alternatives and value choices.

But such a challenging and academically demanding experience for the students led to its own shortcomings. Greater coherence was clearly needed in the subject matter, and a different emphasis will be taken when the course is offered again. Rather than attempt to deal with both the American agricultural economy and developing agricultural economies, future emphasis will be placed upon agriculture in developing countries, the American role in global food economy, and nutritional topics especially relevant to the developing world. In addition, the new course will be introduced more systematically with a stronger emphasis upon the major areas to be explored and their interrelationships. Finally, explicit discussion of policy issues will take place throughout the course rather than relying upon oblique references made during the original course, many of which were missed by the students.

In spite of these suggested revisions, the staff viewed the course as a success in its attempt to heighten critical awareness of food issues and to strengthen skills in analyzing food policies. Student evaluations were very strong and reinforced the faculty belief that the course did indeed realize its chief goals.

Finally, the QUILL grant facilitated a degree of cooperation within the teaching team which was indispensable. Weekly working luncheons helped prepare all members of the team for discussion sections, made possible the cooperative development of quiz and examination materials, and generally strengthened their confidence as a teaching-learning unit. It is often said that team-teaching—when the elements are right— provides such intellectual stimulation among colleagues that it becomes its own justification. Although this course demanded a lot more than merely the faculty's own sense of satisfaction at working creatively with each other, this group of IWU professors would not deny that this has been a special reward from the experience.

Contact: John D. Heyl
              Associate Professor of History
              Illinois Wesleyan University
              Bloomington, IL 61701
              (309) 556-3046

Indiana State University

Development of an Interdisciplinary Course on
"Aging: Fulfillment or Frustration?" for the
University Studies-Contemporary Issues of
Value and Choice General Education Program

(January - May 1979)

While many educators have been concerned with the aging process for some time, the last two decades have seen a rapidly expanding volume of research and writing on the subject. The objective of the QUILL project at Indiana State University was to create a general education course which would bring together four groups of people to address the most current problems in the aging field and to consider divergent views on the appropriate solutions to these problems. Participants in this course included second-semester freshmen, a team of ISU faculty from history, humanities, and sociology, participants from local Community Senior Citizen Centers, nursing homes, and projects for the elderly, as well as local community health workers.

Although fewer students enrolled in the course than had been expected, the interdisciplinary effort met all of its stated goals and was well received by the ISU students. Topics covered by the one-semester course included demographic trends, the aging process, cross-cultural comparisons of aging, social attitudes toward old age, sex and marital adjustment in later life, retirement, death and dying, discussions of the current service delivery programs for older Americans, and other related subjects. Overall, the ISU goal was to improve understanding of this significant issue involving values and the making of choices among all four groups of people involved in the course, and to introduce the students to research and writing principles of use in addressing public policy issues.

The course was divided into four sections. During the first phase, "What Aging Is and What It Isn't," the class identified stereotypes associated with aging and confronted them with factual information. Among the topics examined were the relation of aging to such factors as intelligence and personality change, as well as theories of aging. The first essay required students to examine and express their own attitudes toward older persons or toward their own growing old.

The second part of the course focused upon "Aging in Other Cultures." This brief section offered glimpses of alternative concepts and

31

social patterns of aging. The section also included presentations on interviewing techniques and on twentieth century America to prepare students for essays on how a period of history affected the life of an individual now over 65.

A third section examined "Aging and American Society," focusing on particular attitudes and practices contributing to the frustrations of older people. Among these were factors that inhibit or discourage marriage and expressions of sexuality, and the "double standard of aging," according to which women feel compelled to maintain a youthful appearance long past the age when gray hair and wrinkles have become acceptable for men.

The final portion of the course was devoted to an examination of "Special Problems and Opportunities of Older People." This section allowed for a greater variety of topics such as nursing homes and patients' rights, crime and the elderly, death and dying, with a final focus upon retirement. A field trip to a convalescent and rehabilitation home and five sessions with outside speakers provided more direct involvement with older people and those who work with and for them. The final essay required students to interview an older person about his/her retirement or construct their own ideal retirement situation or ideal culture for aging.

Thus the course ended on themes of challenge and hope: awareness of needs for change, of services presently being rendered, and of the possibility—despite many obstacles—of a fulfilling old age.

One of the greatest strengths of this course was its continuous exposure of students to the experiences of aging. They were constantly confronted with attitudes toward and the experiences of aging which they had to record, analyze and evaluate. Resource material from poetry, drama, fiction, history, art, religion, and the text *Focus: Aging* provided the criteria for evaluation of the experiences.

Student evaluations at the end of the course were positive. Most agreed that they had come to realize there are different ways to grow old and others wished that the couse could have been taught at a much earlier age—if that could happen, perhaps future generations would not have such a stereotyped impression of growing old in this society.

Contact: Elaine L. Kleiner
Director,
University Studies Program
Indiana State University
Terre Haute, IN 47809
(812) 232-6311

Jacksonville University

The Mind: An Interdisciplinary Course Based
   Upon Theories of Mind Originating in
   Philosophy, Chemistry, Psychology and
   Computer Technology

(November 1979 - April 1980)

One of the most significant problems within higher education communities is that professionals in various disciplines have very little basis upon which to speak to one another about substantive issues within their fields. The QUILL-funded project at Jacksonville University was especially designed to address that problem of dialogue by examining one of the most fundamental issues of all, the nature of our thinking apparatus.

Four faculty members from diverse disciplines carefully planned and taught a general liberal arts course for 34 sophomores, juniors and seniors which was designed to consider a number of the following questions: Is thought a very complex biochemical process which is as predictable as a test tube reaction? Is there such a thing as a mind, or is this term simply an outworn euphemism for brain? Is anything extrasensory, or have the senses simply not been objectified conclusively? How do the basic assumptions about the nature of mind lead to logical inferences about the nature of behavior? How do these assumptions justify human institutions, laws, morality, etc.? Does our present knowledge of the mind give any guidelines as to the nature and purpose of human beings, or does it leave us in a highly ambiguous neutral position as a species?

Instructors from the disciplines of psychology, chemistry, computer technology, and philosophy set out to address these issues. The course was presented in a well-organized, sequential manner. The philosopher was responsible for coordinating the separate class sessions, pointing out the over-riding issues, and clarifying purely terminological differences. The other instructors focused upon the very large issues of their own particular disciplines.

The two major philosophical objectives of the course were to present the ideas of the great philosophers of the past (such as Plato, Aristotle, and Descartes) concerning the nature and operations of the mind followed by contemporary reactions to a dualist view of man, mainly behaviorism and the identity theory.

The philosopher presented a variety of common sense meanings of the term "mind," the fundamental views of the human mind in the Judeo-Christian Western tradition, and some contemporary philosophical analyses of the mind. The psychologist demonstrated the rapid advances made in the physical sciences, emerging from the philosophical approach and addressing the human mind scientifically. He focused upon the scientific method of psychologists, visual perception, learning, and higher mental capacities. The more abstract and technical approach of the neurobiologist focused upon the nervous system, brain, neurons, and information processing that goes on within organisms. The computer scientist addressed the questions of whether computers think and are conscious.

The greatest problem for this course and its four distinct sections was in providing continuity. Although each faculty member was responsible for a self-contained section of the course, all were present for every class. Each faculty member was responsible for drawing connections among the sections, and two class periods at the end of the course were set aside to review, summarize, identify key issues, positions and problems, and point out relationships and connections. Four separate tests marked the end of each of the distinct sections. Students were also responsible for writing two short papers addressing the topic "Human Nature, Science and Computers: A Personal View".

The success of the course grew from the quality of the dialogue and the atmosphere in which it took place. The free, open, honest, and sometimes critical remarks faculty members made to each other as well as the exchanges between faculty and students was a unique experience for most of the students. In addition, success was achieved in the manner of presentation of each separate section. Each faculty member was able to present his or her material in an orderly, clear, yet interesting manner. Because of the structure of the course, students were able to see more immediately the connections and relationships among four distinct disciplines, each with its own methodology, interest, issues, positions, and difficulties.

Failures of the course were disappointing. The philosophy and neurobiology texts were too difficult; simpler reading materials must be found or less of the more difficult texts used. On the other hand, there was too little reference to such interesting topics as parapsychology, the occult, and oriental thought. Because of the academic calendar at Jacksonville, it was difficult for teachers to give cumulative final exams which were needed in this course to help relate the four sections. One of the greatest shortcomings of the course evolved from the nature of interdisciplinary efforts (or lack of) at Jacksonville. Each faculty member participated in this venture in addition to carrying a full teaching load. Each professor was individually responsible for his or her own discipline's approach to the human mind and since they respected the other's expertise, they tended to be hesitant to criticize and make judgments about what the others had done.

Clearly, however, this interdisciplinary teaching effort was extremely valuable for both students and faculty members at Jacksonville and will serve as a strong beginning for more courses of its type. In addition, these four individuals are anxious to offer the course again, with modifications in the text selection and coordination of the topics covered.

Contact: Thomas J. Pauly
            Associate Professor of
              Philosophy
            Jacksonville University
            Jacksonville, FL 32211
            (904) 744-3950

Knox College

Redesigning a Required Interdisciplinary Course for Freshmen: Opportunity for Crossing of Disciplinary Barriers

(November 1979 - September 1981)

The QUILL project at Knox College concentrated on the development of new content material for an established interdisciplinary course required of all Knox students. Following a curricular revision in 1974, three "Freshman Preceptorials" were created to reaffirm the strengths of a liberal education through interdisciplinary courses and provide all students with a common intellectual experience early in their undergraduate careers. This plan recommended that certain specific curricular revisions be implemented immediately to put interdisciplinary teaching and learning at the heart of the general education program and was expected to be most effective if faculty members could be encouraged to overcome their habit of approaching everything they taught from the point of view of their particular disciplines.

Initially, the QUILL project set out to redesign the second part of this three-part Freshman Preceptorial, "History of an Idea." However, halfway into this effort, the Knox faculty decided to shorten the Preceptorial sequence to two courses. Consequently the faculty committee reorganized and expanded its membership to meet the new objectives and concentrated upon the development of the course "Perspectives on Nature and Culture."

The creation of this new course had the following objectives: (1) integration with the first part of the sequence, "Perspectives on Being Human"; (2) use of primary sources; (3) consideration of some of the epistemological questions inherited from the third portion of the sequence, "Ways of Knowing"; and (4) attention to some contemporary issues such as genetic engineering, technology and human values.

The interdisciplianry committee which was created to meet this challenge included faculty members with specialties in American literature, American studies, economics, philosophy of science, art history, Greek philosophy, and mathematics. In designing the course, they addressed the following questions: To what extent, and in what sense, is nature to be regarded as knowable? How does culture determine our understanding of what is natural, what is artificial, and what is art? Are humans a part of nature or do they transcend it? Do men and women have different relationships to nature/culture? What models or types of explanations give us an understanding of nature and culture?

During the summer of 1980, this faculty committee met weekly to select books for the course, develop a syllabus and decide on lectures, draft a set of writing assignments, write discussion manuals for the instructors and study questions for the students, and find suitable audiovisual material. The committee's procedures were considered successful in selecting material that was both flexible and rich.

When the course was offered during the winter of 1981, the students were enthusiastic about most of the readings and even the more difficult primary sources, such as Galileo's *Dialogues Concerning Two World Systems*, held up well. Only one crucial text on art history appeared weak, which was disappointing since it had been selected to tie together several themes of the relationship between ideas of nature and culture.

The faculty who taught the course clearly enjoyed the interdisciplinary effort, maintained a high morale, and expressed confidence that it would be even better the second time around. Clearly good primary sources were found which reflected some of the most significant ideas in a liberal education; and students were able to come to grips with the challenges of liberal education by reading the works of Sophocles, Galileo, Darwin, Wordsworth, and Poe.

Finally, the staff shared pleasure with the course emphasis on writing, and its part of the course. The preceptorial program is Knox College's successful attempt to demonstrate that writing counts in all areas of the curriculum.

As the Dean of the College commented at the conclusion of the project:

> The creation of an interdisciplinary course, for a large staff and from scratch, is an immensely difficult task. Each individual brings to the task a different set of baggage: views on education, familiarity with literature, professional experience with interdisciplinary efforts, teaching style, departmental interests, personal concerns. The process of course formation is time consuming; it is also personally and professionally trying. The process . . . at Knox revealed the best—and a bit of the worst—of the efforts of a large group of strong, individualistic, and professionally dedicated individuals seeking agreement. There were honest differences of opinion. There were clashes of personality. There was generous dedication of time to the common cause. In all of this, the QUILL grant was immensely valuable; the ability to compen-

sate faculty for their time, however little the amount in wages per hour, was often both grease on squeaky wheels and oil on troubled waters!

Contact: R. Lance Factor
Associate Professor of
  Philosophy
Knox College
Galesburg, IL 61401
(309) 343-0112

Marist College

Strategies to Accomplish Greater Integration among Components of a New Core Curriculum

(September 1978 - May 1979)

The QUILL project at Marist College was undertaken to assist in the adoption and facilitation of a new core curriculum established in September 1977. Developed with the aid of an NEH Consultant Grant, the core curriculum sought to organize general education courses around the theme of values confrontation. Rather than using general interdisciplinary courses or simple distributive requirements, the Marist core program organized new separate disciplinary courses around the common theme of values confrontation. Each core course was expected to fulfill four criteria: (1) expose students to value issues appropriate to the subject area; (2) give students awareness of the scope and limits of the methodology of the discipline; (3) develop skills related to the discipline; and (4) present content appropriate for a beginning student.

All students began the program with a two-semester sequence in a foundation course taught by members of the philosophy department. The first semester concentrated on the development of different modes of knowing and students proceeded to study core courses in areas other than their own major field: natural science, language and literature, history, social science, business/math, and fine arts. Each course attempted to relate to the foundation courses and to other courses in the program. The QUILL grant was used to meet the need of providing greater faculty development in integrating course aims and contents.

The first aim of the QUILL grant was to achieve greater integration among core courses and to foster interdisciplinary awareness and cooperation among core faculty members. At the outset, one foundation course teacher was paired with a core teacher in one of the disciplinary areas. This team was expected to work together during the Winter Inter-Session and spring semester on course development and on preparation of a report to be circulated to all faculty members within that discipline. This team was responsible for explaining strategies for developing interdisciplinary understanding, teaching exercises, and bibliography for teachers and students in the core program. In addition, special workshops for all QUILL team members were held utilizing scholar-consultants (Dr. Arthur Caplan of the Hastings Center, Dr. A. Novikoff of N.Y.U., and President Leon Botstein of Bard College) to assist in identifying issues and developing strategies for integrating natural science and mathematics into the value concerns and humanistic dimensions of the core program.

As a result of the activities under the first aim of the QUILL grant, formal dialogue has continued on an informal basis between three of the six teams of faculty members. The foundation core courses were revamped as a prelude to reorganizing the entire core structure to provide a more coherent and integrated program. Participants felt that integration would occur more easily if not all disciplines were integrated at once, in the same pattern. One of the most positive results was the development of more spontaneous, more open and more trusting relationships among faculty of different disciplines. They clearly gained heightened respect for one another as well as for their respective fields of specialization.

The second aim of the QUILL grant was to place particular emphasis on the development of core faculty in natural sciences and mathematics since they seemed to have particular difficulty in dealing with the value confrontation portion of the core. A special workshop was held in each of these areas and was attended by the core faculty, all QUILL participants, and all faculty in the two respective areas. Each workshop was conducted by a scholar trained in the particular area, who had a special interest in the discipline's relationship to general education, to value considerations, and to interdisciplinary developments.

The results of these workshops led not only to some course revisions, but also to a rethinking of the faculty's expectations of the role of science and mathematics in the core program. Science and math faculty members offered a critique of certain weaknesses in the core program (e.g. attacks on so-called "positivist" science by foundation teachers with weak or no science background themselves), contributed to new awareness of science and math "illiteracy" among some core faculty, and stimulated among some participants the desire to overcome that limitation.

In spite of these positive accomplishments, there were some disappointments. Certain faculty fulfilled the minimum expectations of the grant but did not continue the dialogue or give evidence of any further interest in the area with which they were paired. Attendance at the open workshops by non-QUILL faculty was very limited, and in fact, several core teachers failed to attend either of the workshops. Certain departments/divisions were conspicuous by the absence of either all or most of their members. Some of the final reports required of each team were less substantive than the project director would have liked.

In the final analysis, however, progress was made toward promoting greater integration among the various components of the new core curriculum and high priority will continue to be assigned to the development of the core program and to encouragement of interdisciplinary dialogue and cooperation on the campus.

Contact: Louis C. Zuccarello
Associate Professor of
  Political Science
Marist College
Poughkeepsie, NY 12601
(914) 471-3240

Medaille College

Developing Applications of Skilled Critical
  Thought in a Multidisciplinary Liberal Arts
  Context

(March - December 1979)

In order to improve students' critical faculties by focusing on thinking strategies that are known to be effective in dealing with questions typical of those encountered throughout life, Medaille College established a new interdisciplinary course within a revised liberal arts curriculum.

"The Art of Inquiry" was developed as a three-hour course composed of three equal modules concerning inquiry as expressed in science, philosophy and literature in order to improve the students' abilities to inquire effectively. Medaille College realized that its students needed experiences that would (1) improve their reading comprehension and their ability to synthesize information; (2) decrease their tendency to make unjustified generalizations; (3) use specific procedures in demonstrating the validity of their conclusions; (4) increase their ability to articulate arguments and arrange evidence; and (5) increase their awareness that in each inquiry there are multiple alternatives to be considered.

Although each module of the course was presented by an instructor possessing a background in the particular content area, the course was not team-taught. Modules illustrated the process of inquiry by actively involving the student in that inquiry process. In order to provide a unifying theme to the three separate parts, the same general model of inquiry was developed in each disciplinary module and then related to the inquiry approach of that discipline. This helped strengthen the students' understanding of some characteristics of the different disciplines and justified the multidisciplinary presentation. The course closed with a discussion of *Galileo* by Berthold Brecht which allowed the students to perceive a common approach to the three content areas treated. Student response was enthusiastic and thoughtful, demonstrating that students had matured considerably in their ability to inquire by the end of the semester.

Each student was evaluated twice within each module through a pre-test and a post-test relating to the content of that module. Additionally, each student was tested on material which might have been included in the course but was not, in an attempt to determine whether skills and knowledge acquired during the semester could be transferred to related but different materials.

On the basis of these evaluations and through informal discussions with students, it was found that the students had significantly increased their ability to inquire by the semester's end. In particular, they increased their confidence in their ability to learn, increased their enjoyment in solving "problems" that arose from the inquiries, developed a keener sense of what information was relevant to an argument, and improved their ability to ask meaningful questions. In addition, they increased their skill in observing, classifying and generalizing, learned to suspend judgments in order to consider alternatives, and increased their ability to apply generalizations to novel situations.

Faculty benefited from this experience as well through a semester-long exploration of each other's unique perspectives on the inquiry process. Not only were they able to better understand and appreciate other disciplines, they were required to reconsider teaching styles and content choices when considering the process of inquiry as a fundamental objective.

A concluding QUILL activity was the training of additional faculty to adapt material from their disciplines to the inquiry course format. A faculty workshop was held to demonstrate the nature of "The Art of Inquiry" and to offer help and advice to those who wished to serve as instructors in future semesters. The workshop was very successful, receiving the enthusiastic participation of about 25 percent of the full-time faculty.

Originally three faculty members were to participate in the classroom at one time in order to dramatize the multidisciplinary orientation of the course, but time and budget constraints made this impossible. In retrospect, this may have been best, for students seemed noticeably subdued and less willing to participate whenever two or three faculty met with the groups. Current plans call for continuing the course in its original modular form, with only one instructor conducting each class.

Considering the scope of the original proposal, the development and presentation of the "Art of Inquiry" was remarkably free of real problems. However, a number of small troublesome areas require further consideration. These include (1) the difficulty of maintaining thematic coherence when using a different instructor for each segment of the course; (2) the tendency of students periodically to neglect to apply critical thinking; (3) lack of student appreciation for this type of course prior to enrollment; (4) isolation of this course from the mainstream programs, and (5) lack of an "official" course coordinator. None of these factors impair the function of the course nor threaten its continued existence, but each will be carefully studied in future years.

In summary, the course was very successful with respect to the effects upon students and the involved faculty. Hopefully, once these students are enrolled in other courses, this experience will beneficially affect the intellectual climate of the entire institution.

Contact: Steven G. Schlosser
            Associate Professor of
              Mathematics
            Medaille College
            Buffalo, NY 14214
            (716) 884-3281

Mohegan Community College

Applied Linguistics in the Social Science
Classroom

(August 1979 - June 1980)

Active collaboration between four Mohegan Community College instructors (two in English, one in history, and one in sociology) was supported by a QUILL grant to develop specific teaching techniques which would increase students' sensitivity to language as an intellectual tool. This project was based on the premise that use of language as an analytical tool—to describe phenomena and problems, to construct explanatory models and hypotheses, and to test possible solutions—served as a common bond between the humanities and social sciences and should be strengthened for future student understanding.

Mohegan Community College is no different from most other open-admission public community colleges, which face a myriad of problems in encouraging students to enroll in many humanities and social science classes: a fragmented existing curriculum, ponderous, unwieldy procedures for implementing new courses and new programs, instructors who are untrained to help large classes of semi-literate students with their basic reading and writing problems; and drop-in commuting students who cannot sustain the type of independent study often found on residential campuses. In spite of these problems, this college set out to develop a dormant resource (existing courses and faculty) into an exciting and challenging experiment to help students with basic skills in existing courses, applying some of the methods of freshman English and reading courses to the content of other disciplines.

The theory behind this project was that liberal learning grows out of the dynamics of a classroom situation—not faculty or committee meetings, consultants or publications—and the place to begin enhancing liberal learning is in the classroom. Two English instructors received released time to participate in two social science classes as students—one in sociology and the other in American history. As "students" they identified specific areas ("target areas" of lecture presentation, assigned textbook reading, discussion, preparing for quizzes, library research, etc.) that could be clarified or made more accessible to students if these skills of applied linguistics could be either assumed or concomitantly demonstrated and practiced. The English instructors were able to identify these specific target areas because of their unique vantage point, experiencing a situation in which some course content is new, but as experienced instructors familiar with day-to-day procedures of generating and teaching courses to open-admission community college students.

During this joint effort, all four QUILL instructors prepared special handouts for students in the two classrooms (models, instructions, supplementary readings, exercises) which were then assembled into a student manual along with other suitable material from other instructors. By the fall semester of 1980, all Mohegan students in introductory social science classes were provided with the manual and on the basis of their actual use, it will be revised and improved for future students. In essence, the manual provides a tightly structured framework which individual instructors can tailor to specific disciplines by filling in course textbooks, readings, and assignments; by referring students to appropriate sections when needed; and, in light of issues raised in the course or class, basing discussion on these sections.

In addition to the actual classroom collaboration of these instructors, all four organized a workshop conference for humanities and social science faculty in the Connecticut community colleges which received very favorable response. During this conference, "English Across the Curriculum: Rationale and Methods for Integrating Composition and the Social Sciences," three outside speakers were brought to the campus for general presentations, along with the offering of eight individual workshops and reports on and curriculum materials from the first semester experience of the QUILL project.

Other regional and national presentations are planned by the QUILL instructors and the manual is being reviewed for possible publication as a textbook.

Within the constraints of a regular schedule of classes, Mohegan faculty are continuing to integrate course activities on this interdisciplinary format. For example, during the fall of 1980, an English composition course and an introductory sociology course were linked by joint enrollment of students, by offering the courses sequentially and requiring coordinated reading and writing assignments.

An on-going, cross-disciplinary student tutoring service was also organized to help students with their writing assignments. Through this activity, selected students are available in the library at specific times to assist students who desire help in specific writing projects. Although this activity was not envisioned at the beginning of the QUILL project, it clearly is an outgrowth of the needs foreseen by the faculty members participating in the classroom situations.

Finally, the two English instructors have become officially organized as the "Mohegan Interdisciplinary Writing Project" and, at the request of the Connecticut Humanities Council, are preparing to work with area high school social studies teachers to improve writing skills at that level as well.

At the present time, the major problem in assessing the success of this applied linguistics approach is the lack of adequate tools to measure the effect of the program on students' learning. Although student response has been extremely favorable, a lack of both elapsed time and adequate or reliable testing instruments have not permitted evaluation of the effectiveness of the interdisciplinary effort on students' liberal learning.

Contact: Ellen Strenski
Associate Professor of
English
Mohegan Community College
Norwich, CT 06360
(203) 886-1931

Ohio Wesleyan University

The Twentieth Century Experience: Scientific and
  Humanistic Perspectives

(December 1979 - June 1980)

The objective of the Ohio Wesleyan University QUILL program, to blend disciplinary perspectives around a common theme, was predicated upon the notion that the university's fundamental commitment to the liberal arts could be further advanced by this mode of unifying knowledge. In the recent past, the curriculum and teaching faculty have generally drifted into quite tightly bounded disciplinary tracks and perspectives. To help reverse this trend, a pilot program was initiated, aimed at increasing the ability of students and faculty to think about and evaluate problems and issues across established disciplinary lines.

Three existing courses were coordinated for this purpose: "The Modern Temper" (Humanities), "Science and Society" (Physics), and "Political Development and Modernization" (Politics and Government). These three courses were orchestrated around the common general theme of "The Twentieth Century Experience: Scientific and Humanistic Perspectives," focusing upon an examination of the role and impact of technology upon the quality of life and values.

Content and format of each of the three courses was modified to fit the common theme. Each class, scheduled for the same hour, met separately two or three times a week and jointly once or twice a week. The total number of students involved was 56. Without detracting from the substance of each course, discrete disciplinary perspectives were drawn together and the unity of knowledge was reinforced through the "common hour." Three books (Picig, *Zen and the Art of Motorcycle Maintenance;* Berger, *The Homeless Mind,* and Pacey, *The Maze of Ingenuity)* were read by all students in addition to the regular reading list for each course. These books, reflecting the view that mature technology is a critical aspect of the twentieth century experience, provided a valuable link among the three traditionally separate disciplines and redirected their thrust to emphasize the continual and complex interrelationships of the human experience.

The common hour consisted of several types of activities. All three faculty members attended each session and discussed various themes relating to mature technology which have influenced twentieth century life, including the critical viewpoint that our collective social, cultural and intellectual human history is most valuable in comprehending the present and preparing for the future. The faculty led discussions of the three common readings and tied them into their respective course objectives as well as the common theme. In addition, four outside speakers (historian, poet, professor of humanities, and professor of popular culture) brought outside perspectives to this session.

Preparation for this team-taught, interdisciplinary effort began with an intensive three-week exchange of views, perspectives and suggestions during the preceding winter break. Those meetings continued once a week during the winter and spring term when the course was actually held and served as an evaluation of the efforts already underway.

Given the fact that this was an experimental project, the evaluation tools used were particularly supportive. A student evaluation of the common hour demonstrated not only an acceptance of the combined courses, but also a critically significant enthusiasm for it. Faculty members were also quite positive in their reactions and appeared to have immensely benefited from the experience. Faculty finally had reason for extended discourse which at times resulted in intense disagreement with one another over intellectual issues and matters.

These efforts were continued after the grant by three different faculty members, each from one of the divisions on the campus, joining the courses of "Urban Sociology," "Environmental Chemistry," and "The Modern Temper."

As a result of the pilot experience, however, the following modifications will be made in these future efforts: (a) a special effort will be made to present at the outset an overview discussion of the role which coordinated courses play in a liberal arts setting; (b) the respective faculty involved will rotate among the individual courses thus bringing their own viewpoints forward on a more frequent basis; (c) periodically students will be provided with study guides/questions which would focus on the common hour themes; and (d) the number of common hour sessions in which the three in-house professors present materials and perspectives will be increased while the input from visiting outside lecturers will be decreased.

The major lesson learned from this experience was that intensive discussion of the linking and coordinating of three courses must take place during the initial stages of the general course planning sessions.

Although Ohio Wesleyan felt that while they were blemished

somewhat by first-effort bugs in the pilot effort, the QUILL grant was most successful and the University will commit some of its own funds to continue these efforts through the next academic year.

Contact: Carl Pinkele
            Assistant Professor of
              Politics and Government
            Ohio Wesleyan University
            Delaware, OH 43015
            (614) 369-4431

Oregon State University
College of Liberal Arts

Designing and Implementing an Interdisciplinary
  Orientation Course for the Entering Liberal
  Arts Student at a Predominately
  Technical-Scientific University

(June 1980 - June 1981)

Following upon the work being done at Oregon State University as part of the national Project on General Education Models (GEM), Project QUILL enabled the College of Liberal Arts to design and implement a required one-credit course for all freshmen within the college to spark their interest in learning by introducing them to the realm of ideas through a critical assessment of the present moment in history.

Although the original proposal to Project QUILL requested funds solely for a two-week workshop to design this new required course, the teaching team and the GEM Committee had already thought through many of the philosophical and pedagogical problems inherent in the proposed course by the time the QUILL award was announced. This preparation, combined with a commitment to meet frequently during the last month of the summer, allowed OSU to invite Dr. Mildred Henry, a noted authority on higher education, to conduct a two-day workshop focusing on the developmental stages work of William Perry, and the learning styles ideas of Paul Heist. This, combined with Dr. Henry's direct critique of the course design, enabled the OSU faculty to better adjust their approach and delivery to the cognitive level of entering freshmen.

The freshman orientation course, "Connections," was offered each of three terms during the 1980-81 academic year. Although not all 660 incoming freshmen students participated in the course (since many preferred to defer course requirements until they were certain they would remain in the College of Liberal Arts), the reduced enrollment of 275 proved to be an unanticipated blessing. As a result of these lower-than-expected enrollments, the pilot run of the course became a simpler matter, and a perfect control group for comparison later on with the students who did take the course was created. Next year the entire CLA freshman class will automatically be registered.

As the introductory stage of the entire general education program,

"Connections" was designed to spark the students' interests in learning and alert them to what lies ahead. It was viewed as an orientation to some of the modes of thought common to the liberal arts as well as an effort to call attention to various issues confronting today's world and to how these issues are connected both to one another and to thinking, valuing, feeling individuals. In short, the focus of the course was on the human condition, and its aim was a better understanding of this most vast and complex of all subjects. As students were advised in their syllabus, "If in this brief time we can convey even a bit of the excitement and pleasure to be gained from pursuing this aim, we will consider our efforts successful, for then you will be on your way to a lifetime of inquiry and reflection, of *making connections* which, in turn, may ultimately lead to wisdom."

The classes met once a week for one hour and were supplemented by one or two films each week except when small group discussions were scheduled. The one required reading for the course was George Orwell's *1984* and the supplementary films included "The Limits to Growth," "Hunger U.S.A.," "Harlan County U.S.A.," "The Selling of the Pentagon," "The Time of Man," and "Future Shock."

As a means of on-going evaluation of this initial offering, a very brief (two-question) questionnaire was distributed at random to approximately ten percent of the students as they left each class. Surveys were returned immediately, and across the board all three sections of the course received very high ratings.

In order to maintain the momentum of and enthusiasm for the new course, as well as to provide additional instructors for the teaching team in 1981-82, a two-day retreat-workshop was held for the 36 College of Liberal Arts faculty members who were either most interested in general education issues or so outstanding that it was worthwhile getting them involved. It was here that the QUILL grant made its greatest contribution, for such off-campus activities are practically impossible to fund with regular state monies. Two outside assistants were brought in—one an experienced conference facilitator and the other a keynote speaker (Dr. William Hamilton of Portland State's University Scholars Program).

This workshop proved to be more successful than originally anticipated. Not only was a competent and enthusiastic new teaching team recruited, but many valuable suggestions were also generated concerning both the course and the larger general education program under consideration. In addition, by soliciting this in-depth collaboration of colleagues, the support group within the college was very significantly broadened and a sense of ownership in the project was spread among many participants. The workshop experience contributed markedly to the sense of community and shared purpose of an especially important segment of the college's faculty.

Contact: Richard L. Clinton
             Associate Dean
             College of Liberal Arts
             Oregon State University
             Corvallis, OR 97331
             (503) 754-2511

Pomona College

Computing as a Common Ground for Interdisciplinary Teaching and Learning in a
Liberal Arts Curriculum

(May - December 1979)

The overall objective of the QUILL grant at Pomona College was to make computing skills more central to the humanities and social science curriculum and thereby to renew the institution's commitment to a classic goal of liberal education: interdisciplinary learning.

For years, natural scientists have relied upon computers in teaching and research, but social scientists and members of Pomona's faculty in the humanities have tended to downplay them in their own work. Natural scientists have dominated policy decisions about hardware and staff support and have tended to overlook the special needs of new or occasional users in other disciplines. Thus, with the QUILL grant, Pomona College has attempted to reconcile these perspectives in order to make computing part of the general education of every student.

Three separate tasks were undertaken to accomplish this goal. First, a series of seminars was held to bring faculty together from all three divisions to discuss the role of computing in the curriculum and to define the nature of a future interdisciplinary computing course. Secondly, a library of documentation was established, directed to social scientists who would use the computer in teaching and research. Finally, an interdisciplinary computing course was taught during the spring semester of 1980 to a group of 150 students and faculty.

Initially, the faculty seminar provided two sessions to introduce the QUILL project and continue discussions of computing in the curriculum which had been underway at various levels for the last fifteen years. These seminars, open to all Pomona faculty members, focused on the explicit goal of planning an interdisciplinary computing course, but also ranged into broader consideration of the role of computing in the curriculum. During both sessions, faculty traded information about computer applications in their own fields and quickly concluded that the new course should include a range of applications from many fields. In some cases, specific faculty in an appropriate field were asked to make a short class presentation.

In addition, the participants arrrived at several points of consensus:

the new course should be a general, nontechnical introduction, without prerequisites, that would be useful to students in any major. In addition, the course should equip every student to compute by providing intensive experience at the terminal, reasonable skill in a multi-purpose language, knowledge of the logic and applications of computing, and rudimentary knowledge of the parts of a computer and their purpose.

The seminars were evaluated by all who participated, with special emphasis directed toward the key issue of how humanists, social scientists, and natural scientists could cooperate to encourage computing at the college. Humanists were given the rare opportunity to influence the making of computer-related decisions. However, the evaluators also agreed that the process was far from complete and that dialogue must extend to those faculty who have not already expressed an interest in computing. For Pomona College, this will be a harder task.

The second phase of this project was to establish a Social Science Library with the hope of making it easier for novices to begin computing by providing a source of basic information about how to operate the computer itself and where to find programs and data. A simple format was designed to list information that new users could easily understand and find in a convenient location. With the help of two undergraduate majors in the social sciences and a graduate student in psychology, a library was established which contains the following information: instructions for using both the IBM 4331 and Dec 10 computers; descriptions of computer programs and data sets available on campus; descriptions of programs and data sets available elsewhere; descriptions of information sources of further interest to social scientists; and reference manuals and books available through the library. Every faculty member received a detailed description of the library and early indications are that individual faculty members are beginning to use the resources. In addition, the college's Academic Computing Center has supported the project by assisting in placing it on line on the IBM computer. The Computing Center is also considering facilitating enlargement of the library to cover the sciences and humanities and placing it eventually in its own offices. Finally, information in the library has enabled social scientists to become well enough informed about available resources to participate actively in recommendations to the associate dean about the purchase of software. Currently, ways are being explored to make the library more effective by increasing its transportability beyond the college.

The Introductory Computing Course was offered during the spring of 1980, essentially following the guidelines established by the two faculty seminars supported earlier by the grant. The course was taught by focusing on the solution of practical problems, particularly those arising in subjects not usually considered as mathematical. During the three weeks of the course, students became fluent in one programming language, APL, and obtained a working knowledge of two other popular languages, FORTRAN, and PL1. A graduated series of exercises was prepared to provide students with all of the skills needed to solve more complex problems. These exercises included numerical problems, creating, storing, and accessing bibliographies, economic modelling and plotting. Although the course was initially offered on an experimental basis, it has now been formally integrated into the curriculum.

Project QUILL may not have revolutionized computing at Pomona College, but it did help realize the goal of making computing part of the general education of every student. It permitted faculty not traditionally exposed to computing to be included in the making of decisions about computing courses and allowed the college to create an instrument, the Social Science Computing Library, to make computing easier for new users. Finally, it provided resources to underwrite a course which has become a permanent addition to the college curriculum.

Contact: Elizabeth H. Crighton
            Assistant Professor of
              Government
            Pomona College
            Claremont, CA 91711
            (714) 621-8000

Russell Sage College
The Junior College of Albany

Changing Perspectives on Liberal Education in
the Two-Year College through Creative
Cross-Disciplinary Mini-Courses

(September 1978 - August 1979)

The major aim of the QUILL project at the Junior College of Albany, a co-educational division of Russell Sage College, was to develop a series of interdisciplinary mini-courses offering broader alternatives to students in a confined curriculum. Within this broad theme, the faculty hoped to provide students with interdisciplinary learning through increased liberal arts and sciences electives within a nontraditional setting. In addition, they hoped to stimulate independent thinking by providing a variety of perspectives on a single theme to illustrate how components of different disciplines cross boundaries, directing students toward a holistic view of the educational experience. A side effect of this entire effort was to increase rapport and cohesiveness among a sometimes disparate faculty.

The overwhelming success of two original mini-courses introduced in 1978 encouraged the college to develop and improve these offerings while developing new programs as well. As in most two-year institutions, students generally enroll in courses which are distinctly liberal arts or professional; courses are not particularly interdisciplinary in nature, are taught by appropriately specialized faculty, and are offered within traditional contexts of format, structure, and schedule. Unfortunately, this approach does not allow students to have the opportunity to become motivated to develop a lifelong process of examining ideas, themes and topics from the diverse and more objective points of view inherent in interdisciplinary learning. With QUILL support, three new mini-courses were introduced into the curriculum: "Fantasy: Coming to Know your World," "Masques of Love: The Dynamics of the Family," and "The American 1930s."

These three new mini-courses were designed by the two QUILL project co-directors and implemented by a team of five faculty members. An outside expert, Dr. Eric Rabkin of the University of Michigan, helped refine the interdisciplinary mode and structured each course with the project co-directors and the faculty team. Topics for each mini-course were chosen to build on themes that would attract student interest and/or integrate support, or augment required course work. For example, the second course, "Masques of Love," focused upon psychological, economic, social and intellectual elements in family life and was interrelated with courses in literature, psychology, sociology, arts, history, health and music.

Each mini-course was designed to include a mixture of presentations (lecture, slide/lecture, film/lecture, readings, dramatic presentations, discussions, panels) because of the compression of time and the concentration of subject matter. This was also planned to demonstrate the inter-relationship of disciplines. Music, for example, was always used as a teaching tool, augmenting, supporting, and illustrating ideas and principles of the lecture topic.

Faculty teams of five members from different disciplines were selected on the basis of subject specialization, reputation as teachers, and sensitivity to cooperative teaching methods. Each course was offered for fifteen hours, for which students received one credit.

The project co-directors prepared special program/study guides as a means of assisting students in assimilating and integrating the various perspectives on the subject areas presented, introducing students to the objectives of the project, and presenting data on course objectives, lecture abstracts, evaluation methods, required examination/paper/project, and readings.

Following each mini-course, the co-directors and faculty reviewed examinations, projects, and papers, exchanging ideas for improving the structure and format of the mini-courses. In addition, students in each of the mini-courses were asked to complete a course evaluation form which was modified for each course to reflect questions specifically related to it.

Almost every student stated that he/she would take mini-courses at a future time because of the positive feelings created by this pilot project. In particular, students were receptive to the variation from a traditional course setting, the usual topics, and the interdisciplinary approach and quality of presentation.

Clearly, the mini-courses generated very positive excitement across the campus. Offering of the mini-courses has been expanded to include the Evening Division, and new mini-courses will be offered in future semesters. Other evidence of the college's commitment to ongoing experimentation with the cross-disciplinary mini-courses lies in the fact that all six division chairpersons are studying the feasibility of planning their schedules so that one week each semester could be set aside for the suspension of afternoon laboratories and studio art classes to allow for scheduling mini-courses during times when greater numbers of students would be free to enroll without conflicts with required course work.

Contact: Christopher R. Reaske   S. Charles DeMatteo
Provost   Chairman
Russell Sage College   Humanities Division
Albany, NY 12208   The Junior College of Albany
(518) 270-2000   Albany, NY 12208
(518) 445-1711

Saint Lawrence University

The Humanities Semester in Modernism

(February - May 1980)

For several years faculty members at St. Lawrence have questioned whether the "cafeteria curriculum" of the 1970s provides students with a sound liberal arts education. While the present system of distribution requirements allows students a high degree of choice in course selection, it offers minimal direction and guarantees no coherence to their general education.

The Humanities Semester was designed as one way of providing students and faculty an opportunity to cultivate connections between disciplines. Offered during the spring of 1980, the Humanities Semester included a newly-designed core course in European intellectual history from 1870 to 1945, and five regularly taught courses, geared to a common theme of "modernism," including "Twentieth-Century Art History," "Asian Religions in the Modern World," " Modern Political Theory," and special studies courses in French and English literature.

In addition to the regular credit-hour courses, six extra seminars were scheduled during the semester which focused on topics central to all the courses. Some of these were "Relativism," "Normality and Neurosis," and "The Revolutionary Character of Modernism." The six faculty members and twenty-four students divided into two groups for these seminars and were able to reflect upon some of the key issues of "modernism" and to see how these issues were addressed in works of art and literature, in religion, in political theory, and in mass movements.

Originally the faculty hoped to attract sophomore students who would take three or four courses in the program (including the core course which was required), but in the end, most participants were upperclassmen who took only two or three courses. The core course in intellectual history ensured a degree of coherence for these students, and the syllabus and lecture schedule was designed to coordinate with material in each of the other five courses. There were a few common readings and three of the participating faculty members lectured in the core course, and all but one attended regularly.

The core course served as organizational headquarters for all aspects of the semester program; discussion questions and reading materials were passed out, announcements made, and special events planned. However, because the core course, like the others in the program, was not restricted to Humanities Semester students, the non-participants on occasion felt neglected or feared that their opportunity to "do well" in the course was diminished. In the future the core course will be restricted to Humanities Semester students while the satellite courses will remain open in order to prevent a drain on participating departments. A spin-off of the program was that a number of students not participating in the program were nevertheless prompted to do interdisciplinary papers and to attend some lectures and seminars on their own initiative. The faculty felt that some of these "hangers-on" were clearly profiting from the experimental model, even though they were not full participants. Since one of the university's goals was to show how to plan student schedules so that one course could mesh with another, they were pleased with such spin-off activity.

The intellectual excitement generated in students and faculty by this program was exceptional for St. Lawrence. The special seminars provided stimulation for the students, encouraging them to mull over among themselves various topics relevant to all their course work and, indeed, to their lives. In addition, the students enjoyed and benefited from seeing the faculty participate in a similar activity; they saw them disagreeing with each other and arguing from quite different perspectives. Both students and faculty learned a great deal about how to work in such seminars—how to focus on an issue, how to stay with a topic, and how to see a point from several perspectives in the course of an evening. The faculty may have benefited from the program even more than the students, for they would meet together before each seminar to thrash out the issue and develop discussion strategies. Here occurred the most significant interdisciplinary activity—each was exposed to the other's teaching methods, and by having to mesh them, they learned how to draw on a wider range of discussion skills than any had possessed before.

During the weeks that the evening seminar did not meet, lectures and films were scheduled to complement the program. Three lectures were given by SLU faculty on Einstein and relativity, trends in modern philosophy and theology, and modern film. In addition, two guest lecturers spoke on "Dislocation and Modern Writing" and "Malraux and the Popular Front." These lectures, plus two films and a trip to Ottawa to see *Mother Courage* were reasonably well attended and provided fresh blood and diversity to the program.

To ensure that students had a sustained, concentrated experience in pulling together the materials and viewpoints of different disciplines, each was required to write a term paper (15-20 pages) for his or her core course plus one satellite course. Some elected to write papers which satisfied the requirements of three courses. In addition, the students were required to write take-home interdisciplinary exams which in some cases were extremely perceptive. These exams demonstrated that the students had learned to think about literary works, paintings, religious traditions or philosophical positions in the context of the whole culture.

Student evaluations provided very positive comments and a good deal of enthusiasm about the experience. Virtually all found the topic of "modernism" to have been especially stimulating as an integrating experience, and felt that many of the issues considered in the seminars could be connected with personal experience.

The success of the pilot program suggests that SLU should continue to develop this model, and work is moving ahead to interest other faculty members in doing a Women's Studies Semester during the spring semester of 1981. In addition, a second Humanities Semester in Modernism will be offered in the fall of 1982, which will draw upon both the original and new faculty members. Substantive changes will probably include the offering of the seminars for academic credit and more assigned readings to focus the discussion. The seminars could become discussion sections for the core course, or perhaps become the core course itself. In general, the participating faculty believe that realistically a two-course program is all that most students will want to elect at St. Lawrence.

Contact: Patricia A. Alden
              Assistant Professor of English
              St. Lawrence University
              Canton, NY 13617
              (315) 379-6175

Southwestern University

Divergence and Convergences Between Academic
Disciplines

(May 1980 - May 1981)

Southwestern University sought QUILL funding to support the evaluation and redesign of several interdisciplinary and team-taught courses
which had previously been offered in its University Studies Program.
With the assistance of this grant, two courses entitled "Darwin, Marx,
and Wagner," and "Chicago, 1883-1933: Urban History and Urban
Sociology" were revised and taught during 1980-1981. In addition, a
course entitled "You Bet Your Life: Statistical Analysis in the Study of
Human Biology" was planned and will be offered during the academic
year 1981-1982.

The purpose of each of these courses was to aid the student in developing criteria to judge claims made by specific academic disciplines, and in
developing conceptual tools by which these claims, when they diverge
from other disciplines, could be reconciled. The project was based on the
assumption that the ability to interrelate various areas of inquiry and to
utilize the tools of one area to assess claims in other areas are central in-
gredients to a liberally educated person.

In each course the means towards achieving this goal included analysis
of the phenomena examined by two or more disciplines, a clarification of
the presuppositions and methodologies of those disciplines, a consideration of the degree to which these presuppositions and methodologies reflect larger, historical and social developments, an enunciation of the
claims made by the disciplines, and a demarcation of areas of conflict
and possible synthesis.

"You Bet Your Life: Statistical Analysis in the Study of Human Biology" was thoroughly evaluated by the biologist and mathematician who
had been teaching the course in the past. One of the professors resigned,
however, delaying actual implementation of their recommendations until the 1981-82 academic year. When offered, this six-hour course,
designed for non-majors in science and mathematics, will emphasize
elementary descriptive statistics and the human cardiovascular system,
enabling students to learn how data is gathered and analyzed in a natural
science and how a specific statistical design is informed by the
phenomena being studied. Students are expected to read extensively in

journal reports of research on the cardiovascular systems and analyze and critique the data and conclusions. They will perform laboratory work on animal cardiovascular systems, collect data on their own hearts, and develop a research project using this or other data to be analyzed statistically. The modified course will provide more effective integration of both disciplines through the earlier establishment of a sound background in the statistical and cardiovascular topics. Additional time will be available for evaluation of research studies, additional laboratory experiments, and a variety of field trips and/or outside lectures. Part of the difficulty in establishing this basic background in the past has been the very weak math/science background of the students. Apparently Southwestern students tended to think that interdisciplinary courses were easier than the traditional ones and hence some weak, insecure students felt that this was their best chance of "getting by." In the future, instructors will make clear to potential students the expected level of work.

"Darwin, Marx, and Wagner," a three-hour course, was designed and implemented by three faculty members from the departments of biology, economics and music. During the evaluation stage of this course, various faculty members with expertise in related areas were asked to make individual presentations to the three faculty members responsible for the course. This idea evolved into a faculty seminar on Darwin, Marx and Wagner—to which approximately thirty other faculty members came as auditors and led directly to improvements in the course syllabus and class assignments. This modified course investigated developments within these fields during the 19th century: specifically how they emerged from the distinctive methodologies and histories of inquiry of the several disciplines; how they reflected larger cultural phenomena of the period (and thus were similar); and how they were distinct from and even in conflict with one another. One of the major modifications in this course included a final individual oral examination for each student to develop integrative issues as they arose in conversation.

The final experimental offering, "Chicago, 1893-1933," was a six-hour course in urban history and urban sociology, evaluated and taught by three faculty in history, sociology, and philosophy and religion. The major shortcomings of the previous offering of this course which the instructors sought to overcome included the lack of coverage of the period after World War I and the fact that the earlier course was more nearly American history as exemplified by Chicago, and not urban history. A new unit on the city as space, using new neighborhood histories recently available and relevant map projects, as well as revised writing projects in history and sociology were devised. The course enrolled twenty-one students and was highlighted by a trip to Chicago to visit many of the buildings which had been studied in the section on architecture and many of the neighborhoods covered in the section on the city as space. Another unexpected feature of the course was a presentation by the President of Southwestern during which he described his first trip out of Texas to attend the Century of Progress Exposition in 1933 and how it had impressed him with the idea of confidence in the future and of the larger world.

Although no systematic evaluation was done after these courses were taught, the participating faculty members were sufficiently impressed with what was accomplished to plan to teach the courses on a regular, every-other-year basis. In terms of the aims of the project, each course succeeded in developing criteria by which claims made by specific academic disciplines can be judged, but were not as successful in developing conceptual tools by which these claims could be reconciled when they differ. Progress was made in the latter case, and there is good reason to expect these tools to evolve and be articulated more clearly when the courses are taught again.

In addition, the faculty seminar format used during the planning of the "Darwin, Marx and Wagner" course was used again in May, 1981 in anticipation of a major symposium the University is sponsoring on Gustav Mahler and his Vienna. Nine professors made presentations to a faculty group of twenty-five, meeting daily for an hour and a half over a two-week period.

Contact: Farley W. Snell
            Associate Professor of
               Philosophy and Religion
            Southwestern University
            Georgetown, TX 78626
            (512) 863-6511

65

Stevens Institute of Technology

Pilot Project for Interdisciplinary Seminars at
   Technical Schools on Biographies of Persons
   Whose Lives Span the Humanistic, Scientific,
   and Engineering Disciplines

(December 1979 - December 1980)

In an attempt to highlight values and methods of the humanities for engineering and science students at technical colleges, an interdisciplinary research seminar was developed to focus upon the creative endeavors of Leonardo da Vinci. Through da Vinci's accomplishments, the essential interdependence between the humanities, science, and engineering was shown while each area's separate integrity was stressed. In short, the goal was to close the gap between the technological culture and the humanistic culture. Fifteen students of high academic standards were carefully screened for participation in this seminar, for which they were required to do research, make reports, and produce lengthy, well-documented papers.

When the course was offered in the fall of 1980, special access to the library's Special Collection of Vinciana was provided, along with a special reading room for students in the seminar.

Because the course's format was of a traditional research seminar, there was no syllabus of lectures or reading lists. The class met for two and one-half hours a week and was taught jointly by a humanist, a scientist, and an engineer. At the beginning of the seminar, background lectures on Leonardo historiography and bibliography were provided, in addition to a tour of the Special Collection. Each faculty member discussed the common theme of the seminar and his disciplinary and personal perspective on Leonardo. After three weeks reading introductory materials, students began their own intensive research for their major project, although class activities continued with presentations on Leonardo's mechanics, art work, psychology, and the historical and cultural context of his life, particularly the environment of the Florentine guilds, Renaissance courts, and the intellectual currents of humanism and neoplatonism.

Basically, students' research topics fell under four basic areas of interest in Leonardo, namely his painting, his engineering, his psychology, and his anatomical studies. Fundamental questions considered in research included the following: What was the relation of theories of painting to what we would call Leonardo's scientific activities? What was the relation of Leonardo's artistic training to his work as a military engineer? Was Leonardo articulate in language, particularly Latin, and what effect did this have on his ability to understand classical and medieval science and engineering?

Twice during the semester, two well-known expert scholars on Leonardo visited the campus (jointly sponsored by QUILL, NEH, and SIT) and met informally with the seminar students in a special afternoon session. In addition, they delivered public lectures for the SIT community as a whole.

In an evaluation of the research seminar, the faculty was very pleased with what they perceived to be a more lively interchange of ideas as compared with interdisciplinary lectures in other courses. In addition, the faculty felt that the length and duration of sessions led to crucial questions being addressed and answered in a number of interesting interdisciplinary ways—although not always to everyone's satisfaction.

Given the relatively small number of liberal arts courses taken by engineering and science students at technical schools, student evaluators judged that they had insufficient preparation for a strict research seminar format. They would have preferred summer reading assignments and more formal lectures by the participating professors before the research aspect of the seminar began.

Both students and faculty, however, considered the format much more rewarding for teaching and learning than regular formats; students were particularly appreciative of learning research techniques and how to write lengthy, well-documented papers. The evening sessions of the seminar were considered essential to accommodate the heavy schedules of students and professors at technical schools.

The evaluation committee found the biographical subject matter well suited to investigate the interfaces between the liberal arts, the sciences, and engineering. As opposed to wider subject matters such as wars or industrial revolutions, biographies were amenable for sharper focusing on crucial issues involving scientific or engineering research and methodology in a human context. Future biographical subjects for study were suggested as Galileo, Einstein, Bertrand Russell, and Frederick W. Taylor.

To improve the quality of seminar discussions for both students and faculty, the evaluation committee also suggested that selected students from neighboring liberal arts colleges be invited to take such seminars at technical schools for credit. A comparable exchange of both faculty and students could be developed for technical personnel to attend classes on liberal arts campuses, thereby adding depth, variety, and quality to the perspectives of all concerned.

In assessing the quality of the research papers produced, the project director felt that some papers were too narrow in focus and that more time should have been spent clarifying the interdisciplinary aims of the course. Moreover, in a number of cases, the papers were well researched but poorly written. It is thought that improved screening of students or the proposed exchange with other campuses would upgrade both conceptual perceptions and set standards for writing papers.

To establish such seminars on a regular basis would add quality to liberal learning at technical schools, but at a high cost. SIT feels that periodic use of this format using some outside funding would be the most desirable way to continue this effort. However, the Institute's administrators felt that such a format was of such value that individual proposals for such interdisciplinary seminars should be reviewed for implementation in the future.

Contact: Geoffrey W. Clark
                Associate Professor of
                  Humanities
                Stevens Institute of
                  Technology
                Hoboken, NJ 07030
                (201) 420-5398

University of Hartford

Integrated Clusters of Independent Courses: A
Prototype and a Manual

(January - December 1980)

The QUILL project at the University of Hartford sought to address the particular needs of Arts and Sciences students who must meet minimal distribution requirements by introducing a curricular model which preserved the discipline, integrity, and departmental structure of traditional courses as well as the excitement of nontraditional interdisciplinary teaching. In essence, this model took three traditional courses from different academic departments and modified their presentation so that overlapping themes were emphasized in each course at a parallel level of development. Synthesis of ideas across disciplines was further encouraged by a one-hour per week seminar taught jointly by the three course instructors.

Although the current system of distribution requirements recognizes that a liberal education must include information from diverse fields, it assumes that students will have the ability to integrate the material and discover the richness of the inter-relationships and patterns on their own. A common way to encourage this integration has been through the creation of team-taught, interdisciplinary courses, but recently the University of Hartford made a conscious effort to reduce those offerings for two reasons: first, they did not replace existing departmental courses but were viewed as supplemental by most faculty who considered departmental courses the best way for students to develop an in-depth understanding of the knowledge, attitudes and methodology of a discipline. Secondly, it was felt that since most successful interdisciplinary courses are team-taught, they are very expensive courses to offer.

Therefore, in order to overcome these problems, the cluster course model was introduced as a hybrid between the traditional and interdisciplinary course approaches. In order to achieve as great a diversification as possible for the prototype cluster, one course was selected from the humanities, one from the social sciences, and one from the natural sciences. All three courses focused on twentieth century man in the western hemisphere, developing the central themes of man's perception of himself, his relationships with other persons and with his environment. The course explored the evolution of these perceptions and relationships during the twentieth century and the various paths they might take in the future. The prototype cluster consisted of a modified section of introduction to sociology, "Technology and Social Change"; a modified art history course, "Modern Art: Twentieth Century"; a new introductory level non-science major physics course, "Twentieth Century Technology"; and a one-credit, team taught seminar, "Man in the 20th Century."

Prior to the offering of the courses in the fall semester of 1980, all three participating instructors met to brainstorm on topics of interdisciplinary connection and exchange relevant bibliography. Their discussions revolved around landmark events in history and their ramifications for the three disciplines involved. Presentations were given to prospective students which allowed the instructors to develop a specific area of study (art, technology, and social change) with an eye toward subject interrelationships, thereby becoming familiar with one another's thought processes and teaching techniques.

Additional planning time during the summer was devoted to a four-day trip to Washington, DC, to gather information at the Smithsonian Institution's museum facilities. This time providing constant exposure to information in the multiple forms of displays, artifacts, art objects, films, audio presentations, bookstores and discussions with experts in the field proved to be the single most important experience in consolidating plans for the program.

Toward the end of the summer, the instructors contacted prospective students, sharing with them reading material on the interrelationship of technology, social change and art in the twentieth century, an assignment for the first meeting, and postcards from the Smithsonian Institution. Plans were also made for each seminar meeting which was directed toward a different technological subject area and individual course syllabi were organized in coordination with the seminar schedule. During the actual teaching of the courses, the instructors continued to meet weekly sharing highlights of class experiences as well as intensive consideration of the progress of the seminar students.

The specific courses focused directly upon the common themes. The "Twentieth Century Technology" course was designed to cover both the history of technology and how technology works. "Modern Art: Twentieth Century" was designed as an upper level chronological survey of the work of major artists and art movements from 1900 to the present in Europe and America, with emphasis given to the fine arts (painting, sculpture, and mixed media creations), and where relevant, architecture, furniture and fashion design, advertising images and illustration. "Introductory Sociology: Technology and Social Change" emphasized the comparative use of structural, functional, and conflict theory orienta-

70

tions toward the societal impact of technology through an examination of the five basic social institutions of the family, education, polity, economy, and religion with reference to the technological revolution in the twentieth century. Finally, the one-credit seminar for the students taking all three of the cluster courses summarized, integrated, and expanded upon the topics covered each week in the three main courses.

The strengths of this cluster model centered upon the ability to discern the interrelationships between art, technology and social change, as well as the enhancement of the ability to transfer skills among normally diverse subject areas. An unexpected bonus of this model was that as student performance was gauged by multiple instructors both separately and together, the students felt they had to keep up with their work and perform well in all four courses, resulting in more lively classes and above average student performance.

Suggestions for course improvement included the limiting of the courses to only selected underclassmen so students are all at the same level and participation confers a prestige value. In addition, guest lecturing by all instructors in each other's courses would help make the linkage among the three courses even more apparent. Students would benefit from receiving questions a week in advance on subjects to be covered in the seminar, as well as from group excursions early in the semester which would help consolidate social links and facilitate later class discussions.

Overall, student and faculty evaluation of this experimental cluster was very positive, demonstrating that cost effective alternatives that combine the best features of interdisciplinary team-taught courses and a traditional academic course structure are not only possible but exciting. Published results of this prototype are available directly from the project director.

Contact: Craig E. Daniels
Associate Professor of
Psychology
University of Hartford
West Hartford, CT 06117
(203) 243-4546

University of Maryland

"The Anatomy of Knowing: The Domain of
  Knowledge and the University Curriculum," a
  Proposed Course for Freshmen

(January - August 1979)

Project QUILL on the University of Maryland campus concentrated upon the development of a freshman-level course taught from a common syllabus by eight faculty members representing a full range of disciplines. The ultimate aim for the students was to develop a sense of the purpose of the university and its curriculum in order to help formulate coherent and relevant academic plans. For the faculty, the project provided an occasion for a great deal of intellectually integrating and academically exciting interdisciplinary interaction. Success was much greater with the faculty development than with the student course.

Initially, a group of thirteen faculty members, representing ten different departments and all five academic divisions, attended eight seminar sessions led by an outside consultant, Dr. Peter Caws of Hunter College, during the spring semester of 1979. Drawing upon Dr. Caws's experience in offering a course with similar purposes in a large lecture format, these sessions included presentation and discussion of the intellectual principles upon which the course was based, the rationale for its organization, the main ideas of each of its parts, and the pedagogical techniques and problems involved in such an offering.

Of the regular seminar participants, eight were fully involved in the planning and teaching of the course, "The Anatomy of Knowing." These instructors came from the departments of zoology, mathematics, government and politics, sociology, health education, philosophy, English, and Germanic and Slavic languages. In addition to participating in the seminar, these teachers met for a full week at the end of the spring semester to finalize plans for the course and almost weekly during the offering of the course in the fall of 1979.

The most successful aspect of the project was the intellectual excitement generated in these meetings. Each staff member was responsible for helping the others understand the specific material all would be teaching. This effort of mutual education integrated new ideas about both substance and process at higher levels of abstraction than those required by other teaching responsibilities and were enlivened by the excitement of new discoveries.

Six sections of the course were offered to new freshmen with the hope of reaching students at the beginning of their academic careers in order to give them an idea of a university's academic purposes so they might better understand the inherent values and relate their goals to the special character of such an institution. In addition, students were expected to understand the value of a general education and thereby obtain the necessary background and guidance to plan their own academic program. Students also received instruction and practice in the basic intellectual skills.

The greatest effort was directed toward helping students understand the characteristics of the three major disciplinary fields: the sciences, the social sciences, and the humanities. Although the students clearly recognized this major course goal, there is some question as to whether it was achieved. The great majority of freshmen at a large public university have been trained to master the content of certain designated materials and to demonstrate that mastery by repeating back to the instructor major facts or arguments contained in the material. Few have developed the habits of mind that lead them to relate these readings to their own experience or ideas encountered elsewhere. Fewer still have learned to consider the implications of this material and understand it in larger, more abstract relationships. The faculty in this course found that neither their techniques of presentation nor the students' level of preparation allowed much progress toward developing an understanding of the world implicit in the intellectual strategies of the sciences, the social sciences and the humanities. Thus they were left with some question as to whether the course was appropriate for the audience for which it was intended.

The most significant contribution to the students came in the area of intellectual skill development. The design of the course, the nature of class discussions, and the essay assignments guaranteed that these skills would be stressed. Less success was attained in helping students understand the nature of academic institutions and the purposes and value of a general education, perhaps because these discussions were concentrated toward the end of the course, assuming the students had grasped all the material leading up to these discussions (which they had not) and with too little time allocated.

Finally, little success was achieved in helping students plan their own future academic programs. Not surprisingly, they could not see the relationship between the specific majors and courses which in a practical sense defined the university curriculum and the higher-level abstractions about kinds of knowledge with which the course dealt. In the end, most instructors chose not to try to make the connection for them.

The greatest weakness of this undertaking was in overestimating the intellectual development of freshmen students and the difficulty in finding an appropriate pedagogy to meet their needs. These mistakes stemmed from the faculty's own heavy involvement in mastering the material and the organizing concepts, leaving too little time or energy to devise alternate ways of making the material clearer to students.

Although a new general education program makes it impractical to offer this course to freshmen again, it will be modified for inclusion in a series of required upper-division courses designed to satisfy another part of the new program. In the meantime, two faculty members who participated in this QUILL project taught a General Honors Program seminar that grew directly out of this experience, and had excellent results with a more appropriate audience.

The time, energy, and money invested in "The Anatomy of Knowing" was well spent. If nothing more had been done than to put together and circulate a course syllabus, there would have been a significant impact on a faculty that does not often think in terms of such offerings and in many cases cannot imagine them. The concept aroused considerable interest and had a major influence on the inclusion of a "ways of knowing" requirement in the new general education program. The faculty involved had a splendid learning experience, both intellectual and pedagogical. The students had an unusual experience, learned something, if not what they expected, and had their minds stretched, albeit sometimes painfully. "The Anatomy of Knowing" led the way in a serious effort to renew the spirit of undergraduate education which is a remarkable undertaking in a multiversity setting.

Contact: Robert E. Shoenberg
             Dean for Undergraduate
                Studies
             University of Maryland
             College Park, MD 20742
             (301) 454-2530

University of Rhode Island
College of Arts and Sciences

Improving Liberal Education through the
Development of Generic Skills

(May - November 1980)

As a follow-up to a general curricular reform supported by a long-term grant from FIPSE, the College of Arts and Sciences at the University of Rhode Island undertook an evaluation and integration of four experimental skills-oriented courses that had been taught for the past three years. Under this general education curriculum revision, certain broadly defined generic skills had been established as essential to liberal learning: (1) the ability to communicate effectively; (2) the ability to think critically; (3) the ability to understand and deal with quantitative data beyond elementary arithmetic; and (4) the ability to learn through aesthetic modes.

Convinced that these skills were not adequately addressed through traditional content-oriented courses which assumed that the acquisition or sharpening of skills would occur as a by-product of the study of subject matter, the college designed four new team-taught, transdisciplinary courses to complement the discipline-based courses. These special courses were "College Communication Skills," "Quantitative Thinking Skills," "Analytical Thinking Skills," and "Experiencing the Arts."

After three years of experience, Project QUILL provided the resources for summer workshops for evaluation of these courses while addressing the following issues: (1) the possibility of integrating the experimental skills courses into a unified skills curriculum which would serve as an option for students within the standard general education curriculum; and (2) the development of mechanisms for encouraging the transfer of the generic skills approach to other courses.

Four two-member faculty teams representing each of the experimental courses met on an individual basis throughout the summer of 1980 to design approaches for transferring the methods used in the individual skills courses to the regular curriculum. All eight faculty members (plus the associate dean of the college) also met regularly in a larger forum to share information about the individual projects and prepare a proposal to link the skills courses into a unified curriculum.

Within the individual workshops, each team devised a plan for developing materials which were specifically suited to teaching the skills the team believed to be most important. The result was that four teams developed materials for transferring the skills approach which were quite different from one another in scope and content. Some produced materials which could be directly transferred to another course; others used the philosophy behind their experimental course to produce materials which could be used in aiding faculty to evaluate students or having faculty review strategies for addressing skills in other classes.

The College Communication Skills team designed a prototype for defining institutional standards and establishing mechanisms through which the speech and writing faculty could work closely with the faculty in other disciplines to develop consistency in communication skills. Specifically, they worked with the College of Nursing and conducted a series of workshops with a representative group of nursing faculty to help strengthen the communication skills component of their courses.

The second team of Quantitative Thinking Skills faculty sought to develop modules to illustrate the use of a problem solving approach that encouraged students to confront a problem through a series of steps rather than simply applying a memorized formula to solve the problem. One module was designed to introduce students to the theory underlying multiple regression analysis in a sociology course and another was designed for use in psychology which offered a step-by-step approach for teaching analysis of variance. Because of the complexities of these modules, special workshops are planned in 1981-82 for a pilot faculty group to prepare exercises designed to teach quantitative thinking skills in existing social science courses.

The Analytical Thinking Skills team designed a new logic-based composition course to be offered through the philosophy department. Instead of the traditional approach of asking students to identify various forms of argument, this course would require the students themselves to produce these forms. The philosophy department has agreed to incorporate these communication strategies into their introductory logic courses and a new course will become part of the University's communication requirement beginning in fall 1981.

The fourth team, Experiencing the Arts (ETA), sought to develop students' creative capacities in traditional learning situations. The objective of the ETA team project was to isolate the tasks, goals, and purposes which make up the ETA environment in order to develop ways of encouraging the growth of students' creative capacities in other learning situations. It became evident that this approach encouraged an active learning environment in which students could develop their creative potential in new ways and the team is now developing a workshop series to introduce students and faculty to the kinds of strategies that need to be adopted to stimulate a more active learning process in the traditional classroom.

Within the larger group workshops, each team shared information about its own individual projects so that each team could benefit from the others' experiences and prepare a proposal to link the skills courses into a unified curriculum. These workshops revealed that the links between the experimental courses were indeed more pervasive and subtle, yet at the same time more substantial than originally assumed. Although specific activities were quite varied, a crucial link between the courses emerged. In spite of the major differences in the type of skills and subject matters addressed in the each of the courses, the instructors had discovered quite independently that the most important determinant of success was whether the teaching team succeeded in encouraging and enabling students to become "active learners" in the classroom—to take risks, to stretch their abilities, etc. In other words, the success of the courses depended on the extent to which the faculty capitalized on the very differences between these courses and other more traditional content courses.

As a result of these workshops, the faculty decided that the experimental skills courses should be continued in the general education curriculum. In addition, the instructors felt that at the present time these courses did not lend themselves to a unified curriculum. The faculty decided that it might not be desirable to encourage the same students to take all the skills courses. Rather, a number of strategies would be tried to increase the teaching and learning of skills in undergraduate instruction. This could be accomplished through special summer institutes to orient students to an active learning approach and faculty team planning seminars in which faculty teaching similar kinds of courses would meet regularly to design materials and exercises to facilitate the teaching of skills.

Contact: Gerry S. Tyler   M. Beverly Swan
            Associate Dean, College of   Associate Professor of
               Arts and Sciences   English and Director of the
            University of Rhode Island   College Writing Program
            Kingston, RI 02881   University of Rhode Island
            (401) 792-2566   Kingston, RI 02881
                                          (401) 792-5931

University of Wisconsin—Green Bay

Reexamining the Intellectual Underpinnings of a
Core Program in Liberal Education

(September 1978 - August 1979)

During the 1977-1978 academic year, the University of Wisconsin at
Green Bay revised its core curriculum and general education requirements to build a more tightly integrated and more meaningful program
for all university undergraduates. This new program entitled "All
University Requirements" (AUR) consisted of interdisciplinary courses
structured around three basic aims: (1) study in the humanities, social
sciences, and natural sciences with attention to their distinctive methods
and procedures; (2) sustained engagement with value questions as they
are inherent in societal problems, with particular attention to cross-cultural perspectives; and (3) integration across traditional disciplines.

The university then requested a QUILL grant to offer assistance to
faculty members who were now required to combine their usual subject
matter with a treatment of values, other cultural comparisons, methodologies and epistemology in the same course (or two-course sequence).
The mechanism chosen through which assistance would be provided was
a workshop for program faculty to be offered in the week before the end
of the spring term and the onset of the summer session. Grant funds supported the direct costs of the workshop at a location off-campus for approximately 35 persons, evaluation of the workshop, and the equivalent
of one course release time for each of four participating faculty Fellows
to develop and offer the workshop. The project director was an un-
funded participant throughout the year.

Meetings were held every two to three weeks during the fall term, with
each Fellow submitting an essay for critique on the structure and goals of
the All University Requirements. Topics included one's understanding of
liberal education, the structure of knowledge and the nature of each of
the three domains, each Fellow's concept of the ten books most essential
to a student's baccalaureate education, a similar study of experiences
essential to that education and the beginning of a never-resolved debate
on the role of experience in education. Sessions ran from three to four
hours each.

During the spring term, each Fellow prepared a paper on some specific
aspect of the AUR program to be critiqued formally by another Fellow

and discussed by the group. Topics included values, other cultures, and each of the three domains of knowledge. After the examination of the nature, potential and limitations of each of the elements separately, the program was scrutinized from two perspectives: (1) What would an ideal core program in liberal and general education contain? and (2) How best might such a program be structured? Subsequent sessions dealt with the structure of the workshop itself and the development of concepts to be introduced.

Participation in the workshop held for three days in early June in Bailey's Harbor, Wisconsin, was extended to all faculty who either had taught or were scheduled to teach in the program, faculty review committees, and academic administrators responsible for reviewing the program. Although space in the lodge was limited, necessitating a trade-off between faculty and students, three student representatives were invited to participate.

The workshop was designed to flow from a consideration of the broad general goals that underlie liberal education to a focus on the various component features of the AUR program. It then progressed to a focus on the "ideal" six-credit sequence. The final session was to consider whether the "ideal" sequence possible within the existing program was adequate given the understanding of liberal education generated at the beginning of the workshop. Any mismatch indicated a need to revise the program itself.

Comments of the Fellows and other participants indicated the workshop was a success because it served as a catalyst for significant changes within both the humanities and natural science portions of the program, changes which might not have been made otherwise. Most participants valued the specific insights and ideas they had gleaned from colleagues. They were particularly grateful for the freedom from distraction in this off-campus setting which provided the opportunity for interaction with colleagues from other fields, something the faculty perceived as not adequate in a normal setting. The small honorarium of $50 per participant seemed to have no bearing on their incentive to become involved.

Disappointments were two-fold: (1) there was less student involvement than would have been ideal, and (2) some participants were more concerned with the specifics of course development than with the broader philosophical issues.

As for the Fellows, all found the year's activities to have been such a rewarding experience that they will try to carry the effort forward (on a limited basis at least, due to the absence of release-time), even as an overload. Many faculty wanted to know how they could become Fellows in such a project.

Most important of all, this QUILL project has demonstrated that a great deal of liberal learning and planning can be accomplished with a modest amount of money.

Contact: Forrest H. Armstrong
             Dean
             William James College
             Allendale, MI 49401
             (616) 895-6611

Part II

Projects Which Improve Continuing Education

Beaver College

An Interdisciplinary Program of Courses in
Liberal Studies for Continuing Education
Students in Business Administration in a
Liberal Arts College

(February 1979 - January 1980)

In response to the needs of an increasing number of continuing education students who have entered Beaver College within the last two decades—and a program in Business Administration that had grown to accommodate them—QUILL funds were used to develop two core courses in the humanities and natural sciences as a component of general education. Since this program had grown so rapidly, the college found itself with a body of students and a curriculum in the major field of business administration before consideration had been given to the special requirements in general education.

Because of its commitment to the liberal arts, Beaver clearly wanted rigorous requirements in the liberal arts for these adult students, but realized that their traditional undergraduate approach and course structure had to be modified. Although the proposal for QUILL support originally included a core course in the social science area as well, financial restrictions permitted the funding of only courses in the humanities and natural sciences without much loss in overall objectives since students in business administration were normally exposed to a good deal of material in social science as part of their major program.

The students in Beaver's evening-weekend college are mature adults whose primary motive for returning to college is a desire for professional advancement. Beaver has been committed to its obligation to provide general education courses specifically designed for students of mature years who have experienced the world of work. For such students ties between "high culture" and the real world are of the utmost importance since they will not lightly suspend disbelief in the virtues of abstract scholarship. Traditional disciplinary courses are inadequate. Knowledge must be integrated rather than fragmented; it must be related to personal experience rather than presented abstractly. The QUILL program was designed to fill those needs.

Shortly after the QUILL funds were approved, two committees were formed—in humanities and natural science—to develop the courses to be offered during the academic year 1979-1980. Unfortunately, the Beaver faculty voted not to require the core courses of all candidates for the degree, allowing those students who had had some previous work in the liberal arts to substitute any courses in humanities and natural sciences for the core. As a result, the enrollment in each of the pilot courses was generally too small to permit formal evaluation of attitudinal change and cognitive growth, though all students participated with a high level of interest.

"The Humanistic Perspective," the humanities survey course, offered a cogent, integrated introduction to the unity and diversity of humanistic ideas and expression, and to different ways of viewing and interpreting the world and "man's" place within it. Among the specific purposes of the course were: (1) to present an integrated introduction to the disciplines within the humanities; (2) to establish the relevance of the humanities to life; (3) to offer contexts in which to understand the role of the humanities and their role within society; (4) to increase student understanding of and appreciation for art, music, literature, language, and history; and (5) to encourage creativity and flexibility of thought.

This course was divided into two interrrelated segments. In the first half students were introduced to three forms of artistic expression (abstract painting, poetry, and architecture) to illustrate the characteristics and purposes of humanistic expression. These included creativity, exploring and expressing human values, and critiquing society. The second half of the course concentrated upon an examination of humanistic expression during 1905 in Europe. This helped students focus upon a historical study to apply some of the principles learned in the first segment; to study the function of "humanists" in a situation that allowed students to maintain their objective—i.e., to be able to see how ideas, art forms, and controversies "turned out."

"Science and Technology Today," the natural sciences survey course, was a two-semester non-laboratory course presenting basic interdisciplinary science concepts in an integrated fashion to help students understand the application of these concepts in the form of the technological advances that influence their standard and style of living outside of the academic world. It was hoped that by understanding how technologists apply scientific knowledge to meet human needs and desires, the students would appreciate both the positive and negative results that occur when humans exploit their natural environment, and thus become capable of making informed decisions about the future role that science and technology will play in their lives and in the lives of their children. The course consisted of a major unit dealing with basic physical, biological and earth science concepts intended to provide a fundamental background for application in four later units which focused upon population dynamics, pollution of the environment, the role of energy in human life, and the potential for alteration of the human organism in the future via the recent revolutionary advances in biology.

In both the humanities and natural sciences survey courses, students were extremely enthusiastic and actively participated in the class discussions. Students described both courses as eye-opening, enriching, and tantalizing. Although the courses will continue to be the core courses for those adult students who have not had basic liberal arts courses in the past, they are still not yet required of all students. The faculty members involved in this project are optimistic that the enthusiasm generated by the first group of students will help attract a larger number of students who are not required to take the courses in the future.

Clearly this program has demonstrated that it is possible to project central ideas in both science and humanities to mature students through interdisciplinary courses. They were not watered down surveys; rather they rigorously dealt in some depth with the key ideas that were presented. Although these activities were not intended as substitutes for systematic work in the traditional disciplines, the students who participated should become better citizens, more capable of making decisions in their work, and lead more enriched lives.

Contact: Bernard Mausner
             Professor of Psychology
             Beaver College
             Glenside, PA 19038
             (215) 884-3500

Bloomfield College

A New Entry into the Liberal Arts for Adult
Evening Students

(December 1979 - June 1980)

In view of the apparent unmet needs of a growing adult student population within the Evening Program at Bloomfield College, an attempt was made to fashion a new entry-level English course as a more effective and appropriate introduction into the liberal arts. Instead of appearing as a conventional composition course, this new course was modeled upon the humanities/social sciences components of the Freshman Core Program. This also served as a model course that could be used for other entry-level courses and would help strengthen the liberal arts in the Evening Program by motivating these students to elect further liberal arts courses.

The overall objective of the course, taught during the spring semester of 1980, was to increase the students' literacy levels. Course planners believed that literate individuals should be able to read difficult, nontechnical material intelligently and to write clear, coherent, concise, and correct English prose. Furthermore, they should be expected to have developed general cognitive skills such as the ability to perform analytical problem solving on an abstract level with reflective, critical, judgment. They should be able not only to summarize the thinking of others, but generate their own ideas effectively. They should also have achieved literacy in the sense of being familiar with several dominant conceptual schemes that have influenced the modern world. And finally, they should have a developed sense of self, an awakened sense of curiosity about the world, and the confidence to continue exploring and learning in areas that are new to them.

To meet the objective of literacy, three fundamental conceptual schemes were chosen for the course: a Darwinian sense of evolution, a Freudian conceptualization of unconscious motivation stemming from unresolved conflicts in personal development, and a radical socialist view of class struggle and prejudice associated with Marx. The three texts chosen were Stephen Gould's *Ever Since Darwin*, George Orwell's *Road to Wigan Pier*, and Sigmund Freud's *Introductory Lectures on Psycholanalysis*.

Teaching methods were carefully structured to move sequentially from simple to more complex tasks, within a small class framework (sixteen students). Class discussions focused upon the assigned materials and students were required to write short papers each week. This method concentrated upon making explicit the ways intelligence operates in constructing a reasonable argument. The course was not meant to give a liberal education in concentrated form, but rather to provide an effective entry into humanistic learning at the college level.

Specific goals set forth sequentially the stages of cognitive operation that were to be emphasized. Students were to be taught how to (1) find the main point of an assignment (categorize and discriminate); (2) see how sections of an argument fit together and find evidence that supports the argument (analyze); (3) develop their own ideas about how authors build arguments (generalize); (4) defend their interpretations with evidence (apply their ideas); and (5) develop mastery of writing mechanics and express their ideas in a well organized paper (communicate effectively).

Evaluation of the course was based upon teachers' review of student performance and progress, students' assessment of the course provided in an end-of-semester questionnaire, and quantitative and qualitative analyses of these materials in view of the overall course objectives. The faculty members clearly felt that students improved their basic reading skills (comprehension) and writing techniques. They also felt that the students made considerable progress in improving their reasoning skills, though more attention should still be given to the development of analytical reasoning, so that it can be more effectively used in their lives outside of the course. This conclusion directly points toward the need for additional courses of this type.

By both objective and subjective standards, students indicated that they had been challenged by great thinkers and had improved their ability to understand difficult ideas. More than 80 percent of the students registered deep satisfaction with the course and with themselves as a result of it. Most students were unusually challenged, and learned to appreciate the kind of challenge provided by difficult reading and writing assignments.

The final objective, of institutionalizing this course by having it serve as a model for other English introductory courses and strengthen the liberal arts component of the college was not met. Regular faculty members in the Humanities Division were reluctant to adapt this approach to existing courses. However, the same instructor planned to offer this same course again in the fall of 1980, which would provide an opportunity for improving it more and bringing it to the attention of other faculty members for examination again. Although the faculty at Bloomfield College is reluctant to expand its use of this model of teaching for adult students, it is clear that a majority of the students affected by this course benefitted from it and will seek more liberal arts courses in several divisions in the near future.

Contact: William A. Sadler, Jr.
       Chairman, Division of Inter-
        disciplinary Studies
       Bloomfield College
       Bloomfield, NJ 07003
       (201) 748-9000

Kalamazoo College

Cultural Revolt in Modern America: The 1920s,
the 1960s, and Beyond: A Program for the
Non-Traditional Student

(September 1979 - June 1980)

With the hope of creating new links between the local community and
Kalamazoo College, a new interdisciplinary course on "Cultural Revolt"
was taught by an historian and a sociologist within the Non-Traditional
Student Program. Meeting for ten weeks in the living room of the Stry-
ker Center, the course attracted high school students, college students,
and adults from the local community ranging in age from mid-30s to 70s.
Given the nature of the setting and the diversity of the students, discussion was facilitated and there was an overriding sense of conviviality.

The course focused upon two decades in twentieth century America—
the 1920s and the 1960s—which were characterized by much cultural
conflict. In both periods, commonly accepted values, conventional social
roles, and lifestyles were challenged. Although each period had its own
unique characteristics, both evoked a sense of change and a quest for
new identity, especially among the youth.

The first objective of the course was to clarify what happened in each
period: who challenged the conventional culture, on what grounds, and
with what result? Secondly, the course examined the extent to which the
cultural conflict of the 1960s was unique and the extent to which it was
foreshadowed by the revolt in the 1920s. The students discussed how
much cultural revolt in America was itself infused with certain traditional American values. And finally, the interplay between cultural and
political issues and movements in the 1960s was analyzed with special
emphasis upon its implications for Kalamazoo.

Although the subject matter of the course was inherently interesting,
for any given session it was also personally significant to at least some
and often many of the students. For example, in the sessions dealing with
the 1920s, some of the older students recalled their adolescence during
that decade and enriched the material for everyone. Since there were
students in the course who had "come of age" in the 1960s rebellion, and
students who as adults themselves had been activists during that decade,
this focal point of the course was of wide interest. Moreover, the sessions

on women and feminism seemed especially appropriate since fifteen of the twenty-one students were female, and it was this issue above all which seemed to generate a great deal of intergenerational sharing and enlightenment. The broad age span of the students thus helped to provide diverse perspectives on the theme of cultural revolt.

Outside consultants played a major role in the success of the course as well. A sociologist from the University of Michigan-Dearborn and an expert on jazz in the 1920s gave a fascinating talk about race and jazz during that period. Furthermore, the visit by Professor Sara Evans of the University of Minnesota was a high-point in the course as she elaborated significantly upon her book, *Personal Politics,* which was used as a text for the course. In addition, one of the main goals of the course—to link national events in the 1960s with local Kalamazoo developments—was substantially achieved through visits to the course by a leader in the local black community (who among other things, provided a taped interview with his son, who had been a "militant" in Kalamazoo in the late 1960s) and by a well-known local feminist, who talked about a successful drive to eliminate sexual stereotypes from school textbooks.

There were, inevitably, occasional problems. Many of the students were far removed from an academic setting and sometimes noticeably reticent. Moreover, on occasion, a few persons both monopolized discussion and digressed wildly from the issues at hand. At times, the faculty members felt that the larger theoretical perspective they were attempting to convey was lost in the details.

Nevertheless, based on the overwhelmingly positive student evaluations and faculty observations, it was generally concluded that the few problems were far overshadowed by the successes. Neither professor had had much experience teaching "non-traditional" students and now both feel the attempt was clearly worth the effort. Following discussions with a number of their colleagues at the college, during which time they described the experience of the course and its positive conclusions, it is apparent that their enthusiasm encouraged more interest in this area at Kalamazoo College and that other colleagues will offer courses for a non-traditional audience.

Contact: David Strauss
Professor of History
Kalamazoo College
Kalamazoo, MI 49007
(616) 383-8434

Robert Stauffer
Associate Professor of
  Sociology
Kalamazoo College
Kalamazoo, MI 49007
(616) 383-8429

Meredith College

Can This Be Love? A Liberal Look at Tragic
Passion

(November 1978 - April 1979)

Although the targeted audience for this continuing education course offered at Meredith College failed to materialize, this QUILL-funded project opened the way for interdisciplinary, team-taught courses which would appeal to adults.

Because many of the residents of Raleigh and the Research Triangle area are especially highly educated in science and technology, the faculty involved in this program hoped to provide a course grounded in the humanities to expand the interests of the science-oriented population. Unfortunately, the course enrollment reached persons already interested in liberal learning, but did provide this group with a structured learning experience and introduced them to the overall program of the college.

The ten-week, interdisciplinary, team-taught course provided a genuine depth of content beneath its attention-catching title. Faculty members from four disciplines—literature, philosophy and religion, music, and French—focused their attention on the theme of romantic passion in western culture. The course began with a modern film, *Love Story*, and raised questions such as the nature of love, the meaning of tragedy, and the difference between a perceptive and sentimental response to the tragic and heroic in love.

Following this introduction, the course assumed an historic perspective. Ancient roots of love, such as the myths of Orpheus, Theseus, and Phaedra, were followed by an examination of great loves such as that of Antony and Cleopatra and views of love by persons as different as St. Paul and Paul McCartney. Medieval romances were examined for the concept of courtly love and its religious-social implications. Tristan and Isolde, Abelard and Heloise, Deirdre, and *The Divine Comedy* were viewed in their literary, musical, and religious dimensions. Near the end of the seminar, modern novels and films were viewed as continuations of the ancient and medieval themes, emphasizing psychological and anthropological content in addition to the major approaches.

The overall objective of the course was to demonstrate that from ancient Greece to the present time, there is a lasting value in liberal studies.

Although the seminar highlighted the value of understanding the origins of conventions pertaining to sex and love, it attempted to develop in the participants a higher regard for humanistic studies.

The successes of the experiment lay in the effectiveness of the interdisciplinary approach. Although the teaching team was a little ragged at times, it provided an opportunity for team teaching and made the faculty members eager to try it again. The students also had their first experience in an interdisciplinary class organized to examine a central theme and found it stimulating, interesting, and valuable.

The course might have reached its intended scientific and technological population had cooperation been sought with a co-sponsoring professional group in the target area, and this approach no doubt will be followed in the future. Nonetheless, Meredith College definitely plans to follow up on the success of presenting a liberal learning course organized around a theme and will pattern more continuing education courses on this model.

Contact: Sarah M. Lemmon
             Dean, Office of Continuing
                Education and Special
                Programs
             Meredith College
             Raleigh, NC 27611
             (919) 833-6461

Saint Joseph's College

Liberal Arts for Health Professionals:
Strengthening the Liberal Learning
Component of Continuing Education

(January 1979 - March 1980)

By its very nature, adult continuing education tends to have a professional emphasis, with the unfortunate result that students are often deprived of the essential skills and understandings long associated with the liberal arts. Contributing to this situation is the view held by many students that the liberal arts portion of the curriculum is an irrelevant frill—less appropriate than professional course work for the attainment of success in their chosen fields.

Such was the case within the Division of General Studies at St. Joseph's College, which offers highly individualized degree options to persons living in the metropolitan New York area. While possessing the capacity to meet the needs of a diverse professional population, the program is most fully developed to serve those engaged in the health professions: of the 1200 students currently working toward the B.S. degree in Community Health and Health Administration, the majority are R.N.'s, Black, female, middle-aged, and foreign-born.

The QUILL project at St. Joseph's helped this Division of General Studies create four new courses which would both link the liberal arts more directly with these two programs and assist students in acquiring generic problem-solving and critical thinking skills with a direct application to the health care field.

Initially four curriculum teams of adjunct faculty members were established to design each of the four new courses. For each two-person team, one faculty member had a liberal arts orientation and the other came from the health field. Although the teams worked primarily alone on course development, they had two joint meetings to listen to the remarks of outside consultants who discussed the general skills of critical thinking and problem solving. At the end of that summer preparation period, two sections of each course were tested on the main campus: "Problem Solving for Health Professionals," "Critical Thinking for Health Professionals," "Community Health and the Liberal Arts," and "Health Administration and the Liberal Arts." In some cases, a variety of teaching methods and syllabi were tested, but for the most part, the two sections of each course were identical.

By the fall of 1979, additional faculty members had to be trained to meet an expanded demand for the courses. This training was accomplished on a one-to-one basis between the experienced instructors and those just joining the project. For spring, the increase in the number of sections was even more dramatic. This was primarily due to the college's registration of more structured programs in Community Health and Health Administration—both of which had the QUILL courses as part of the core curriculum.

To gear up for the coming semester, the entire faculty was invited to attend three training sessions, during which the QUILL faculty explained the nature of the courses, followed by a concentrated immersion in the specific courses the new faculty members wished to teach. During that semester, thirty-six sections of these courses were offered at the main and branch campuses, in addition to off-campus extension sites.

Overall evaluation of the experiences involved in preparing, teaching, and expanding these courses were very positive. The single most pivotal factor in the project design centered on the composition of the faculty teams. Health professionals and liberal arts faculty truly pooled their resources. Although the original proposal was the idea of one individual, all faculty participants worked together, understanding the common objective and the necessity for a single unified course.

Another important factor in the planning and development stage was the heavy reliance on adjunct faculty. The most pleasant aspect of the faculty members' work was their enthusiasm for the project. Once they agreed to the initial premise of the course, there was little obstructionism over issues so significant to members of entrenched departments. On the other hand, because of their part-time status, it was an administrative nightmare scheduling time for the teams to work together on a regular basis. The degree of unity between outlines was directly correlated to how often the teams met together.

Because of the interdisciplinary nature of this effort, the problem of providing written materials to the students was very large. Particularly in the liberal arts courses, copyright laws prevented the photocopying of much necessary material, so students were required to purchase a limited number of inexpensive paperbacks while the college bought multiple copies of the hardcover works. Eventually, it is hoped that the original faculty teams can prepare their own anthologies for publication.

Another objective of the original proposal was to create workbooks to foster replicability of the courses, both at St. Joseph's and elsewhere. As with the unevenness of the course outlines, the nature of the workbooks varied greatly among the courses, but for each course at least one met with the minimal standard of replicability. It is anticipated that selected outlines will be added to each workbook to add depth and foster development of materials for future instructors.

The division did make great strides in improving communication skills of its students. A writing committee was formed to improve students' writing skills and a new course was added. The new and more basic writing course has been subsequently coupled with the "Problem Solving" course to form the first semester program for students admitted to the college on a "conditional" basis.

Minimal success was achieved in improving student enrollment in traditional liberal arts courses. The primary reason for this is that many students transfer into the program with large amounts of credit, much of which satisfies the liberal arts requirements of the program. Consequently, these students become almost immediately involved in their major coursework.

Ironically, the college underestimated the impact of the QUILL project on its academic program. As indicated, during the period of the project the college registered majors with the experimental courses as part of the core curriculum. While difficult to ascertain, it was the feeling of the administration that the quality and significance of the experimental courses was a positive influence in the State Education Department's eventual endorsement of the majors.

The other benefit of the project resulted from the above-mentioned increase in sections and the consequent necessity to train large numbers of the primarily adjunct faculty. Because these individuals, mostly health practitioners, wanted to be competent to teach as many courses as possible, they attended these sessions in great numbers and with keen interest. Accordingly, the pedagogy of generic skill development has been internalized by the majority of the faculty who are not only teaching one of these specialized courses but are using that knowledge and applying it in their other courses.

Contact: Thomas A. Travis, Director
Division of General Studies
St. Joseph's College
Brooklyn, NY 11205
(212) 622-4690

Saint Mary's College of Maryland

Institute for Liberal Learning in Retirement (ILLR)

(September 1979 - May 1980)

In combination with Title I funds from the State of Maryland, the QUILL project at St. Mary's College was designed to encourage retired persons in its rural community to return to the classroom, lecture hall, or seminar room for formal academic participation in the liberal arts and sciences, but under conditions structured to build confidence and give pleasure. Through this positive reinforcement it was hoped that some participants might be induced to develop a continuing and lifelong habit of exploring the world of ideas, first, through special programs designed for them, and later, by taking existing liberal arts courses at the college.

After the program was publicized and promoted with the help of the County Commission on the Aging, an organizational meeting was held to determine the course content and format which would be most responsive to participants' desires. Approximately 80 senior citizens attended this meeting and expressed their preference for film and slide presentations coupled with discussions, necessitating abandonment of the original plan for formal lectures and rigorous subject matter.

After evaluating surveys and discussions of the senior citizens who attended the planning sessions and served on a Community Advisory Committee, the top three areas of liberal studies of interest to the group were formed into programs and presented during four separate sessions at the college during the first semester. These included lectures on psychology, county history and the colonial Chesapeake region, and the Shakespearean tradition.

Because of the great diversity of students attracted to this program (most of whom had less than a high school education), two sessions were developed during the second semester following a unified program during the first semester.

The second semester program included a Tuesday morning session which attracted approximately 40 less-educated senior citizens for film series and a hot lunch at various locations throughout the region. Tuesday evening sessions were held at a local church and since some of these participants had at least some college experience, the subject presentations were slightly more rigorous. This spring program focused upon

Kenneth Clark's "Civilization" film series and was offered in thirteen separate sessions.

Given the wide range of educational background of the senior citizens, the St. Mary's College staff felt the project was very successful and that the interest of the participants in subjects ordinarily studied by upper-division college students was surprising. The greatest strengths of the program were the ability of the participants to select the subjects, the program approach as compared with the course approach, and the variety of sites for presentations.

A project of this sort is probably best suited for rural areas since opportunities for cultural programs are limited in such areas. As a result of the stimulation provided by the project, it is believed that many of the participants did increase their knowledge of history and culture, did enrich their lives, and will consider additional enrichment experiences as they become available.

Contact: Christine Cihlar
Assistant to the President
St. Mary's College of
    Maryland
St. Mary's City, MD 20686
(301) 863-7100

University of Iowa
College of Medicine

Enhancing Liberal Learning in an Academic
  Health Sciences Center

(September 1980 - June 1981)

The Office of Continuing Medical Education at the University of Iowa's College of Medicine sought funds from Project QUILL to enhance the liberal learning available to a sizeable number of health science students and professionals, and especially to the public that populated its large multi-faceted Health Science Center. Based on the belief that humanities were all too often relegated to secondary importance in society, this program attempted to underscore the continuing importance of liberal learning and to bridge the gap traditionally perceived between it and the sciences.

Specific goals for this project included (a) exposure to liberal learning subject matter for persons associated occupationally or educationally with the Health Science Center and for the public in general; (b) stimulation of participating health care professionals to continue an interest in liberal learning throughout their professional careers; (c) role modeling for students who see their professional faculty support an interest in the arts and humanities; (d) extension of personal horizons of the lay citizens who participate; (e) appreciation of the value to society of the humanities and, therefore, of institutions of higher learning in general by the public; and (f) provision for the possibility that other health science centers, upon learning of this program, may take the initiative to use the facilities available to them in their parent or nearby academic institutions.

In order to implement this program, a steering committee composed of individuals representing the interests of the hospital administration, the patients, the arts and the humanities, mapped out the best strategies for accomplishing the stated goals and acted as a review and planning resource once the program was under way. In cooperation with the director and his assistant, this committee provided valuable ideas for making the program both entertaining and educational, insightful suggestions for potential problem areas and promotional possibilities, and broad-based support for the project even before it began.

Three main activities were accomplished under this program. Two of the programs were noon-hour activities and conducted in a lobby of the hospital that was open to all patients, visitors, staff, students, and faculty. Film and lecture series were included under the umbrella title of "Learning at Lunch." While most of the presentations in the lecture series were given by faculty members from the University of Iowa, a few were delivered by people from other institutions. Sample titles of these presentations include: "Scientific and Religious Ethics," "Shakespeare and the Sonnets," "A Very Liberal Rabbi Looks at the Doctrine of Original Sin," "Women and Politics in Historical Perspective," and "Architectural Triumphs of Iowa." The film series was procured from the large collection within the University's audiovisual library and included films from the "American Short Story" series, the "Humanities: Bridge to Ourselves" series, and an original series on comedy of the early film industry entitled the "Clown Princes of Hollywood."

Methods used to publicize these two presentations included master posters which appeared weekly at strategic locations in the Health Science Center as well as fliers which enumerated the entire film or lecture series for the month, announcements sent to the University and local news agents, and public address announcements made in the lobby preceding each event.

Another program partially supported by Project QUILL funds was the Midwinter Reading Retreat, designed to further not only the cardiologic education of internists and family physicians, but to provide a stimulus and opportunity for them, along with their spouses, to expand their general liberal education. Works of physician-authors (Chekhov, Maugham, Selzer and William Carlos Williams) were read and discussed with particular emphasis placed on the links between the authors' medical work and literary creativity. Evaluations by participants in this retreat were extremely enthusiastic.

In this same vein, a literary writing contest was also supported by the QUILL grant and conducted by the College of Medicine student newspaper. Entries from medical students consisted of poetry, satire, essay and fiction, and the winning selections were printed in the newspaper as a part of its regular production.

Evaluation of these varied programs was accomplished in several ways. For "Learning at Lunch," a head count was taken at each event and a brief evaluatory questionnaire was distributed to those in attendance. A description of the program will be prepared for presentation at national meetings and in appropriate medical and hospital journals which reflects these evaluation efforts. In general, the evaluative feedback was very positive, with the most negative comments describing the actual physical conditions associated with the program which were dictated by the constraints of the location.

Perhaps the highest honor of all was a request from Iowa Lutheran Hospital, another large medical complex in Des Moines, Iowa, for information about, and help with, setting up a program in their hospital similar to this one. Based on the university's notions of success and enthusiasm at providing a model for other medical institutions, application has been made for funding from the Iowa Humanities Board in hopes of continuing the efforts at infusing liberal learning into the clinical setting for at least another year.

Contact: Richard M. Caplan, M.D.
             Associate Dean for
                Continuing Medical
                Education
             College of Medicine
             The University of Iowa
             Iowa City, IA 52242
             (319) 353-5763

University of Oklahoma

Liberal Learning and Individual Educational Planning: A Holistic Approach to Adult Education

(September 1978 - August 1979)

Since 1961 the College of Liberal Studies at the University of Oklahoma has offered the Bachelor of Liberal Studies degree through nontraditional procedures designed especially to meet the needs of adult students. Project QUILL provided the resources to review and renovate this established curriculum and make it more responsive to faculty and student needs of the present day.

The College of Liberal Studies offered flexible instructional procedures that were adapted to the individual student in terms of time, location and sequence. Instructional strategies included a combination of extended independent study directed by faculty tutors, intensive short-term seminars taught by interdisciplinary teams, major written assignments and comprehensive examinations. The program had always adhered to a strong concept of core liberal learning.

Immediate objectives of this QUILL project were to regenerate and strengthen the base of liberal learning in the Bachelor of Liberal Studies program in the curricular areas of humanities, natural sciences, and social sciences, while at the same time establishing the means for design and evaluation of individual educational planning more responsive to the unique interests of the learner and to individual cognitive styles. Four steps were planned to meet these needs: (1) definition of revised core studies in liberal education in each of the three curricular areas; (2) exploration of the processes of individual educational planning and development of procedures for designing individual educational programs; (3) solicitation of faculty input on curriculum design and orientation of faculty to newly developed curriculum and procedures; and (4) testing of the new curriculum and individual planning procedures through two student weekend advisory sessions.

Initial efforts were made to redefine the core curriculum through the cooperation of three faculty members representing each of the disciplinary fields—natural sciences, social sciences and humanities. These three faculty consulted widely with other faculty teaching in their areas and based on that consultation, developed new curriculum proposals. Essentially, they sought to establish a central coherent theme, to select reading materials that were current and relevant to that theme, and to reflect the range of disciplines in each of their areas as well as the interconnections between the disciplines.

During this planning phase, two outside consultants visited the campus to advise on experiences at other institutions that combined core learning with individual planning. In addition, a faculty retreat was held away from the campus for three days at which time teams of faculty worked on the three area study proposals, selecting from among options and revising recommendations. By the end of the retreat, the core curricula were compiled and subsequently adopted by the College Executive Committee.

Individual educational planning was assessed by another group of three faculty, from each of the divisions of the college. The intent of the revision was to permit each student a portion of elective space within his/her program for which the student could develop a personally designed study experience, using a variety of content, instructional procedures and resources. In the course of this study, two faculty members visited other institutions to observe programs in operation and a consultant was invited to the campus. As a result of this groundwork, the college initiated the use of Student Learning Contracts for the elective portion of individual student planning, and materials were developed for the use of faculty advisers, the orientation of students, and the designing of study plans.

In order to orient students to the new materials and the procedures for individual program planning, two weekend seminars were held for students at which the new features were presented and explained. So far, the new programs have been well received by students who find the curriculum materials interesting and challenging, and who respond well to the opportunity to form individual learning contracts.

Follow-up sessions with the faculty have also been held to discuss their experience with development of the learning contracts. In addition, printed study guide materials are being prepared to accompany the curricular materials, and there will be examinations based on the new materials.

All of the activities planned under the project have been completed and the new curriculum is in place. It appears to be working successfully and to be well accepted by both faculty and students. Operations of the individual student contracting will continue to be monitored in order to perfect it further, especially in terms of providing more individual counseling to the students during the formation of their learning contracts.

Contact: William H. Maehl, Jr.
Dean, College of Liberal
   Studies
University of Oklahoma
Norman, OK 73037
(405) 325-1061

University of Toledo

Strengthening the Interdisciplinary and Individualized Aspects of the Adult Liberal
Studies Program at the University of Toledo

(September 1978 - June 1979)

The Adult Liberal Studies Program at the University of Toledo is designed to meet the needs of adults over 25 who desire an accelerated
degree in the humanities. Wishing to improve the program, the University requested a grant from Project QUILL to assist in accomplishing three
goals: (1) to strengthen the academic and interdisciplinary quality of a
series of nine topical seminars in the Adult Liberal Studies Program; (2)
to assist students in individualizing their programs to meet occupational,
professional, or personal goals; and (3) to heighten the community's
awareness of the value of a liberal studies degree.

The major body of coursework consists of a series of nine topical seminars, three each in the social sciences, humanities, and natural sciences.
The program, offered at times convenient for working adults, in-
corporates a strong component of individualized study and permits a
high degree of flexibility in terms of choosing the accompanying electives. QUILL was requested to provide a team-teacher for the social
science series, and funding for guest speakers for the social science, humanities, and natural science seminars. These speakers, from the departments of history, anthropology, physics and astronomy, economics, Far
Eastern and Asian history, art, English, American studies, and foreign
languages, as well as class participants representing special areas of community expertise, provided multiple points of view in each seminar.

In attempting to assist students in choosing their electives, the program
offered a course entitled "Career Choice and Contemporary Ethical Decision Making." This course focused first on contemporary ethics from a
global perspective, stressing the interdependence of humankind, based
on such texts as Reinhold Niebuhr's *The Nature and Destiny of Man*,
Mihajlo Mesaronic and Edward Pestal's *Mankind at the Turning Point*,
and Robert Heilbroner's *An Inquiry into the Human Prospect*. The second part of the course, utilizing the Richard Bolles/John Crystal method
of career life planning, based on careful individual value clarification and
self assessment, helped students weigh their own personal interests

against their needs to incorporate marketable skills for broadening future employment possibilities.

The third and final program under the QUILL grant was the sponsorship of a two-day conference at the completion of the seminars which addressed the question of the value of liberal education versus technical and vocational training. Continuing education specialists from seven states, as well as many from diverse areas of Ohio, joined university faculty, students, and representatives from the areas of employment and human resources in sharing information and ideas. Panel discussions followed by workshops on innovative programs for continuing education were devoted to providing models which could incorporate vocational, technical or professional coursework into humanistic degree programs without violating the academic integrity of the liberal arts.

Although there was a feeling among some students in the topical seminars that guest lecturers sometimes took too much class time for their presentations, cutting short the professors' opportunities for emphasizing what they felt was important, student evaluations of guest lecturers were extremely positive. In fact, the social science classes quickly became over-subscribed, and two extra sessions of the spring seminar had to be arranged due to demand.

"Career Choice and Contemporary Ethical Decision-Making" received extremely favorable evaluations. Some students had difficulty in relating Reinhold Niebuhr's readings to their own lives and this part of the course may have to be restructured. Overall, the course filled a definite need and many students asked for a longer version. Part of this may have been due to a "panic" reaction which sets in when it becomes apparent that there are no "magic wands" in any effective career planning course, and that only hard work and tenacity will bring results. It was felt by the instructor that the adult student is perfect for this course, since he or she has had enough life experience to profit by it.

The conference on Liberal Arts and Lifelong Learning benefited professionals in continuing education by bringing them together to share ideas and discuss problems. It did perhaps attempt to cover too much ground, in too short a time, leaving the audience somewhat frustrated when issues and concerns were left hanging. There were problems, too, in that some speakers did not deal with the specific topics assigned. The highlight of the two days revolved around discussion of the Richard Bolles/John Crystal method of career/life planning. Proceedings of the conference are available for those interested.

The QUILL grant for the Adult Liberal Studies program has resulted in increased enrollment in the program and a faculty committee's working with the Dean of the Graduate School on the possibility of a Master of Liberal Studies Program.

Contact: Shirley Leckie
             Associate Dean for
                Continuing Education
             Millsaps College
             Jackson, MS 39210
             (601) 354-5201

University of Wyoming

Strengthening Liberal Learning in Continuing
  Education through Our Alumni—A Statewide
  Project

(August - December 1979)

As the state's only four-year institution of higher learning, the University of Wyoming has a responsibility to illustrate the significance of liberal learning throughout the state. A grant from Project QUILL was requested to establish continuing education courses/activities in the traditional liberal arts by using university alumni who form the strategic link between the college community and the community-at-large.

Three thousand copies of a booklet entitled "The Liberal Arts and Lifelong Learning: A Report to Alumni" was published in August 1979 and sent to the College of Arts and Sciences alumni within the state, Wyoming community college liberal arts faculty, University of Wyoming faculty, members of the University Board of Trustees, state legislators, and other interested individuals. This report on the College of Arts and Sciences conveyed both the spirit of the faculty, students, alumni and friends that makes academic excellence possible as well as explaining the interdependence of activities on-campus and off-campus. It also presented a new program, a "mini-college" for alumni which was to be held during Homecoming Weekend.

The mini-college took place on an afternoon in early October for the dual purposes of informing alumni about the present programs underway in the College of Arts and Sciences as well as to give the college an opportunity to receive suggestions from alumni as to what kinds of outreach programs in liberal learning might be possible in Wyoming communities. The president's proposal for a distinguished lecture series throughout the state was one of the well-received ideas. There was also considerable discussion on specific topics, potential discussion leaders, and possible formats for delivering liberal learning in communities.

Following the mini-college session, the participants met with Alumni Association county directors and other interested individuals in eighteen communities throughout the state to develop specific topics of continuing education classes/activities in their communities. Professors from the departments of physics, botany, theatre, zoology, history, English, mathematics, chemistry, and computer science each joined one or more of the community meetings to illustrate on-campus commitment to the projects. Approximately one quarter of the community meeting participants were alumni of other University of Wyoming colleges, or of liberal arts colleges out-of-state. In several communities, the college dean or project director participated in radio talk shows. On four occasions, leaders of major industrial plants were included in discussions on applied research opportunities for faculty and graduate students, internships, and other projects in the liberal arts of special interest to business.

The results of this community outreach program were varied. It enabled the university to identify qualified leaders of continuing education courses or activities in the liberal arts throughout the state and led to the establishment of an Advisory Council, for which the university is seeking alumni participation. It also resulted in the creation of a college faculty Committee on Alumni Relations which will be combined with the state-wide Advisory Committee on Liberal Learning. Perhaps most important of all, there has been an increased public awareness of the value of liberal learning derived from the radio talk shows in some of the smaller communities. A course on the United States in the twentieth century is scheduled for Farson (pop. 50) and the Eden Valley of Sweetwater County; a social science research project is planned for Wyoming's newest town in Campbell County; a three-course core in the fine arts will be offered in Teton County; a traveling exhibit of college collections in anthropology, art, botany, geology, physics, and zoology is being prepared, and a history department-sponsored Wyoming Historical Survey with alumni involvement is underway.

There was one disappointment along the way. The participation in both the mini-college on campus and at some of the community meetings was lower than expected, considering the comprehensive publicity campaign. Possible reasons for this include (1) a lack of clarity as to precisely what the University hoped to accomplish in these meetings, (2) the relative novelty of this sort of project, and (3) the fact that residents of smaller communities are sometimes deluged with meetings.

But in general, the project met with success, largely due to the active participation of the university faculty, both on and off campus, the staff of the UW Alumni Association and the County Directors of the Association. This outreach project indicates that there are ways and means by which alumni associations can assist their schools in academic as well as non-academic ways.

Contact: John F. Freeman
            Assistant Dean
            College of Arts and Sciences
            University of Wyoming
            Laramie, WY 82071
            (307) 766-4106

106

Part III

Projects Which Combine Career Education and Liberal Learning

Carthage College

The Future and its Implications for Career and
Educational Planning for Liberal Arts Students

(September 1978 - February 1979)

An experimental interim-session course developed especially for freshmen provided the framework for this QUILL-funded program to address the concerns of students, parents, and faculty about the applicability of liberal arts training for career preparation. A full semester of work provided the planning for this course which was offered to 33 students during the month of January 1979.

The pre-course planning was extensive. The project director investigated other career preparation projects at nearby colleges and the college hired an outside consultant to help plan the format of the course. Since the course was designed to use a wide variety of information sources, a great deal of time was spent talking with prospective speakers, reviewing films, readings, and tapes, analyzing texts of vocational interest and individual values, and arranging trips for the students. A major effort was undertaken to recruit students, with the result that the class was somewhat larger than expected.

The course itself met daily for five hours between January 3 and January 24, with the theme of each week focusing upon a particular section. The initial period dealt with an investigation into an expected future society and the anticipated changes in American and global society. Through a series of lectures, films, readings, and discussion of Alvin Toffler's *Future Shock*, students were asked to consider not only the future in general, but specific changes likely in a particular institution or group.

The second section of the course addressed the question of careers more directly. The emphasis was on general values and rewards students desired from work, rather than specific job preparation. Students were asked to clarify what they wanted out of work, what skills they possessed, and the problems of job satisfaction. They each took personality inventory tests and vocational interest exams. Field trips were arranged to observe and interview individuals in a variety of work environments and meet with specialists on career planning and placement. Guest speakers addressed the class on the topic of career preparation and the liberal arts. In addition, students read and discussed Studs Terkel's book *Working*, and wrote essays on their objectives from work, their values, and lengthy accounts of their interviews with various workers.

The final third of the course concentrated on individual career and academic planning. The Carthage College directors of placement and testing met with the class for four days to work on exercises in decision-making, skill assessment, research of particular careers, resume writing, interviewing, and academic preparation. Students read and discussed Richard Bolles' *What Color is Your Parachute?* At the conclusion of this section they met with the dean of the college to discuss the liberal arts curriculum at Carthage and its application to career preparation.

Course evaluation was carried out through anonymous critiques of each phase, and individual meetings with the instructor. Responses were overwhelmingly positive. The minor criticism focused on specific speakers, readings, or approaches, rather than the general philosophy and intent of the course.

The success of the course led to a number of possible follow-ups. Carthage is considering making the course a regular offering, using some of the original students as "para-professionals" to work with their peers on career planning. Materials purchased especially for the course have already received wider use by the entire student body, but most importantly, the grant and resulting course stimulated a new interest among both students and faculty in the general question of career preparation and the liberal arts.

Contact: Thomas J. Noer
             Assistant Professor of History
             Carthage College
             Kenosha, WI 53141
             (414) 551-8500

College of New Rochelle
School of New Resources

Where Can We Go with the Liberal Arts?

(January 1979 - January 1980)

As one of the three major emphases of adult education at the School of New Resources, the Project QUILL grant concentrated upon enabling students to transform traditional liberal arts into arts that relate to a better and more human life. The project began by assisting faculty to clarify the integral connection between learning and work skills, and, more specifically, between a given academic discipline and the skills and attitudes required for successful careers.

The School of New Resources is committed to the liberal arts as the most suitable vehicle for the education of adults because of the broad perspective and depth of understanding they provide. The school recognizes the special needs and strengths of the adult learner and has designed a program which enables these students to become responsible for their education and take an active role in the learning process. Each semester students and faculty work together in curriculum development to assess learning needs and design new seminars to be offered the following semester. The seminars are then offered if they meet academic standards and have an enrollment of at least fifteen. In addition to the group learning experience of the seminar, each student is expected to initiate and carry out an independent learning project, the results of which are shared with fellow students in a formal presentation. This project offers opportunities for exploration of life/career directions.

Recognizing that adults return to college for the purpose of effecting changes in their lives, preparing for new careers, or rethinking life plans, the need for career education must be addressed within the framework of the program. This QUILL-funded project developed a form of career education appropriate for adults pursuing a BA degree and intrinsic to the liberal arts program.

Seven of the most competent instructors from a variety of disciplines rethought their teaching methods and modified their course content to meet the desired goal. In a series of workshops prior to and during the spring semester these faculty (a) identified skills required for their disciplines and saw the relevance of these skills to various work settings;

(b) developed a plan to utilize independent study projects (called Life Arts Projects) for students to gather information about professionals in careers related to academic disciplines; and (c) devised means of aiding students to create new academic courses which would serve their career needs. Although these workshops were meant to be a process of self-insight for the faculty members, they became more of an intellectual exercise given the fact that faculty were unfamiliar with the process and in some cases subliminally resistant. Although no standard formula for integrating career development principles into the liberal arts courses emerged, the faculty demonstrated a revitalized and specifically oriented teaching style.

The second stage of this project was the actual instruction of students, sharing with them the value of liberal arts for life and career, and providing them with the ability to translate learning from the classroom into new career and life directions. It was hoped that students would change their understanding of the term "skill" from a definition involving credentials and knowledge or ability to one where activities are described which involve skills which are transferable from one situation to another.

Pre- and post-course questionnaires were distributed to students as part of the evaluation of this segment. Although there were no controls to determine whether such changes occurred in other classes within the same liberal arts courses (i.e. those not included in the QUILL project), the results remain significant. In order of change (most to least), the ranking of seven classes were: statistics, oral communications, math, logic, abnormal psychology, sociology, and fiction. Unlike what might have been expected, the most change did not occur in those courses which have traditionally been considered most applicable to the world of work (i.e. sociology and psychology).

Finally, this project disseminated these models for integrating career concerns into liberal arts courses to faculty in related disciplines, staff and faculty of other campuses of New Resources, and also to staff of alliance colleges (adult college programs with similar educational philosophies). The dissemination to New Resources faculty was accomplished through a meeting to introduce faculty to career/planning concepts and to facilitate discussion with participating QUILL project faculty about their successes and failures. More than 97 percent of those attending indicated their intention to integrate some aspects of career/life planning into their courses. The dissemination to Alliance colleges was accomplished through a booklet entitled "Where Can We Go With the Liberal Arts," available through the School of New Resources. It summarizes the experiences of this project in addition to reprinting "The Transferable Skills Map" (an adaptation of Bolles and Zenoff) to help students identify skills they use and enjoy.

Contact: Muriel Dance   Sister Ruth Dowd
             Director of Curriculum   Director
             School of New Resources   School of New Resources
             College of New Rochelle   College of New Rochelle
             New Rochelle, NY 10801   New Rochelle, NY 10801
             (914) 235-3066   (914) 235-3066

City University of New York
John Jay College of Criminal Justice

The Ethics of Law Enforcement

(February 1981 - January 1982)

While long-established fields like law and medicine have already integrated ethical components into professional education, the newer academic disciplines, still struggling to develop their basic identities and orientations, have been less responsive to the need for emphasizing values. In the belief that police education should include in its required curriculum a thorough consideration of the ethical dilemmas and value decisions of police work, John Jay College of Criminal Justice requested a grant from Project QUILL to develop an interdisciplinary course and accompanying textual materials on the "Ethics of Law Enforcement."

John Jay College is a fertile ground for the proposed implantation of ethical awareness within the framework of liberal learning, because a large proportion of the students are either already civil servants (in police, fire, corrections, and parole departments) or are preparing to enter civil service careers. The impact of such a course would, therefore, be felt not only by the students themselves, but by the communities they will be serving.

On delving into the content he wished the course to cover, the project director decided it would be impossible to include all the material in a single course, with the result that two courses were devised. The first, Philosophy/Criminal Justice I (Police Ethics) will be offered for the first time in the fall of 1981. The second will examine issues in judicial and correctional ethics.

These courses will not provide students with panaceas for all moral choices, but will aid them in perceiving the variegated nature of ethical dilemmas, in recognizing the appropriate ethical theories, and in developing an analytical style of thought. The courses will assist police officers who make critical, often life-or-death decisions, to grasp the wide range of moral issues encountered in police work, and to apply the tools of ethical analysis to the practical problems they face. The non-police student will acquire a deeper awareness of the diverse and difficult value choices police officers must make to perform their duties effectively.

While the exact content of the courses may vary from term to term,

113

some proposed areas to be covered include discretion (the justification and ethical hazards of discretion, professionalism, and codes of ethics), deadly physical force (justification for the necessary use of force, responsibilities inherent in the exercise of authority and power, the shoot to wound-stop-kill dilemma), misconduct (cynicism and its effect on police misconduct, a sequential perspective of the erosion of ethical values, combative techniques, and ethical awareness/workshop training), politics (political interference, internal and external influences on ethical conduct, pressure groups), discrimination (the justification of affirmative action programs, police-community relations, stigmatization and police morale), and civil disobedience (ethical grounds for civil dissent and public violence, moral distinctions from other types of dissent, police as participants and as defenders of public order).

The course, while under the sponsorship of the philosophy faculty, will be taught, in various terms, by professors from the departments of philosophy, theology, and police science. Guest lectures by law enforcement officials and by faculty members in allied disciplines will illustrate the different facets of moral conduct which relate to criminal justice. The aim is to achieve a true symposium, supplemented by small discussion groups, and hence to foster a mature and rounded understanding of the morality of law enforcement. Participation by members of the sociology, psychology, and government departments will also be encouraged.

The text for the course will be an anthology on police ethics which will be developed by the project director. In addition, the Institute for Criminal Justice Ethics, located at John Jay College, is sponsoring a national conference on police ethics, to be held in New York City in April 1982. The proceedings of the conference will be published by the John Jay Press, and will be useful in criminal justice education programs throughout the country. The topics to be treated include privacy issues in police surveillance, selection of undercover targets, women in policing, whistle-blowing, and deadly force.

Members of the John Jay faculty who have experience in measuring student values will participate in designing an evaluation survey for the course. Faculty observations and reports by the instructors will also be used in determining the impact of the course on student thinking.

Contact: Timothy Stroup
John Jay College of Criminal
Justice
New York, NY 10019
(212) 489-3598

Dartmouth College

The Integration of the Teaching of Ethics in Professional Education: An Institution-Wide Program at Dartmouth College

(September 1978 - August 1979)

Based upon the principle that the field of ethics clearly demonstrates
the need for and value of cooperation between liberal arts and professional education, two Dartmouth faculty members from the departments
of philosophy and psychiatry began testing their theory of ethics in a
number of the college's professional programs. Under QUILL sponsorship, the cross-disciplinary teaching of ethics was expanded in the Dartmouth Medical School, and started in the Tuck School of Business Administration and the Thayer School of Engineering. In addition, extensive conversations were begun with a group of nursing clinical specialists
which led to spontaneous development of that program as well.

This project set out to overcome the separation between liberal arts
education and professional education, which was constantly reinforced
by institutional structures, language, and curriculum. If liberal arts
education has as its goal the training of the individual to think clearly, to
judge and act wisely, and to communicate effectively, then successful
liberal arts education is a part of successful professional education. Both
must instill the habit of critical thought and self-education, not just a
given body of knowledge.

Nowhere is the commonality between liberal arts and professional
education more clearly demonstrated than in the field of ethics. The ex-
plosion of knowledge, the growing interdependence of economic and development decisions, the increased complexity of modern industrial
society, and the capabilities of modern science have made the improved
and expanded teaching of ethics a national need in professional as well as
undergraduate liberal arts education. The location of a number of professional schools on the Dartmouth campus created an ideal situation for
the testing of the proposed model.

Since resolution of most moral disputes depends primarily on becoming clear about the relevant facts of the case, the theory espoused by
these two professors helped to determine what facts were morally relevant, but called upon experts in the individual professional fields to
determine the actual facts of the case. Thus, in all efforts launched by this

grant, joint teaching and research was undertaken with experts in medicine, business, engineering, and nursing. Lecture series were provided as part of the required curriculum in both the Dartmouth Medical School and the Thayer School of Engineering, and developed for the Tuck School of Business Administration. All three series are being incorporated into the ongoing curriculum of these schools.

Over a six-month period, the two project directors met with a group of nursing clinical specialists to lay the foundation for an extensive program in ethics for nurses. Reception of these ideas was so enthusiastic that additional outside funding is now being sought to establish an on-going program and several members of the nursing faculty are beginning research on their own in this area.

In general, the QUILL project at Dartmouth College helped to promote the concern for ethical issues in professional education and developed a core body of material, methods, and faculty to supplement and enrich the efforts to teach ethics within each professional school. Case materials were developed for use by other institutions and closer substantive relationships were established between the liberal arts faculty and professional school faculty. Important insights gained from this multi-field approach have proven its value not only for increasing the awareness of the importance of ethics in the professions, but also for developing a more adequate ethical theory to deal with a multitude of situations.

Contact: Bernard Gert   Charles Culver
            Professor of Philosophy   Professor of Psychiatry
            Dartmouth College   Dartmouth College
            Hanover, NH 03755   Hanover, NH 03755
            (603) 646-2022   (603) 646-2214

East Tennessee State University

The Professional Imagination: An Introductory
  Required Course in the Pre-Professional Core
  Option Program

(September 1980 - June 1981)

As part of a much larger effort of curriculum redesign, Project QUILL supported the efforts of the College of Arts and Sciences at ETSU to promote interdisciplinary studies within a distributive core program currently dominated by disciplinary thinking. Since the majority of students preparing for professional careers often chose majors outside the liberal arts and sciences, it became obvious that many such students did not perceive, until too late, the value of traditional core requirements. Therefore, to meet the needs of these students intending to pursue professional careers in such fields as law, medicine, business and industry, a complete program of optional instruction is being created with the new course "The Professional Imagination" at its core.

Specifically, this multi-format interdisciplinary course was designed to incorporate lectures, films, panel discussions and debates as means of realizing its five stated goals: (1) to trace the history and development of modern professionalism; (2) to explore the world of professional education including its achievements and limitations; (3) to analyze the language of professionalism, especially with regard to problems of communication in a pluralistic society; (4) to define the role of the professional individual in a democratic society; and (5) to set professional theory against practical economics.

Planning for both the new pre-professional option and the specialized introductory course was undertaken during the fall semester of 1980 by two distinct groups—the Pre-Professional Task Force which pursued the overall planning objectives for the program and the Interdisciplinary Teaching Team which established the curriculum, determined the course objectives and prepared the examinations and supplementary readings for the course.

"The Professional Imagination" was offered during the second semester of the 1980-81 academic year, to 32 underclassmen. This coordinated team-taught course involved professors from five disciplines: physics, philosophy, history, political science and English. The ultimate goal of this course was to show each pre-professional student the various ways to integrate the diverse subject matters customarily presented in a general education program. Part of this integration resulted from the work and consultation of the teaching team, and part depended upon the student's ability to draw together the loose ends. This course attempted to demonstrate that the concerns of historians, political scientists, literary humanists, philosophers, and scientists essentially overlap and that various disciplines are not separate compartments or pigeon-holes in which disparate knowledge can be found. On the contrary, these disciplines provide different perspectives in the pursuit of the total knowledge needed for the education of the whole person.

The ultimate objective, therefore, of this introductory course was to foster a new set of positive attitudes toward general education in the sciences, the social sciences, and the humanities. This objective is the hardest to achieve and is not measurable in any sense of the word.

Following actual presentation of the course, the teaching team agreed that a little more time should have been devoted to tracing the historical roots of the major professions, and general background material on professional education should have been presented toward the beginning of the syllabus. This initial emphasis upon educational demands and requirements would have provided a needed focus for students whose first concern was basically vocational, and then the humanistic dimensions of the course would have been stronger if predicated upon the students' primary interests.

Student evaluations demonstrated that they felt the course was extremely valuable as an introduction to professional career education. Several reacted adversely to generally low grades on the examinations and others felt the course was disorganized, attributing part of this difficulty to the lack of a textbook. Most students experienced difficulty in working in a predominantly critical and analytical mode, and some thought the course was too advanced for sophomore students. Only a few students consistently contributed to class discussion.

The planning, conduct, and teaching of "The Professional Imagination" were part of a larger effort to design a core option for students pursuing professional career education. Funds obtained from Project QUILL were augmented by the acquisition of a Consultant Grant from NEH thereby permitting the Task Force to continue its efforts to float a pilot program for the 1981-82 academic year, with plans to implement the whole program in a three-year period from 1982-1985.

As a result of modifications made after the initial year of this effort, "The Professional Imagination" will be team-taught by three professors (a humanist, a social scientist, and a natural scientist), with the program coordinated by the project director. The Task Force has already appointed subcommittees to work with officials of the College of Medicine to plan coordinated activities between the colleges and to provide further experiences in terms of continuing medical education.

Contact: Edward F. J. Tucker   Frederick O. Waage
              Head   Department of English
              Department of English   East Tennessee State
              The Citadel   University
              Charleston, SC 29409   Johnson City, TN 37601
              (803) 792-5012   (615) 929-4339

Ferrum College

Innovative Approaches for Integrating
Humanities Programs with Career
Education in the Classroom

(September 1979 - May 1980)

In an attempt to increase the awareness of and interest in the humanities on the Ferrum campus, a highly unusual and successful project was
undertaken to present forty dramatic portrayals of significant issues and
ideas of important historical figures along with a number of other live
theatrical performances. With a modest grant from Project QUILL, in
combination with other small funding sources, Ferrum College sponsored three plays, three major addresses by distinguished outside
visitors, nineteen interdisciplinary seminars on major themes of Western
thought, seven debates focusing primarily on historical topics, nine live
performances of music or dance, and the screening of five films.

This innovative approach to bringing the humanities to life was designed to help strengthen the relationship between Ferrum's humanities
minor and the career majors in human services. In 1974 Ferrum initiated
a fully accredited baccalaureate program for career education in the human services after a long history as a two-year institution. Coupled with
this professional training, a strong humanities core curriculum required
eighteen credit hours in the junior and senior years. Therefore, each Ferrum student graduates not only with course work and field experience in
some area of professional study in the human services, but a mandatory
minor in the humanities as well.

Designed around this year's college theme, "The Quality of Life: Alternatives in the Global Village," the QUILL project explored this concept
from two directions. The first examined the theme from an historical
perspective, calling upon the greatest minds of the past for their insights.
The second approach attempted to reach out into the contemporary
"global village" and bring to Ferrum representative samplings of the
finest in non-Western culture.

Selected presentations demonstrate the variety of activities and concepts encompassed in this program. Debates were staged between faculty
members representing Niccolo Machiavelli and Sir Thomas More, as
well as Booker T. Washington and W.E.B. DuBois. Seminars were offered on topics such as "Science and Human Understanding" featuring

Charles Darwin, Karl Marx, and Richard Wagner, and "Democracy: The Eternal Illusion?" involving Plato, Benito Mussolini, and Andrew Jackson. Among the films shown were "Hamlet," "Pride and Prejudice," and "The Seven Samurai." Live theatrical performances, classical concerts, demonstrations of Indian and Japanese dance, as well as appropriate excerpts from longer plays were presented.

The original proposal envisioned video-taping each of the scheduled programs in a library facility that accommodated 50 persons; however within two weeks of the project's inauguration the programs had to be moved to a facility accommodating 200 and certain special occasions were scheduled for the college chapel.

One reason for this surprising response to this experiment was the faculty's eager support of the project. Though Ferrum's faculty of 70 each offered 15 hours of classes a semester, 50 of them took part in QUILL programs with a few appearing as many as four times. Another factor contributing to the success of the program was the planning and coordination engendered by the grant. The advent of the QUILL project caused virtually every academic department to participate in planning programs around the project theme and coordinate its plans with the other disciplines.

Other sections of the Ferrum community contributed spiritual and financial support. The college's Campus Programs Council, for example, devoted much of its own budget to adding five major performances of music and dance. The student government officers volunteered to underwrite the cost of showing four of the five films planned for the series and by the end of the second semester, volunteered a substantial portion of their remaining budget to pay for a major speaker to address the project's theme at the end of the year (former Senator James Abourezk of South Dakota). A final, unanticipated source of support, was a HEW Title III grant in October 1979, $1500 of which was earmarked to help defray the cost of costume design, technical services, and five of the more costly programs.

Although enthusiasm was extremely high for this project, a number of problems were encountered as the original proposal was being implemented. The 40 small programs envisioned in the proposal could not be "mass produced" in long sessions before television cameras for subsequent classroom use. Instead, limitations of faculty time and the advantages gained by presentations before student audiences dictated that the programs be presented on a regular basis throughout the year. This meant that one QUILL program was planned, publicized, and executed nearly every week of the academic session. In addition, insufficient attention to the technical details of video-taping so many events, and the need to move the "stage" to larger surroundings resulted in spotty productions—often with poor lighting and soft voices.

In spite of the vexing technical problems, faculty and students were virtually unanimous in their approval of this undertaking and insisted that it be continued and a future theme selected—"American Culture: What Do We Cherish, What Do We Share?" Funding of this effort will come from increased Title III sources and a local foundation. It was anticipated that the number of events would be reduced to 20, allowing for improved quality and avoiding the danger of oversaturating the potential audience with too many programs on the same theme. Even with this more modest approach, demonstrated student interest was shown by the request that they be permitted to research characters for the program and present them in debate with the faculty. Programmers were delighted with the prospect of student volunteers and planned to use them in such sessions as those on Indian policy and the justification of the Spanish-American War.

Contact:	Douglas Foard
	Professor of History
	Ferrum College
	Ferrum, VA 24088
	(703) 365-2121

Furman University

The Humanist in the Working World

(January - October 1979)

With a combination of funds from Project QUILL and the National Endowment for the Humanities, Furman University launched an innovative program placing six humanities faculty members in summer internship positions to help them better understand the relationship between their academic disciplines and the employment situations their students would face upon graduation.

Based on the assumption that liberal arts students are the least likely to seek guidance for careers and the liberal arts faculty have at best a vague comprehension of the relationships between their academic disciplines and career education, this project successfully opened the minds of many in the Furman community.

The internship program was introduced in May 1979 with a luncheon and workshop led by John R. Coleman, president of the Edna McConnell Clark Foundation and author of *Blue Collar Journal.* During his remarks at both events, Dr. Coleman spoke directly about possible experiences that might be anticipated on the job, as well as the implications of non-academic work experiences for all members of a college faculty. His remarks provided the future interns with a perception and understanding they would not ordinarily have had, and at the same time inspired enthusiasm in faculty members not initially undertaking internships. In addition, his appearance at Furman provided a focus for public announcement of the program in the local press.

In June 1979 six members of the Furman faculty began their internships: an English professor worked in corporate communications for Springs Mills; the chairman of the history department researched and edited at the South Carolina Historical Society; an associate professor of French wrote and produced radio dramas for National Public Radio; a political scientist assisted the Greenville Solicitor; an art historian developed programs for the new Andrew Wyeth collection at the Greenville County Museum of Art; and a Spanish professor worked in creative services for the local NBC television affiliate.

Each internship was successful. Although they immediately shared their enthusiasm for their experiences with their Furman colleagues, the culmination of this program occurred at the "Humanists in the Working World" convocation and full day program on October 17th. All humanities departments were invited to actively participate in these activities; each assigned a departmental coordinator to assist the QUILL director in relating the events to the needs of their disciplines, and each of eight departments invited three to five relatively recent graduates to return to Furman and provide information about careers related to their college major.

All faculty, returning graduates, and approximately 1400 students attended the university convocation at which time the summer interns related their experiences. During a "talk back" session informal questions were encouraged that focused on the moral questions facing humanists who worked in a "bottom line" oriented world.

Following the convocation, the alumni participated in a luncheon for which each department had its own table. The informal structure provided time for the graduates to tell their former instructors about the courses they wished they had taken, and the books they were glad they had read. Even the most traditional faculty members responded favorably and were ready to admit that in-class learning must have had some effect on students' lives after college. The afternoon featured career programs sponsored by the eight departments and attended by twenty to sixty students each.

The overall benefits from the program were very positive. Furman obtained a high degree of visibility in the community it serves and in the academic world generally. In addition, it gained six faculty members who became better career advisors, more convinced of the values of experimental education and the values of the humanities disciplines they teach.

At this point it is unclear whether there will be actual curriculum change as a result of this program, but clearly there will be more emphasis on writing and speaking skills and more realistic examples woven into class discussion.

For the students, the benefits were significant. Following the convocation, the participating faculty members received notes not only from their own majors or students they knew, but from students who were excited about career possibilities they presented.

As an institution, Furman moved from a slightly defensive attitude toward the liberal arts to a stance which is positive and affirmative. Although new courses or majors have not been added, applications have increased with only a limited slippage in the enrollment in traditional major fields. By approaching the problem of educating students for living as well as training them for a livelihood, Furman is seeking a balance which provides for a realistic assessment of competencies and skills with a full fledged continuing commitment to the liberal arts mission of this small selective university.

Contact: Judith Gatlin
            Director of Career Programs
            Furman University
            Greenville, NC 29613
            (803) 294-2106

George Washington University

Integration of the Humanities into a Program in
   Pre-Professional Education for Liberal Arts
   Graduates

(January 1979 - January 1980)

Two important issues in contemporary higher education supplied the background for the QUILL project at George Washington University: (1) the so-called new vocationalism among undergraduates that leads them to discount the traditional liberal arts curriculum, and (2) the criticism of the professional schools for failing to ground their students in good professional ethics.

In order to meet these challenges, this grant was used to expand the required weekly seminars for liberal arts undergraduates engaged in internships in pre-professional off-campus settings to include not only members of the appropriate professional school faculty, but also members of the humanities faculties as co-teachers. By the end of the second semester of the grant, the following faculty teaching teams had been active: philosophy/medicine; English literature/education; history/law; religion/gerontology; American literature/arts administration; American studies/urban planning; and Romance languages/law. In addition, the project director formed a core of 20 - 25 faculty from a wide range of departments and schools who participated in a very sharp, ongoing debate centering upon the relationships between the educational resources of the humanities and preparation for meaningful career lives in modern society.

In addition to the regularly-scheduled seminars for interns, George Washington sponsored a regional conference entitled "The Humanities, Education and Working." Although this conference was in essence a self-evaluating summary meeting, more than 90 individuals attended, including most participating faculty, selected students, other interested George Washington faculty, and administrators from colleges and universities throughout the region.

For several years a group of work-study courses, known collectively as the Service-Learning Program (SLP) had been a means of experimental education for undergraduates in all departments. Originally under the sole supervision of faculty members from the five professional schools, the courses focused upon such areas as Urban Legal Services, Issues in

Education and Human Services, Issues in American Health Care, Issues in Managing the Arts, Community Planning and Development, Social Issues in Engineering, and Society and Aging—all enabling students to incorporate off-campus pre-professional work placements into their liberal arts program. Students chose sections according to the general professional area of their field placements, working roughly two days a week in their placements and attending a weekly seminar in which readings and discussions focused on the social, personal, moral, and intellectual implications of a particular vocational choice.

Although the SLP courses had been to some degree humanistic in their emphases by encouraging self-conscious inquiry into the values as well as the methods of various professions, the introduction of trained humanists not only facilitated the adopting of professionally relevant materials from historical, philosophical, and literary sources, but also brought a different point-of-view to bear on professional questions. Although there was no one clear meaning for "humanism" and the "humanities," this experiment excited speculation about both the vocabulary and the values of professions and the humanities.

As faculty members continued their discussions and made plans for the regional conference, all expressed surprise that there was so much common ground between professionals and humanists. Most faculty teams found that their seminar discussions tended to cluster around large interrelated questions of values and terminology. (What is Justice? What is Art? What are the implications of calling someone a "patient," a "senior citizen," a "schizophrenic"?) The humanists' large investment in language and definition dovetailed nicely with the professionals' concerns. Several participants commented upon the high degree of student enthusiasm in the courses and suggested that "real world" placements might be made a regular part of the degree program in all academic departments.

In assessing the impact of QUILL on the George Washington campus there are certain clear measurements of its success. A number of faculty members are undertaking specific research projects to pursue interests awakened by the team-teaching experience. A number of the team-taught efforts continue beyond the time of the grant period and further team-teaching experiments in other courses are being planned.

Less easy to quantify are individual perspectives. Students have testified to the way the SLP courses made much of their earlier academic coursework "come together" into an intellectual unity. They have also claimed that certain habits encouraged by the humanities—the analysis of problems, the analysis of language, the consideration of social and ethical implications of action—will shape the way they regard their future professional pursuits.

The QUILL project also made a modest impact on faculty relationships. Faculty members from different divisions of George Washington University had seldom had extensive professional dealings with each other. These collaborations have promoted an intercollegiality, a dialogue across professional divisions that may be fruitful in bringing about further interdisciplinary activity.

Contact: Judith A. Plotz   Roderick S. French
              Associate Professor of English   Director, Division of
              George Washington   Experimental Programs
                University   George Washington
              Washington, DC 20052   University
              (202) 676-6515   Washington, DC 20052
                                                  (202) 676-7565

Gonzaga University

Incorporating Liberal Learning Values into Professional Decision Training

(June 1980 - May 1982)

Realizing that students in the University's various professional schools
sometimes perceive liberal learning to be unrelated to their career-
oriented training, and watching these students become unwittingly chan-
nelled into pursuits which stifle the philosophical and cultural tendencies
acquired in earlier years, Gonzaga sought QUILL support to provide a
practicable and pragmatic approach for integrating liberal learning into
the professional curriculum of the School of Business Administration.
Under this proposal, Gonzaga will introduce a liberal arts base into management decision-making processes in a logical, yet rigorous, manner
consistent with contemporary analytical trends in the business sector.

The project introduces a series of instructional modules into a required
management course offered to undergraduate students enrolled in Gonzaga University's School of Business Administration. Stressing the
importance of ethical/societal issues related to real-life business situations, the modules focus on a value-oriented decision-making process
which uses utility theory concepts. Utility theory techniques afford an
avenue for incorporating liberal learning value concepts into the
analytical decision-making framework currently employed by modern
business managers while also providing a means of measuring the
relative preference that individuals have for various choices available to
them.

The instructional modules will be designed by a professor of ethics and
a faculty member of the School of Business Administration. The case-
study situations will describe potential business situations which involve
ethical and/or societal implications which can not be ignored. Individual
students will be required to make their own business management decisions, and to explain or defend their positions. Different choices, made
by other participants, will also be discussed and examined. Students will
then be acquainted with techniques for quantitatively measuring the
utility, or preference of their decisions and will be required to make utility based decisions. Each situation will conclude with a critique during
which the professor will highlight key business and ethical/societal issues

129

which should, or could, be taken into account in the decision-making process.

The faculty members involved in this project have already reviewed current literature and developed a bibliography concerned with potential applications of utility theory to characteristic business/management decisions having ethical/societal issues. They have undertaken preliminary development and field testing of an assessment methodology, and have begun development of forms to be used by students when recording the preference for one course of action in comparison with other alternatives. At the present time, they are developing decision scenarios which reflect potential conflict situations in priorities and values. During the summer months of 1981, the assessment methodology and decision scenarios will be refined and prepared for use in an instructional setting for fall or spring term use.

The instructional modules will serve as a vehicle to evaluate the methodology and pedagogy chosen by the project director. If the individual utility functions adopted by the students reveal a logical consistency of choice, the method will evidence validity. In this regard, the expression of student preferences must not only incorporate their own values in a rational way, but it must also be reasonable and understandable to them and to others. If significant inconsistency exists, the approach will have to be modified.

A survey will also be conducted among the student participants to determine the extent to which the utility theory methodology permitted them to incorporate aspects of their own value systems into their decision processes. These same students also will be asked to comment upon their reaction to extending this participative mode of instruction on decision making to other classes.

Contact: Joseph G. Monks
             School of Business
               Administration
             Gonzaga University
             Spokane, WA 99258
             (509) 328-4220

Hiram College

Exploring the Feasibility of Dual Degree Programs in the Humanities and Social Sciences
at Hiram College

(January - May 1980)

As a cooperative effort to combine a strong liberal arts education with well-defined career preparation, Hiram College explored the possibility of establishing a number of new dual-degree programs to permit students to transfer into professional schools for their senior year and to earn a Hiram B.A. while, in essence, beginning their careers. At the time of its QUILL proposal, Hiram currently offered cooperative programs in three areas, all related to the natural or physical sciences: engineering, nursing, and medical technology. Through Project QUILL, a means was being sought to undertake an exploration of the feasibility of dual-degree programs in the humanities and social sciences as well.

The most compelling reason underlying the feasibility study for dual-degree programs in the humanities and social sciences was based upon the anxieties that today's undergraduates experience due to the vicissitudes and constraints imposed by the American economy. Students fear that a liberal arts education will not train them for any particular type of work; understandably, they wish to acquire skills that they can sell on the marketplace. But professional schools have a different interest. They seek students who are literate, intellectually mature, versatile, and discriminating. They seek, in short, liberal arts graduates. In an effort to combine these interests and condense this process, the QUILL project at Hiram hoped to accelerate education by juxtaposing general and specialized education in a complementary manner.

Throughout the course of the grant, reception to this idea was mixed. An agreement was signed with the Graduate School of Public and International Affairs at the University of Pittsburgh which combines, on a 3-2 format, Hiram's liberal arts program with their programs leading to master's degrees in international affairs, public administration, and urban and regional planning. A proposal for a dual degree program in journalism was not feasible, although a "guaranteed admissions" relationship with the S.I. Newhouse School of Public Communications at Syracuse University was achieved.

In the area of international business, negotiations were proceeding (rather optimistically) with several schools, including the American Graduate School of International Management in Glendale, Arizona. Unfortunately, it was impossible to work out a dual-degree program with an architecture school.

Although not included in the original QUILL proposal, Hiram broadened its area of focus and moved to establish dual-degree programs in other areas. An agreement was consummated with the School of Applied Social Science of Case Western Reserve University, leading to a master's degree in the field of social work. Conversations were also begun with the Weatherhead School of Business Administration at Case Western Reserve University and the Kogod School of Business Management at American University. In addition, programs were investigated with Boston University School of Forestry and Environmental Affairs, and the Rhode Island School of Design.

Although students were not yet aware of these opportunities for career preparation, faculty response to the programs was mixed. Initially the project aroused suspicion among the faculty members, but in many cases faculty were cooperative, even enthusiastic, about programs planned in areas related to their fields. In every case, the college's Committee on Educational Planning and Policy approved the programs with little or no dissent.

As a result of this research/investigative effort, the project director offered two generalizations of interest to others who might pursue this type of cooperative effort. First, success is possible only in an atmosphere of mutual respect. In other words, strive for cooperative arrangements with schools interested in your students, while at the same time being discriminating of professional programs. Secondly, interinstitutional programs need to be reciprocal endorsements of academic *programs*, not individual *courses*. This is the underlying reason for insisting on the simultaneous awarding of the bachelors and master degrees, instead of simply transferring individual courses through the registrar.

Contact: Kenneth Kolson
             Coordinator, Inter-
                 Institutional Planning
             Hiram College
             Hiram, OH 44234
             (216)569-3211

Johnson County Community College

Topical Integration of Humanities and Career
Education

(August 1978 - March 1979)

In a broad sense, Johnson County Community College requested
QUILL support in order to advance already initiated efforts to bring humanities education or liberal learning to students enrolled in career preparation programs. The college had settled upon a strategy for accomplishing this which enabled the humanities faculty to work with career
program faculty in developing units on specific humanities topics which
would be integrated into current courses in the selected career programs.

Since most community college career programs are designed to prepare their graduates for immediate employment and are therefore highly
concentrated with regard to the amount of technical or vocational
courses required, little or no room remains for exposure to humanities or
general education courses. Recognizing this fact, JCCC believed that the
most feasible avenue for exposing students in these programs to humanistic education was through judicious integration of clearly focused
humanities issues into existing career program courses.

Specifically, QUILL provided support services for the development of
two new efforts through travel funds for staff research and consultation,
support of outside consultants on campus, and development of television
tapes of classroom lectures and conversations with the consultants.

Two areas of specialization were the focus of these activities. An instructor in philosophy developed materials pertaining to ethical issues in
nursing and in business, while an instructor in history developed materials and presentation on the history of law enforcement in America.

Although individual courses were not prepared with the support of the
QUILL grant, presentations and materials on specific topics in humanities were prepared for future integration into existing courses in career
programs in business, nursing, and administration of justice.

Within the area of ethics, three consultants were brought to the campus who conducted public lectures and/or were interviewed in the television studio so that permanent tapes would be available for use in pertinent courses. The most notable of these consultants was Dr. John
Conklin of Tufts University who spent two days on the campus meeting

with faculty from the humanities area, business and economics division, and the administration of justice program.

In addition, seven case problems on ethical issues in business were developed posing real-life situations which involved ethical choices of both personal and social dimensions. These case problems were introduced to students in management courses and were very well received.

Finally, a one-credit hour course, "Ethical Issues in American Health Care," was developed in consort with the nursing faculty, which focused on issues such as patients' rights, life and death, scarcity of resources, and professional concerns in health care. This team-taught course was to have been offered on an experimental basis during the Fall 1979 semester.

The second area of concentration, Law Enforcement and History, funded an outside consultant who made live and video-taped presentations on women in crime and women's prisons. In addition to traveling for research purposes, a JCCC instructor developed four classroom presentations on (1) the history of the police and the political machine, (2) the history of changing definitions of crime, (3) the history of vagrancy laws, and (4) the Bill of Rights. Each classroom presentation was video-taped for future uses as well.

In general, this attempt to integrate humanities issues into existing career courses was highly successful. The energy given to the project by two professors was infectious, and other liaisons developed between career and humanities faculty which resulted in planning and development of additional integrative schemes.

In other respects JCCC learned a great deal about making integrative efforts more successful. Both instructors felt that the absence of release time from their regular teaching loads while implementing the modules caused difficulties. The coordination with career program faculty was difficult due to schedule and time concerns and there was not sufficient time devoted to the lead-in and phase-out periods framing the presentations. Therefore, the burden of integrating the presentation was placed upon the career program instructor which was not satisfactory.

The impact of these efforts on students was not as influential as originally hoped, but since initial problems have been identified, it is expected that future modules can be implemented more smoothly. More effort needs to be made on the part of the career program instructor to place the presentation in a continuous context of instruction if the integrative schemes are to be successful. In addition, career program faculty members need to be involved at a much earlier stage of the development of the humanities module.

Contact: Landon Kirchner
Director, Division of
Humanities and Social
Sciences
Johnson County Community
College
Overland Park, KS 66210
(913) 888-8500 ext. 156

Juniata College

Integrating Career Education and Liberal Learning through Improved Academic Advising

(April 1979 - June 1980)

In order to improve the integration of liberal learning with career and professional education at Juniata College, a QUILL award was made to underwrite the costs of a week-long faculty development workshop. Specifically, this program called for improving the advising skills of the faculty members who in turn could help students broaden their educational objectives in order to meet both the specifics of career education and the breadth of liberal education.

In 1971 a new curriculum was introduced at Juniata College which replaced the traditional departmental major with a Program of Emphasis (POE)—a student written statement which included individual objectives, a listing of fifteen courses, and a rationale explaining how the fifteen courses would achieve the student's stated objectives. Students were required to construct their own POE in consultation with two faculty advisors, each of whom would make written comments about the plan which then became part of the student's permanent record.

Recently, two specific concerns had arisen about the POE concept which were addressed specifically by the QUILL-sponsored faculty workshop. The first concern was that students were not taking the exercise seriously. Often a hastily constructed draft was submitted without serious thought or attention, merely to fulfill the requirement of submitting the form. Secondly, many POE's were excessively vocational and faculty members felt that students might have been making premature judgments about particular career choices without adequately exploring the alternatives. In addition, there was faculty confusion about the extent of their role as academic advisor.

The week-long summer workshop focused on faculty advising as a way of dealing with academic, career and personal decisions facing students. The first part of the workshop focused on interpersonal advising skills. An important function of a good advisor lies in recognizing that the student is often looking for more than basic curricular information. He or she is also looking to establish a relationship within which there can be confidence in the results of the advising. Specific advising behaviors were suggested and demonstrated and particular problems discussed. It was strongly suggested that an explicit advising contract be established so that both the faculty and student know what each of their responsibilities would be.

The second part of the workshop concerned career choice and career development theory. A new developmental tool, the Self-Directed Search (SDS) was introduced as a process to encourage students to actively think about career choice. The SDS instrument was to be administered to freshman to enable them to answer questions about their career preferences as well as to become familiar with the Career Planning and Placement Center to discover what career options exist. Students were introduced to the idea that their career options may change over time and hopefully through the use of the SDS students would not make premature choices. Faculty members as well were introduced to the Juniata Career Center at this time, many for the first time, and found useful information to have for their advising function.

The concluding part of the workshop dealt with issues peculiar to advising at Juniata. Issues discussed included the merits of having two rather than one advisor, new graduation requirements, development of a faculty/student advising work sheet, faculty options in reviewing POE's and student evaluation of faculty advisors.

Participating faculty evaluated the workshop immediately upon its conclusion, and student evaluations of the revised procedures were made after the system had been in operation for a year. In general the workshop received favorable comments and all involve hope that it served as a first step in moving Juniata from good to excellent in advising. But this is a long process and will involve a continuing process of monitoring and modification to meet the need of students.

Two important results of the workshop were noticed immediately, however. First, a much smaller percentage of students failed to complete the POE on time compared with previous years, indicating the revised early advising and SDS encouraged them to take the process seriously. Secondly, most advisors required their students to write goal statements for the POE well in advance of a first submission, thereby encouraging the students to actively think about their goals and to conceive of them as more than job choices. Students informally indicated that SDS helped in this regard.

Contact: James J. Lakso
             Associate Professor of
                 Economics
             Juniata College
             Huntington, PA 16252
             (914) 643-4310

Mercer University/Atlanta

The Philosopher and the Businessman:
Ethical Imperatives in Business

(June 1980 - March 1981)

The Mercer University/Atlanta QUILL project was conceived for the primary purpose of stimulating M.B.A. students toward moral reflection within the world of business. To achieve this goal, texts from classical and contemporary moral philosophy were combined and edited to provide the content for a critical discussion of the basic terms in the vocabulary of ethics such as rights, duties, ends, choice and conscience. This compiled text served as the main resource for sixty adult M.B.A. students who participated in a team-taught course for ten two-hour sessions, offered by the chairman of the Division of Business and Economics and an assistant professor of religion and philosophy.

A basic assumption underlying this project was that the case approach to business ethics, although attractive and engaging on the surface, was limited because it failed to accomplish the decisive task of answering the question "Why be good?" Since this method of teaching ethics seemed most widespread, the project director at Mercer undertook a direct challenge to this approach.

The initial portion of this project was devoted to three months of research and preparation of an outline and selected readings. The following sections served as the divisions of the final collection of readings that were prepared for the students: Ethics in general; Ends and Purposes; Choice and Responsibility; Rights and Duties; Virtue and Character; Avarice and Dishonesty; Property Rights; Justice; and Humaneness: a Model for Business Ethics. This outline contained general concepts in ethics, specific concepts particularly suited to business ethics, and the inclusive concept of humaneness to present an integrated model of ethical behavior. The material was presented to emphasize both an internal consistency and the possibilities for a concluding synthesis.

Each section of the outline included readings from three or four sources in an effort to assure selection of a text that would "click" for the students. Later evaluation revealed that this was a mistaken judgment since neither the amount of time students had to read or the classtime which could be devoted to discussion of the readings were adequate for the quantity of the material.

On the whole, students found the readings intelligible and helpful, after an initial period of adjustment to the strangeness and density of the philosophical style and a reminder that such reading would benefit their overall verbal skills. The greatest appreciation was shown for the last group of readings organized under the topic of humaneness. In fact, the response to this section was so positive that future work in this area will probably be expanded.

Among the authors considered most relevant by the students at the end of the course were C.S. Lewis, Josiah Royce, John Rawls, Soren Kierkegaard, Simone Weil, Charles Fried, William James, Adam Smith, and Jacques Maritain. The material by Aristotle and Aquinas was not easily assimilated because of its difficulty.

As the course progressed, many students began to profit from the class in a variety of ways. The quality of the discussion prompted by the readings and lectures was surprisingly high. Based upon class discussion, reflection papers, exams, evaluators, and conversations with students, the majority of the class read the texts and participated in the thought processes, while a significant minority resisted to the end, although even some of these found themselves drawn into class discussions at times.

Time in the classroom was used primarily for discussion of the reading material. The class was divided into different groups which were taught separately by two individual professors. Although the faculty members benefited by being able to teach the new material twice and compare reactions of the groups, the students felt a lack of integration between the two halves of the course. The faculty member responsible for assembling the text of readings was also responsible for dealing with moral theory in the course, while the second professor taught the specific topics in the relationship of business to society—law, unions, ownership, employee relations, business history, and social responsibility. In retrospect, each professor treated his half of the course as the whole and thought that fuller integration could have occurred if only the pace had been relaxed.

Revisions to be made in this effort in the future involve both the text and the course itself. Required readings in moral philosophy will be limited to one or two selections to insure adequate time for class discussion and some addition of case studies. One presentation of this type would be offered at the end of each of the major discussion areas thus preserving the primary focus on moral concepts. The two faculty members will have to become more proficient in areas of the other's expertise to encourage integration of the course as well as build trust in the business students toward the material. Finally, one section should be added to the text to discuss the concept of law which will link the notion of natural law with civil law.

Contact: Deal W. Hudson
Assistant Professor of
Religion and English
Mercer University/Atlanta
Atlanta, GA 30341
(404) 451-0331

Michigan State University

Writing in Business and the Professions:
   A Skill-Utilization and Placement Program
   for English Majors

(January - December 1979)

The Michigan State University English Internship Program was established to counter a situation under which English majors had not been trained to think in terms of career goals in fields other than teaching. The first three months of this program were devoted to preliminary contacts with both employers and prospective interns and establishment of procedural guidelines and course requirements. Placement of interns began in the spring of 1979 and has continued since that time. The main goals of the program included career awareness; practical, professional experience; knowledge of the "usability" of the skills of the English major; employer education as to the effectiveness of the liberal arts major; and facilitation of entry into the job market for English majors.

To be eligible for the program, students had to be at the junior, senior, or graduate level and maintain a high grade point average. Writing samples were required so that the intern director could assess the students' writing and analytical skills. Each student had to obtain a professor's recommendation to gain entry into the program. Final acceptance was determined after a personal interview with the director in which career interests and goals were discussed. Often the major had no specific "career" in mind, so the director of the program helped determine possibilities through discussion of skills and interests, as well as recommended reading materials. Once the area(s) of interest had been established, the director began his or her placement contacts.

Potential employers were deliberately not contacted until student interest areas had been established and definite plans could be made. Interest in individuals was a much greater motivation to the employer than interest in the "program." Interviews between student and director followed at which time responsibilities were firmly outlined and work schedules established. Since the student received between three and five academic credits (quarter system), depending upon the number of hours on the job each week, the internship director made certain that the responsibilities involved the use and growth of research, writing and speaking skills.

The internship experience was a graded course, determined by employer evaluation and director evaluation. The student maintained a log of his/her professional activities which was submitted to the director twice a term. Personal appointments with the director followed the submission of the log to discuss areas of concern and to further the intern's career pursuits.

Placements of students varied each term, but have included the Chamber of Commerce, Legal Aid of Central Michigan, Michigan Dental Association, Michigan Citizen's Lobby, Michigan Council for the Arts, 4-H Youth Programs, the State Department of Education, medical centers, and non-profit associations. Experiences varied from pre-professional activities to technical writing in the sciences.

Originally the English Internship Program established workshops on resume writing, interviewing, job application procedures, and business writing techniques, but responsibility for these activities was turned over to the College of Arts and Letters to free the program director for more personal consultations for each of the interns.

Initial student and employer response was excellent and there was no problem in obtaining appropriate internship experiences. The main problem in the career process centered on determining the student's goal—not the implementation of that goal. In fact, this was the main benefit of the English Internship Program—it enabled students to consciously identify and develop specific career goals combined with a professional experience which enabled them to identify their skills and their areas of expertise, and to establish self-confidence and pride in those skills. Thus, the students could optimistically go to a business knowing that what they had to offer would be of value; as a result of their internship, they could offer a definite recommendation which would testify to their performance and contribution in a similar situation.

Project QUILL initially funded the English Internship Program which is now being carried on through a grant from the All-University Research Initiation at Michigan State University. Gradually, the English department itself is incorporating the costs of the program into its own budget as the value of the program is identified.

The program is by no means a panacea for all the problems that beset the liberal arts major in seeking employment today, but it does offer a way to more effectively enter that job market with the advantage of a firm goal and knowledge of the value of one's skills. This, along with the experience of the professional interview and employment itself, makes the job search much more effective and rewarding. As the program matures, ideally the English major will be consulted much earlier in the academic program so that elective and cognate areas can be used more effectively to implement future career goals.

Contact: Linda Wagner   Karen D. Nelson
          Professor of English   English Internship Program
          Michigan State University   Director
          East Lansing, MI 48824   Michigan State University
          (517) 355-7570   East Lansing, MI 48824
                                        (517) 355-7570

Mount Vernon College

Professional Applications of the Arts
   and Humanities

(September 1979 - June 1980)

As part of a much larger effort at Mount Vernon College, Project QUILL underwrote support for the management component of a new interdisciplinary major, "Arts and Humanities: Cultural Management and Human Creativity." This new major was designed to blend professional and liberal courses in a model program that demonstrated avenues for professional application of the arts and humanities by enabling students to acquire competency in management of cultural institutions, awareness of career opportunities, and professional outlets for their intellectual and artistic development.

The theme of "human creativity" strengthened this interdisciplinary program through expanded course offerings in studio art, art history, cultural anthropology, history, writing and literature, and the performing arts. Students are able to explore the nature of creativity, major creative accomplishments, and the historical conditions under which creativity has flourished. Requirements for the major include a broad overview course, "The Artist, Humanist, and Society," a distribution of courses focusing on the creating process, the created work, and the social or historical context in which creativity is nutured; selection of two courses from those which explore a special topic; and selection of either a creative project or a management component to express that which has been learned. The creative component will require students to produce substantial works of art or criticism, while the management component will focus upon the management of cultural organizations, drawing upon the curriculum of the college's other professional programs, particularly business administration, communications, and public affairs and government.

Specifically under the auspices of the QUILL grant, the college strengthened the "management component" of this new major by developing internship placement opportunities, offering an arts and humanities management seminar under the direction of a professional arts administrator, acquiring a core library collection, developing an advisory committee to the program, and consulting with professionals in the field of arts and humanities management to develop further the curriculum for the program.

Although only one student initially participated in the internship opportunity (at the National Endowment for the Humanities), initial contacts were made with various possible field supervisors for future internships. Five students preregistered for this option for the following semester, and placements were expected at the Wolf Trap Foundation, Capital Children's Museum, Renwick Gallery, and the National Geographic Society.

The new course, "Arts and Humanities Management," was offered by an adjunct professor, an expert formerly associated with the National Endowment for the Arts, and provided an introduction to general administration, operation and organization, operating problems, personnel and staffing, grantsmanship, income and audience development, and public relations. Each student developed a research paper in collaboration with an arts or humanities administrator affiliated with a local museum or association. Although initial enrollment in the course was small since students had to meet a number of prerequisites, student evaluations were very positive and the course will continue to be offered in the future.

Other activities directly related to the QUILL grant included the addition of thirty-eight library holdings which helped develop a core collection in arts and humanities management. The Professional Advisory Committee in Arts and Humanities, representing leading members of the Washington arts and humanities community, was established to advise the College on the needs of the profession and career opportunities for Mount Vernon students. Additionally, course requirements and curriculum were revised and strengthened under the guidance of three outside consultants.

Another area of curriculum development was the program, "Junior Year in Arts and Humanities Management," designed to make available the arts and humanities management courses and internship opportunities to students from other colleges and universities. Although not specifically supported by the QUILL grant, the college developed this year-long program and advertised it widely. Although no students have enrolled so far, feedback from faculty and administrators at other institutions is quite encouraging, and this program is expected to begin drawing students in the near future.

Assessment of the entire new arts and humanities major was undertaken by three independent consultants who evaluated the progress of the project and made recommendations for further development of the curriculum. Each visited the campus separately, and brought a special perspective of their assessment. Overall evaluations were quite positive and specific recommendations have been incorporated into the program.

At the end of the first year of the program, an evaluation retreat was held for those faculty and administrators actively participating in the program. Areas for expansion and further development were discussed and included the Arts and Humanities Junior Year program, an adult education program directed toward local residents, a cooperative MA/BA program between Mount Vernon College and The American University, and further development of foreign language study within the curriculum.

Additional funding has been secured to continue development of the Arts and Humanities Program beyond this year to enable further expansion of the curriculum along with necessary outside evaluation.

Contact: Judith Weiner   Philip Bolton
           Vice President of Academic   Chairman, Arts and
              Affairs   Humanities Program
           Mount Vernon College   Mount Vernon College
           Washington, D.C. 20007   Washington, D.C. 20007
           (202) 331-3414   (202) 331-0400

Saint Anselm College

Development of an Interdisciplinary Course
in Bioethics for Undergraduate Nursing
Majors in a Liberal Arts College

(June 1980 - June 1981)

Support from Project QUILL was used by St. Anselm College to provide a one-week summer workshop in which faculty from the nursing, philosophy and theology departments reviewed together the basic moral, ethical and legal principles involved in bioethical decision-making to prepare themselves to teach an interdisciplinary course in bioethics to students of nursing. This interdisciplinary approach was consistent with the aims of the college as a liberal arts institution, and reinforced its philosophy which emphasizes human values as they relate to life in its personal and social dimensions. This orientation demands that a liberal education concern itself primarily with the fundamental questions of human existence, i.e. those which lead to the formation of a view of the ultimate meaning of human life.

To achieve this primary goal, Saint Anselm College has pioneered an interdisciplinary approach to the core curriculum for all students (aided by a grant from the National Endowment for the Humanities). This program concentrates on joint faculty-student discussion of value questions and principles within the context of the development of our Western culture with a major focus upon ethical and moral issues.

Within this context, it was natural for the departments of philosophy and theology to work together with a professional discipline (nursing) in teaching ethical issues. For the past three years, faculty from these departments sponsored and voluntarily attended a series of colloquia addressing topics such as "Conscience," "Theological Analysis of Health Care," and "Choice of the Right Path—Values and Decision-Making."

As a result of these colloquia, it became apparent that despite the remarkable increase in publications dealing with ethical issues in the practice of medicine, there was limited published information focusing upon the application of ethical principles and theories to nursing situations. Perhaps more than any other member of the health team, nurses may be confronted on a daily basis with a variety of procedures and problems which present ethical implications. In order to provide these students with the necessary additional knowledge and expertise in the

147

area of bioethics, fourteen faculty members participated in this intense summer workshop.

During this one-week seminar for faculty from the departments of nursing, theology, and philosophy, two experts in medical ethics from Boston College gave presentations on "Morality and Ethical Theory," "Professionalism in Health Care," "Justice and Health Care," "Death and Dying," and "The Beginning of Life." Extensive readings were done in conjunction with these presentations and there was opportunity for group discussion and reaction. Evaluation of this workshop indicated that although it was extremely successful, follow-up sessions were needed in which the group could explore ethical approaches to concrete problems presenting ethical dilemmas in nursing situations. In addition, more time was needed to develop case studies with model guidelines which would be helpful to students in applying moral and ethical principles.

Although additional funds were not obtained to actually develop specific interdisciplinary courses in bioethical decision-making, faculty members immediately began constructive use of their new expertise by applying ethical and moral principles to situations encountered in the clinical area. Seminar and group learning sessions which focused on topics involving bioethical decision-making were enriched and seminar participants used their knowledge in many different classroom situations, in supervision of students, and in developing "learning packages" for the various nursing syllabi.

The next step for this workshop group will be to conduct some interdisciplinary teaching relative to bioethical decision-making within the existing courses at the college, prior to or instead of initiating a new interdisciplinary course in bioethical decision-making. This will give the faculty the opportunity to become more proficient in interdisciplinary teaching before undertaking an extensive curriculum revision. Some progress has been made in this regard, and it is expected that greater strides will be made during the next academic year.

In summary, the goals and expectations at Saint Anselm College exceeded their resources and capabilities. However, through this intense, interdisciplinary experience, faculty members have identified many ways in which they are (and will continue) enriching their teaching of bioethical decision-making to nursing majors.

Contact: James McGhee   Mary R. Bruton
            Chairman, Theology   Chairman, Nursing
              Department   Department
            Saint Anselm College   Saint Anselm College
            Manchester, NH 03102   Manchester, NH 03102
            (603) 669-1030   (603) 669-1030

Saint Edward's University
New College

Integrating Liberal Learning and
   Career Education in a Non-Traditional
   Adult Degree Program

(February 1979 - January 1980)

New College at St. Edward's University is a non-traditional, competency-based adult degree program offering a Bachelor of Liberal Studies degree. Within its curriculum design, New College offers a variety of ways to learn and obtain college credit—assessment of prior learning, challenge and CLEP exams, traditional campus classes, and individualized learning activities. The individualized learning activities are formalized through learning contracts between students, instructor/facilitators, and the dean of New College. They are designed especially for students who travel extensively in their jobs, are housebound, or live quite a distance from the campus.

Recently, New College developed curriculum materials in the form of mobile Individualized Learning Packages (ILPs) to accompany the learning contracts. ILPs include carefully prepared and very specific course syllabi, audio-cassettes, filmstrips, slide-tape presentations, and other material pertinent to the content of the learning package.

In an attempt to strengthen the New College curriculum and integrate liberal learning with career and professional education, Project QUILL assisted in the development and pilot testing of two ILPs within a broad theme of Values in a Pluralistic Society—"Humankind's Search for Meaning" and "Business and Social Ethics." Traditionally, college courses exploring basic human questions had used a theoretical and/or philosophical rather than an applied approach to questions such as "Who am I?" "What is Truth?" Recent research with adult students had shown that the most common motivator for learning was some anticipated use or application of the knowledge learned. The New College faculty, therefore, was convinced that liberal arts courses related to ethics and the valuing process had to address also more practical concerns and provide realistic guidelines for resolving problems.

Since a large number of the New College students major in management, business administration, and related fields, new ILPs were prepared for adult students to examine, compare and evaluate basic existential questions and answers in the light of their own personal experiences. "Humankind's Search for Meaning" was developed by the chairperson of the Department of Religious Studies and pilot-tested by 27 students during a three-hour colloquium; "Business and Social Ethics," developed by a professor of philosophy and religious studies, was also pilot-tested in a similar colloquium by 45 students. Each adult student who attended one of these colloquium sessions evaluated the presentations in writing and generally found them to be thought-provoking and stimulating.

The new ILPs are now in use and available to all New College students for the equivalent of a three-hour credit course. Those students who used the new programs immediately offered informal evaluations during discussions with their respective instructors. In general, students felt some stress and/or discomfort in having to think in terms of different cultures and different values, and having to analyze and re-evaluate their own values. As a result of this student feedback, "Business and Social Ethics" now includes a more comprehensive glossary of terms and additional material on ethical theories. The other ILP, "Humankind's Search for Meaning" has remained intact, as originally prepared.

The new ILPs are available to other St. Edward's University programs which deal with adults. They can be used by other instructors without any difficulty, and copies of the library materials are available at the university library and the New College office. Audio and audio-visual materials purchased for the ILPs have been incorporated into the audio-visual library and the Learning Resource Center.

Both professors involved in the program development subsequently taught courses which were based on material adapted to their respective courses from the ILPs. Some of these courses are scheduled in the evenings and are attended by adult students who are working in the business and social science areas.

The New College model of Individualized Learning Packages integrating liberal learning with career and professional education can be adopted by other institutions with similar services. The replicability potential of the ILP model is great, and New College staff is available to share their experiences and packages.

Contact: Jean Meyer
Dean of New College
St. Edward's University
Austin, TX 78704
(512) 444-2621

Seton Hill College

Transformation of Persons for Business
through the Study and Practice of Creative
Imagining in a Liberal Arts Context

(September 1978 - December 1979)

Seton Hill, a private four-year liberal arts college for women, created a liberally-grounded educational model to meet the growing market for women in careers in business and management. The project focused upon the development of an interdisciplinary course in imaginative thinking and symbolic transformation.

During the full semester of preparation for this course, two separate plans were formulated. A team of two teachers from the Religious Studies Department prepared a spring semester course, "From Mythology to Madison Avenue: Human Imagination and Creative Problem-Solving" by establishing a resource bibliography, identifying relevant films, books and other course materials, and formulating a detailed course outline. In addition, fourteen businesspersons from the Greensburg area met with the two team teachers, the academic dean and the faculty advisors of business and management majors to develop plans for the cooperative participation of the business community in the implementation of the QUILL project. Not only did this breakfast meeting generate support in terms of interest and personnel from the businesses involved, it initiated the desired dialogue between business and liberal learning.

During the spring semester, the new creativity course was fully enrolled—38 students participated, equally divided among business or management majors and humanities, arts or social sciences majors. The goals of the course were to expand the imaginative horizons through exposure to some pivotal ideas of the twentieth century, while at the same time to train the students—through practice in divergent thinking and other problem-solving skills—in the discipline and methods of creative imagining.

In addition to the basic course requirements, students participated in small group problem-solving tasks, preparation of a viable problem-solving model, and compilation of a journal. The communal activities of the course were stressed to give students actual first-hand experience of the freeing power of liberal thinking—including broadened views of reality, deepened penetration into their own resources, and personal energy and heightened capacity for original thinking.

The course was offered once a week for two and one-half hours. As a result of this scheduling, problems resulted when two sessions had to be cancelled because of bad weather, resulting in a lack of sufficient "incubation" time for ideas between activities occuring during the same session. The longer class session, however, allowed for use of planned group activities requiring an hour or more of time, with time still remaining for discussion and further work in the area.

Generally speaking, the arts and sciences majors were more receptive to both the readings and the problem solving dimensions of the course, while the business and management students found the readings more difficult and were less willing to be imaginative about the process-oriented aspects of the course. This reaction led the faculty involved to conclude that creative problem-solving was indeed necessary for the integration of career preparation and liberal learning.

As a result of the enthusiastic reception for the course, it will be included as an elective for the management program in future years, with a somewhat tighter structure. More readings will be included which deal with creativity and the creative process, and fewer on scientific or mathematical ideas. In addition, a one-credit practical component will be introduced into the course in which business students will work with a management or business faculty member to apply the liberal learning of the course.

The final section of the course took place during the fall semester of 1979. A follow-up, non-credit workshop entitled "Business and Imagination: A Human Enterprise" was aimed at application of the previous course in imagination and creativity to actual situations in business and management. During three specific workshop sessions, nine persons from various local firms participated in discussions of "Communications Problems in Management" and "Personnel and Training Problems." In addition, one entire evening was devoted to a discussion of "Is There a Role for Creative Imagination in Business and Industry?" followed by workshops on "Financial Problems and Functions of Management and Planning" and "Legal Problems and the Role of Government Regulations in Business."

The greatest problem in the implementation of this portion of the program was that nearly half of the students in the credit course had graduated, so the follow-up sessions were not as effective as those which could have been aimed at specific, simultaneous application of course material.

Future continuation of the QUILL Project is a high priority, although staffing limitations presently prevent its immediate rescheduling. When these are solved, the course will be offered again, but with significant changes. The corresponding workshop sessions, aimed at application of course learning, will be included in the course itself, in the form of a one-credit concurrent workshop series. The course itself will carry two credits, and students could opt for a two or three credit program.

Contact:	Sister Frances Stefano, S.C.
	Instructor, Religious Studies
	Department
	Seton Hill College
	Greensburg, PA 15601
	(412) 834-2200

Tougaloo College

Project COPE (Career Opportunities—
Professional Ethics)

(September 1978 - June 1979)

Project COPE was conducted by the Humanities Division of Tougaloo College as an attempt to assist faculty and students in all disciplines to develop techniques for examining ethical issues in the professions and to integrate these concerns into selected courses. In addition, the project provided faculty and students with information about career possibilities, needed skills, and career development strategies for liberal arts students while at the same time disseminating to selected employers and government officials information on the role of the liberal arts as career preparation. Project COPE was a direct complement to Tougaloo's effort to establish an interdisciplinary career-oriented humanities major, a curriculum development effort supported by the National Endowment for the Humanities.

One of the main features of the COPE effort was the Scholar-in-Residence program which brought two outside scholars to campus, each for a six-day period. Thomas Flynn, professor of philosophy at the University of Mississippi focused upon closer integration of ethical considerations into regular course work and met with humanities majors, pre-health and pre-engineering students, honor societies, and groups of "philosophers" (faculty and students). He also delivered a special campus-wide address, "The Uses and Misuses of Human Rights" and actively participated in nine separate introductory classes.

The second Scholar-in-Residence was A.P. Marshall, Director of Libraries at Eastern Michigan University and a consultant with NEH. Although he gave some attention to ethical questions, the focus of his residency was on communication skills. He too talked with student and faculty, visited classes, and gave a campus-wide lecture on "The Humanities in Practice." The ten classes he attended were either part of the English curriculum or focused upon library skills. Both scholars were well received by students and faculty and were responsible for stimulating interest in the issues raised.

Several resource persons who came to the campus for one or two days also assisted faculty and students in exploring career options and ethical

154

issues in career areas. These included the dean of the School of Business at the University of Kansas, the director of the Jackson, Mississippi Office of the U.S. Office of Personnel Management, a para-legal with the Central Mississippi Legal Services, an author, and a teacher. In general these consultants met with students within special interest courses or programs as well as conferring with the Career Planning and Placement staff. They not only addressed career or educational opportunities within their own particular organizations, but also addressed the issues of career alternatives.

The final major activity under the QUILL grant was an All-College Career Conference held in cooperation with the Tougaloo College Career Planning and Placement Office and the Tougaloo/Industry Cluster. A keynote speaker, Dr. Emmett Burns, Regional Director for the NAACP, addressed all participants at a morning assembly program on "Black Institutions of Higher Education: Their Mission—Excellence, Equality and Preparation for Leadership." The afternoon activities were devoted to concurrent workshops in business and commerce, arts management, government and public service, health professions, communications and social and human services.

In order to promote the cause of liberal arts education, a brochure "Employers Be Wise," was developed and sent to over 200 employers in the immediate area and across the nation, attempting to point out career skills developed by the liberal arts colleges in Mississippi. In addition, the project director, a Scholar-in-Residence, and a faculty member appeared on a locally produced public service program to discuss the nature of the liberal arts college and the way Tougaloo is attempting to prepare its students for meaningful careers. A booklet, *The Liberal Arts, Ethics, and Careers*, containing speeches by the two Scholars-in-Residence and the keynote address for the All-College Career Conference was prepared and distributed to selected employers and colleagues in other colleges.

Evaluative resources (questionnaires and personal comments) suggested that the Scholar-in-Residence and resource persons components of Project COPE had positive impact upon faculty and students. Teachers became more aware of ways of integrating ethical issues into their course work and students gained useful information about career possibilities. Reaction to the career conference was also favorable and students felt that such an activity should be held on a regular basis.

As a direct result of Project COPE activities, a journalism professor and a philosophy professor became interested in developing instructional materials to have students attempt to grapple with ethical issues faced by journalists. Support is currently being sought for this activity.

Under a major grant from a private foundation, the Humanities Division will continue to sponsor several Scholars-in-Residence over the next several years to continue the intellectual stimulation begun by the scholars under Project COPE.

Finally, the college faculty will become increasingly sensitive to the role of the liberal arts college in career preparation and will seek to develop the curriculum in such a way that liberal education and career education reinforce each other.

Contact: Ben E. Bailey
Chairman of the Humanities
  Division
Tougaloo College
Tougaloo, MS 39174
(601) 956-4941

University of California—Berkeley

A One-Quarter Course on the
Berkeley Campus—"Integrating
Women's Studies and Careers"

(January - March 1980)

Instructors and ten students gathered in January 1980 on the Berkeley campus for a course funded by QUILL to examine the relationship between the liberal arts major in women's studies and career goals. Seven of the participating students were women's studies majors. The three other students were from the departments of anthropology, English and computer science. Because the majority of these women were only a quarter or two away from graduation, serious consideration of careers was an urgent concern for them.

The second purpose in offering this type of course was to encourage faculty members to make the transition from a concept of the liberal arts as "pure" learning to a more active idea about the value of the liberal arts after graduation, a transition which has been extremely difficult for most faculty members to make.

The course included readings on the social, psychological and economic barriers to success among women, as well as a required paper on one of the issues raised by the readings. But the main focus was on practical assignments: resumés and field work, with oral and written reports on that research. Among the students and their projects were an aspiring writer who interviewed Bay Area women writers, discovering that it is possible to write and survive; an English major who focused on a major interest—women and fitness—and landed an internship with a San Francisco Women and Sports Foundation; and a re-entry woman who developed a re-entry counseling program on the Berkeley campus.

The main issue of concern to the participating students was a value-centered one. There were intense seminar debates on the definition of success, with the feminist women's studies majors insisting that the essence of feminism is a rejection of the world as it is, including the prevailing success ethic. Other students felt confused about the extent to which they would compromise their sense of morality in order to get ahead. Towards the end of the course, the feminists were fusing their idealism with a bit more reality, and the woman who had declared at the first class that she wanted to "make a lot of money" was more thoughtful about the ethical dimensions of her life work.

The class assignment and seminar format were chosen expressly to allow students to exercise some of the skills associated with liberal arts learning (the ability to write well and to speak with clarity and force), and to make it possible for the instructors and a series of feminist guest speakers to point out just how valuable these thinking skills are in the workaday world.

The students felt overwhelmingly positive about the class. They appreciated the opportunity to pursue thinking about career goals within the context of a course, pointing out that the burdens of the normal academic load preclude one's being able to do this. Others said they were glad to be forced to confront their futures after having put it off for so long. In both cases, students felt less anxious about the step from the world of school to the world of work because of the links between these worlds made implicit in the classroom. The field work played a great part in the lessening of these anxieties by providing concrete information about the job market.

The response to the seminar format of the course was more varied. The students were to take turns framing "study questions" for each discussion, and for leading that discussion. But for those who had never led a class discussion during their undergraduate years, this was a difficult and frightening task.

The field projects were put off by students who were reluctant to do the required academic reading essential to thinking realistically about careers for women. But once the projects were defined and the students felt comfortable with each other, the class started to move quickly.

There was a request from all the students that the course be offered yearly. If this happens, the reading would probably be changed somewhat with more emphasis placed on ethics, proceeding to readings on the philosophy of work and leisure, and concluding with readings on barriers to success among women. There would also have to be a discussion as to whether admitting non-women's studies majors who had not been exposed to some basic women's studies principles was a plus or a minus. These students hampered the speed of the course while some remedial work was being done, while at the same time these very students kept the women's studies people from becoming too narrow minded.

All in all, it was an exciting experiment, and one which could be replicated easily on another campus.

Contact: William B. Slottman   Gloria Bowles
            Professor of History   Lecturer and Coordinator,
            University of California—   Women's Studies
              Berkeley   University of California—
            Berkeley, CA 94720   Berkeley
            (415) 642-6302   Berkeley, CA 94720
                                          (415) 642-6302

University of Puget Sound

Professional Ethics
   for a Technological Era

(June 1979 - May 1980)

Although the University of Puget Sound had offered a general ethics course for nearly a decade, a changing interest was discerned among students, reflecting their concern for general ethical issues in relationship to their prospective professions. Under auspices of Project QUILL this original course was modified and expanded into a full program, shifting the focus from the very broad social issues to more professional ones. Separate courses for each profession were not considered, but rather it was assumed that each one had enough in common to warrant treating the issues of the professions generically.

The established program, "Professional Ethics for a Technological Era," consisted of two courses: "Ethics for a Technological Era" offered in the fall term, and "Values: Conflict and Compromise" offered during the January term. The aim of the first course was to teach the art of ethical decision-making, i.e. the styles of ethical reasoning, and to provide a range of ethical issues arising from professional life. The second course applied skills learned from the first to one specific social conflict, bearing on the practice of many professions, for purposes of identifying, analyzing, and hopefully resolving the ethical issues. The courses were united by the sequential theme of theory and practice.

"Ethics for a Technological Era" was offered in fall 1980 to fifty students and team-taught by three members of the university faculty, each representing a different discipline, (religion, business administration, and chemistry). Prior to the actual course, the faculty team spent many hours in the planning of the course—selecting texts, articles, guest speakers, and arranging field trips. The class met for two hours, twice a week, with all instructors present for plenary sessions, and the course was divided for weekly discussion groups led by the individual instructors. The semester was divided into four parts.

The first portion of the course concentrated on the theme of professionals as moral agents and professions as moral entities. Lectures and discussions centered on the definitions of ethics and professional character. Other topics included professions as moral reference groups

160

and the role for professional ethics codes and committees. This portion was highlighted by a showing of the film, *The Seduction of Joe Tynan,* and a visit by four members of the Weyerhaeuser Company's Business Conduct Committee.

The overall theme of the second part of the course was moral decision-making. Definition of a professional ethical issue was investigated and lectures covered topics such as principled character, the concept of triangulation, and a systems approach. Various ethics codes were also studied.

The theme of part three centered upon specific issues in professional ethics. Lectures and discussions began with moral relationships—primary groups such as consumers, clients, customers, peers, employers-stockholders, and employees. Lectures also touched upon social accountability of the professions and professional accountability to global trends.

During the final two weeks of the course, the class concentrated on the future of professional ethics, with the final class session devoted to a course evaluation.

The greatest strengths of this course were the interaction between the teaching team, the use of guest speakers, and the assigned short papers, at which time students interviewed professionals and prepared character studies. Perhaps the greatest weakness of the course was the unrealistically high goal set by the instructors for the students to actually attain and use the skills of ethical decision-making. In addition, students felt that too much emphasis had been placed upon professional ethical problems and not enough was placed on current student ethical problems.

The second course, offered in Winterim (the January intensive term), 1981, was designed to offer students an opportunity to apply ethical decision-making skills to a major social policy program—in this case, the national health insurance proposals of President Carter and Senator Kennedy. Thirty students were enrolled in the course which was taught by a team of three instructors—two of whom had participated in the original course. A biologist substituted for the chemist, who had conflicting duties.

During the first week of the Winterim course, students were introduced to the two health insurance proposals, ethical issues raised by each of the proposals, and application of ethical decision-making skills to the two proposals. The remainder of the course focused upon student task groups doing research on the effects these two plans would have on various special interest groups. Through direct interviewing, telephone interviewing, and study of the literature, the student task groups gathered information in their own special interest groups. One comprehensive research paper was then compiled covering the two proposals and their comparative effects on employers, taxpayer/consumer, labor unions as consumer, private insurers, other organizations as consumer, health care professionals, facilities, government and medical researchers.

In general the students were positive about the course orientation to a specific problem and the results they obtained from their collaborative research. The greatest disappointment arose from the fact that students from the first semester-long course did not enroll in the Winterim follow-up course. Although the PETE program was designed as a two-course sequence for one group of students, in actuality it turned out to be two separate courses for two different group of students.

In conclusion, it was clear that students learn about ethics by exposure to situations or cases presented graphically, by articulating their own responses to issues, and by contact with professionals who were actually involved in the decision-making process. In the future, the format of this particular course must be better defined in advance so students clearly understand what is expected of them, and the issues of professional ethics must be more carefully linked to students' current concerns.

As a result of modifications made following this pilot experiment, a sudden interest in the program grew dramatically. For the second offering of the semester-long course during fall term, 1980, now retitled "Professional Ethics for a Technological Era," the course was overenrolled and was offered again in spring term 1981, as well. In addition, the Winterim course, also retitled as "Public Policy: Conflict and Compromise," received much attention and a large group enrolled in that course as well, including, in this case, several students who had taken the fall term course. Project QUILL clearly allowed the University of Puget Sound to infuse liberal learning greatly into professional studies.

Contact: Darrell Reeck
Associate Professor of
   Religion
University of Puget Sound
Tacoma, WA 98416
(206) 756-3287

Wheeling College

SAIL: Summer Alternatives in Learning
at Wheeling College

(May - September 1980)

The decision to take advantage of the summer weeks to integrate the humanities with professional training resulted in the launching of a program entitled SAIL: Summer Alternatives in Learning at Wheeling College. The purposes of the two six-week sessions from May to August were four-fold: (1) to provide those enrolled in highly technical areas enough time in their crowded schedules for broadening liberal arts courses, while simultaneously providing schedule relief during the normal semester; (2) to provide strongly career-focused or specialized sub-concentrations for liberal arts majors; (3) to improve the performance and retention of conditionally accepted students by strengthening their basic skills; and (4) to improve the quality of the Summer School.

After an evaluation questionnaire distributed to the college community indicated an interest in more innovative teaching and undistracted learning, as well as stronger interaction among faculty and students, the dean of instruction met with the department chairpersons and the director of the Evening Division to discuss the implementation of a new Summer School structure, and to decide which courses were to be made available.

Three basic clusters of courses were set up in each of the two sessions, with different choices available during each six week period. Students could register for all or part of each cluster. Core-fulfilling courses in the humanities were organized around a common focus or specialty, thereby offering minor-concentrations for students in the career-focused disciplines. Career clusters were set up for the traditional liberal arts, social science, or natural science majors to add a supplementary "track" of a specialized nature. These first two clusters of courses offered supplementary activities such as guest speakers, special dinners, field trips, films and performances. The third grouping, a basic skills sequence in writing, reading, mathematics, and study skills, was available for the conditionally accepted students at Wheeling (traditionally about 25-30 persons) as well as area high school students preparing to enter other colleges. Evaluation was achieved by the administration of a questionnaire to students and faculty at the end of the SAIL program. The results were compared with a similar questionnaire administered the previous summer after the less-focused normal summer program.

The number of students choosing to fulfill humanities core requirements increased dramatically from 38 percent to 80 percent. It was determined that there were two basic reasons for this: students wanted to lighten the load of courses during the fall and spring, and they wanted to graduate earlier. The number of students taking liberal arts courses beyond the core requirements also increased in most subject areas. That this interest was carried over into the fall semester was evident with the impressive increase in the total of liberal arts majors. The liberal arts-career connection was most apparent to criminal justice majors who, after enrolling in the summer Spanish classes, traveled to a local prison to interview Spanish-speaking inmates.

The impact of the summer school on retention of conditionally accepted students was less clear. College-wide retention among these students had increased dramatically since the expansion of the basic skills program in 1975. It is too early to ascertain whether SAIL was successful in adding additional positive impetus to this program.

As for the hoped-for improvement in the quality of the summer school program, all indications are that SAIL was successful. The 1980 questionnaire results showed that summer school was perceived as stimulating, demanding, strong, valuable, clear, neat, pleasant and coherent. Most important, perhaps, was the feeling that the sessions were relaxed as opposed to tense in 1979. Some conclusions that might be drawn from the experience of the summer are these: it is possible and desirable to develop a coherent summer curriculum which satisfactorily meets the needs of students and is still educationally sound. The SAIL program, and others like it need to be seen as part of the larger effort to make liberal arts studies more attractive to career students and at the same time provide career options for students who are interested in liberal arts. The need in terms of further refinement is to plan and schedule course selections better, and to examine each course in terms of its relative effectiveness in summer versus the regular sessions. The SAIL experiment will be revised and offered again in the summer of 1981.

Contact: Jeanne Kammer
            Academic Dean
            Wheeling College
            Wheeling, WV 26003
            (304) 243-2349

Wilkes College

Communications in an Open Society

(July 1980-May 1981)

As a response to declining enrollments in the liberal arts, especially in English, Wilkes College adopted in 1977 a number of professional, career-oriented courses in journalism, broadcasting, and communication theory. In 1979, the college developed a new major, Communication Studies, which is strongly centered in the liberal arts. The college requested assistance from Project QUILL to prepare an interdisciplinary seminar for seniors which would focus all previously-learned professional and liberal arts subjects upon the significance of communications in our society. This seminar was entitled "Communications in an Open Society."

There were four major objectives in the attempt to develop in students an understanding of the moral, political, and historical significance of communication acts: (1) to develop a clear understanding of the place and function of communications in American society; (2) to develop the ability to analyze and to evaluate the significance of current events in broad historical and cultural contexts; (3) to develop a sensitivity to various ways in which public opinion can be directed and to the moral implications of such direction; and (4) to challenge the student to put into responsible practice what he has learned through the development of a major media project.

The team of instructors prepared itself through extensive reading and research, and held informal planning discussions during the summer of 1980. The seminar was taught during the spring semester of 1981 by faculty from the departments of English and communication studies, history, political science, and sociology. It was hoped that bringing together instructors from a variety of disciplines would demonstrate to students the interrelatedness of knowledge and the direct applicability of "knowing" to "doing." Fourteen students enrolled in the course and explored topics which included the media and its effects on the individual consciousness and public life, as well as the media as a technological imperative.

The course was taught very much as planned, with only one minor exception. Although several guest lecturers and outside consultants had been counted on for course participation, it was discovered that prominent guest speakers charged more for their services than was available in the budget, and for this reason, only one actually attended. At the same time, much more time and effort was required for the instructors in preparing for the course than had been anticipated, as three of the four faculty members had had little or no training in communications or in the impact of communications on society.

In choosing a term project, the students, after reading extensively, decided to produce a half-hour television documentary entitled "Regional Inferiority Complex: An Investigation of Images of the Wyoming Valley Area—Their Courses and Manifestations."

The experience was evaluated by the students enrolled in the course, by the instructional team, and by an independent committee appointed by the Dean of Academic Affairs. The evaluations were so overwhelmingly positive that the course has become a permanent part of the curriculum.

Contact: Thomas Kaska
             Chairman
             Department of Language
               and Literature
             Wilkes College
             Wilkes-Barre, PA 18766
             (717) 824-4651

Worcester Polytechnic Institute

Museums: A Unique Resource for Integrating
Humanities and Technology in the Career
Education of Engineering Students

(June 1980-May 1981)

Worcester Polytechnic Institute expects engineering and science students to complete part of their degree requirements by doing projects which relate science and technology to some aspect of human life. In 1977, by collaborating with the staff of some of New England's museums, the Institute was able to devise "The Time Machine," a program whereby students do research and projects for academic credit at nine museums in the Worcester area. As a result of the program, science and engineering students have been forced to combine their knowledge of technical specialties with liberal learning. At the same time, these students have been able to undertake projects which the museums could not otherwise do. By 1980, WPI faculty and museum staff had accumulated enough experience to see clearly the strengths and shortcomings of "The Time Machine" program.

A QUILL grant was requested to strengthen two areas of the program. The first aim was to increase the faculty's familiarization with the collections, research facilities, and library holdings of each museum, so as to enhance their ability to advise future museum projects. The second purpose was to increase student preparedness for "The Time Machine" program.

During the summer of 1980, seven faculty members each spent a week at a museum of his choice, immersing himself in his field of interest. Each drew up two proposals for projects, with bibliographies, significant to the museum and which could enable students to explore the complicated interactions among science, technology, and the humanities, particularly literature and history. The interdisciplinary themes of the proposed projects demanded the combined expertise of a professor in the humanities and a person with technical competence.

"The Time Machine" program naturally attracts students whose courses in humanities such as the history of technology already fit them for museum studies. But not all students embark on the program with a background of courses which prepare them to tackle a specific project. To deal with this problem, three faculty members spent a week in the

167

summer of 1980 structuring a course which students could take as partial preparation for working at museums. For logistical simplicity, the faculty decided to present the course to students who signed up for projects at the Higgins Armory, Worcester, Massachusetts, a Museum of Medieval and Renaissance Warfare.

The first of the weekly meetings consisted of a comprehensive tour of the museum with staff as guides. The staff also talked with the students about possible topics for projects. At the next three meetings, the entire group of students explored archery in the Hundred Years War. One of the sessions was led by an historian of science and technology who showed the students the questions they must ask and the sources they must consult to analyze a battle such as Crecy. Extracts from French and English documents of the period of the war, and a contemporary account of the battle of Crecy were assigned to the class. They also read selections from a classic history of the crossbow. A professor of physics helped them analyze the relative merits in battle of longbows and crossbows, using content from the freshman physics course as a foundation. A professor of literature examined the Robin Hood ballads as well as other literature from the period incorporating the archer. Thus the class approached the topic of archery in the Hundred Years War historically, technically, and through literary analysis.

The students also met once a week in small groups with faculty advisers to draw up proposals for the projects they hoped to do at the museum during the next academic year. These proposals were presented to the entire class for discussion and criticism. The course culminated in an evening of archery at a local range, which demonstrated to the students how difficult it is to shoot with skill and accuracy.

The work done by faculty under this grant, and the projects advised by them are being assessed at the present time by WPI's Center for Educational Research and Development.

Contact: E. Malcolm Parkinson
Associate Professor of
History
Worcester Polytechnic
Institute
Worcester, MA 01609
(617) 753-1411

Appendix I

Innovation—How to Create New Programs in Liberal Learning

A panel presentation on QUILL-funded projects, presented at the Annual Meeting of the Association of American Colleges, January 11, 1980, in Phoenix, Arizona. The panel included Shirley Leckie, John D. Heyl, and Landon C. Kirchner.

Strengthening the Interdisciplinary and Individualized Aspects of the Adult Liberal Studies Program at the University of Toledo

Shirley Leckie

In 1971 The University of Toledo introduced an innovation in liberal learning, the Adult Liberal Studies program. Five years later the program was dying; it lacked both institutional legitimacy and faculty support. Since this was the only interdisciplinary, adult degree program in northwest Ohio, those of us administering it genuinely believed that it was worth salvaging. To accomplish this, we were forced to raise some basic questions that, unfortunately, had not been confronted at the time of the program's inception. Once we took this essential step, we were able to make some recommendations to the university administration. These were accepted, implemented, and the results have been beneficial for the program as a whole. Today, the Adult Liberal Studies program at The University of Toledo is highly successful from the standpoint of both student satisfaction and faculty support. My remarks on this panel will be based on my involvement with its changing fortunes. I would like to

Shirley Leckie was formerly director of External Affairs, University College, at The University of Toledo, and is now the Associate Dean for Continuing Education at Millsaps College, Jackson, MS 39210.

begin by making some brief generalizations based on that experience.

First—I think that it is imperative that the need for a new program be clearly established and documented. I know that this sounds elementary but the question of justification arises in every step of the implementation process. Nothing, it seems to me, could be more destructive to a new program's success than the lack of a clear statement of purpose. In the face of budgetary constraints, you must be prepared to argue the merits of your proposal persuasively. To do so, you must be convinced that your innovation fills a vital need.

Second—It is worthwhile to take a long, hard look at the educational institution involved. I think that you need to determine where power lies, how decisions are made, what incentive system exists for the faculty and how your proposed program can fit into that system. At The University of Toledo, the central administration has been very supportive of innovative programs that meet valid needs. Individual college deans, on the other hand, often must be convinced that you are actually attracting new students and not threatening the enrollment in established programs. Aside from administrators, however, faculty committees, especially the Faculty Senate, and the college curriculum committees, wield a tremendous amount of power on our campus. I suspect that this is true of their counterparts in varying degrees at other institutions as well. For this reason I am convinced that a great deal of support can be gained by meeting privately with influential faculty members prior to initiating the process of gaining approval.

Third—I think that those faculty involved with the program, or their representatives, should work with program administrators to formulate objectives that will guide the program in its implementation. These might be subject to modification later on as students' needs become more apparent. From the beginning, however, I think that objectives are essential, especially for innovation in liberal learning which often involves interdisciplinary coursework. It has been our experience at The University of Toledo that when standards and objectives for such coursework are vague, academic quality often deteriorates.

Fourth—I feel very strongly that students who become involved in an innovative program should be made fully aware of its experimental nature at the same time that they are informed of the new program's objectives. While you may discourage some potential students by doing this, the ones that you do retain develop a sense of identity and cohesiveness. Furthermore, if your program actually serves academic needs that are not being met elsewhere, you can count on student support and assistance, both of which are invaluable. Finally, such candor helps to keep the institution of higher learning honest.

Having made these preliminary remarks, I realize that each institution is unique and such generalizations might not apply to the process of creating new programs everywhere. Let me turn now to a brief overview of the history and development of the Adult Liberal Studies program at The University of Toledo and let you judge for yourself how our experiences might correspond to possible situations on your own campuses.

* * *

The Adult Liberal Studies program is designed to meet the needs of those over 25, who desire a potentially accelerated, interdisciplinary bachelors degree. To achieve this it offers credit by examination, topical seminars in social sciences, humanities and natural sciences and one year of electives, chosen by the student to meet personal or professional goals.

In 1971 the need for such a program had been well documented. Even before it was officially instituted a number of adults had enrolled. The program's first coordinator was a highly gifted individual who, from the beginning, emphasized student services. The original seminars were scheduled at times convenient for working adults, and both evening and weekend advising appointments were made available. He also informed the students that the program was new and, therefore, controversial, and that it would take time and effort on the part of everyone involved before it would be totally accepted.

Unfortunately for the program, however, faculty support was minimal. As the program had originally been established, the responsibility for teaching the interdisciplinary seminars was assigned to the various departments of the College of Arts and Sciences on a rotating basis. Department chairmen asked instructors to volunteer to teach the interdisciplinary seminars, and when they failed to do so, specific individuals were assigned. Many of these original teachers thus felt that they had been drafted, and their lack of enthusiasm was conveyed to the students in the program. Moreover, many of these early courses were not taught as interdisciplinary seminars, but instead were presented as modified versions of existing lecture courses. By the spring of 1976 the attrition rate approached sixty percent, and those students that remained complained bitterly. The program seemed moribund.

Those of us administering the program had not been inactive. We were committed to its continuation, if possible, because we knew that when this program ceased to exist many of the students involved would simply leave the university. It appeared obvious to us that the lack of academic quality in the program's major course offerings represented the greatest threat to its existence.

We also understood that there was absolutely no incentive for faculty to participate. At our institution faculty members achieve their promotion and tenure within their individual departments on the basis of departmental teaching and research. When they taught an ALS seminar they received no recognition; indeed many of them were penalized since their participation cost them time and effort that could have been devoted to career-advancing activities. In retrospect, it is surprising that, despite these problems, some of the initial seminars were well-conceived and well-taught. These instances were significant because they demonstrated to students the program's potential.

Given these problems it appeared that the only way to save the program was to improve the academic quality of the seminars. It was also necessary to broaden the base of faculty support. When the university administration was initially approached and asked to provide additional funds for overload compensation as a means of providing faculty incentive, the response was negative. Overall enrollment in the College of Arts and Sciences did not appear to justify increased funding. At this point the ALS program's problems appeared simply insurmountable.

The decision was made to survey all active and inactive students in order to produce more concrete data regarding the unmet needs of ALS students. We were especially interested in learning more about their motivation for enrolling, and we also sought to determine which aspects of the program were least satisfactory for them. The questionnaire was fairly extensive, covering sex, age, income and sources of financial aid, in addition to other questions.

I had not expected that over seventy percent of the respondents would check personal growth, rather than career advancement, as their primary reason for enrolling in the program. It came as no surprise, however, to discover that the educational experiences offered in the topical seminars provided the single greatest source of student dissatisfaction. Many of the ALS students felt so strongly about this matter that they wrote additional comments at the end of the survey. These included such remarks as: "The seminars have an ad hoc quality", "the seminars are uneven" or "we don't know what to expect—they are inconsistent."

The results of this survey were summarized and issued as a report to the Vice President for Academic Affairs. It included the following recommendations:

1. That a Faculty Advisory committee be established to review the program's progress and to establish academic objectives and standards for the topical seminars.

2. That the Faculty Advisory committee be charged with the responsibility for approaching faculty members and encouraging them to submit seminar proposals conforming to these newly established guidelines.

3. That the Faculty Advisory committee review the proposals received and select the outstanding ones, taking into account faculty interest in teaching adult students.

4. Finally, and perhaps most important of all, that the program be given additional funding so that the seminars hereafter would be taught on an overload basis.

This time the university administration accepted these recommendations and awarded the program additional funds on a trial basis. We had already determined that members of the Faculty Advisory Committee should be individuals respected on campus as teachers and scholars and, at the same time, active on the important faculty committees. We were able to involve individuals who met both criteria. One of the members, in fact, was elected chairman of the Faculty Senate shortly after he agreed to serve.

Over the past three years, these individuals have made outstanding contributions. In the winter of 1977 they painstakingly established a set of academic objectives for each of the series of topical seminars. Since then, they have explained the program to colleagues, defended it in the Faculty Senate and encouraged outstanding professors to submit course proposals. Overall, they have helped to give this program institutional legitimacy. The committee is comprised of a group of gifted and unique individuals, but I am sure that their counterparts exist on every campus.

The overload compensation has been set at the modest figure of $900 per quarter for a six hour seminar. Despite this, the number and quality of proposed courses have steadily increased over the past three years. Moreover, every professor who has participated on this basis has resubmitted proposals for the following years. What has happened really, I think, is that the instructors who have taught on a voluntary basis have discovered the many intrinsic rewards of teaching adults. These students generally complete the required readings, often write fairly well and are, almost always, enthusiastic contributors to classroom discussion.

The funds for overload compensations have now become a permanent part of the program's budget. We have conducted no new surveys, in large part because we have been busy advising the new and continuing students in the program. Overall the level of student satisfaction has risen along with the academic quality of the liberal studies seminars.

Last year the ALS program benefitted greatly as the recipient of a QUILL grant. This enabled us to enrich the topical seminars by bringing in outside speakers and introducing a course entitled "Ethical Decision Making and Career/Life Planning" for ALS students. Finally, we were able to host a two-day conference on "The Liberal Arts and Lifelong Learning." All of these activities combined have given the program greater visibility both within the university and the community.

This fall seventy new students entered the program largely on the basis of favorable comments that had been made by students within the program. There is no concern at this point that it will die. Indeed it is now viewed institutionally as a model adult degree program which should serve the University of Toledo well in the decade of the 1980s as traditional student enrollment declines.

American Agriculture in the Liberal Arts Setting: An Interdisciplinary Approach

John D. Heyl

A review of innovations in liberal learning over the past five years would probably identify interdisciplinary teaching as one of the leading teaching strategies of the period. This development has been especially notable at smaller colleges and universities that emphasize their teaching mission and where faculty contacts across disciplines are more common than at larger, research-oriented institutions where specialists have a prior claim to many subject areas with an interdisciplinary potential.

Illinois Wesleyan, a small (1600 students, 125 faculty) central Illinois university combining a Liberal Arts College and four professional schools (art, drama, music, nursing), belongs in the former category noted above. Some of the recent interdisciplinary innovations at IWU have emerged from the easy exchange among faculty from different departments and schools; others have arisen from a recognition that many pressing problems of the day require a team approach if we are to help solve—or even clarify—them with our students. Recent additions to the curriculum at IWU from both these sources include: bioethics; writing and reasoning (a course in essay writing and logic taught by English and philosophy faculty); religion and the liberal arts (a course team-taught by members of the Religion Department and including visiting teachers from four other disciplines); community studies; human growth and development (a course taught by a biologist, sociologist and psychologist for nursing majors); utopian studies; and national food policy—the last named being the theme of a QUILL-sponsored project originally funded in 1978. Depending on educational tradition and patterns of faculty interaction, other institutions may well reflect a different pattern of interdisciplinary efforts, but some thrust in this direction has probably been evident in recent years.

Indeed, interdisciplinary teaching—by one definition or another—is probably even more widespread than is reflected by a listing of new

John D. Heyl is an associate professor in the Department of History at Illinois Wesleyan University, Bloomington, IL 61701.

courses. A recent review at IWU, for example, revealed that such teaching was more common than first supposed. This was especially true in those courses in which one or more instructors from the same discipline raise questions or discuss problems that fall naturally into other disciplines. Such would be the case when an historian raises questions regarding the structure of political revolutions, or when a chemist discusses problems in the media's presentation of alleged pollution hazards. The same review, however, also pointed out that other levels of interdisciplinary teaching, although increasing in number, were still relatively rare. These variants include those courses in which two or more instructors from different disciplines treat different aspects of the same problem from their disciplinary perspectives, or those courses in which two or more instructors from different disciplines treat the same aspects of a problem.

These latter approaches, necessarily team-taught, cross-departmental courses, will probably be the first to go on the defensive in the coming years. Several factors will contribute to this development: the drift back to a curriculum emphasizing "basic skills"; growing departmental parochialism in the face of shrinking resources; waning enthusiasm under the strain of administering such courses; and the relatively high cost of such courses in their developmental phase. At Illinois Wesleyan, a similar wave of interdisciplinary teaching in the early 1960s bequeathed only a single offering (an upper-level humanities course) to the present curriculum. Signs point to an uncertain future for many recent efforts of this sort.

Many elements, of course, ultimately determine the success or failure of innovation in any area. Developing well-defined objectives shared by both administrators and faculty is certainly important. Especially with interdisciplinary courses, however, four other considerations are decisive. First, it must be shown that the offering meets a particular curricular need of the institution. Second, one must demonstrate to both faculty and students that the offering, instead of diluting general education requirements, actually strengthens them through its holistic or problem-solving approach. Third, faculty with strong teaching and scholarly reputations must be recruited into the teaching of the offering. Fourth, support for participating faculty (such as summer stipends or release time) must be forthcoming to foster the development of subject matter competence and to ease the administrative burden involved in planning and implementing such courses.

Interdisciplinary teaching is no panacea for the many curricular issues facing higher education today. In any given case, the goals of specific faculty teaching specific subject matters must dictate the appropriate teaching strategy—not the other way around. But in light of the inevitable pressures that will be brought to bear on them, what will be the fate of recent interdisciplinary efforts on our campuses? Illinois Wesleyan's experience with its QUILL project—"American Agriculture in the Liberal Arts Setting: An Interdisciplinary Approach"—may offer some insights into these issues.

* * *

Illinois Wesleyan is implementing a QUILL grant to develop a curricular role for the study of American agriculture in a liberal arts setting. IWU's geographical location, the background of many of its students, the economy of the region, and the persistence of national and global food issues, all suggest the need for a commitment in this area. Indeed, these have been the same factors that have led some faculty to want to develop their own competence in the subject.

With QUILL support we have been able to study curricular experiments in this field on other campuses, to present a one-day agricultural institute (March 1979) bringing members of the surrounding community to Wesleyan's campus, and to organize a one-week faculty workshop (July 1979) to build an interdisciplinary teaching team (including a biologist, an economist and an historian). A new course—"American Food—Problems and Policies"—will first be offered in spring 1980.

It is too early, of course, to judge the prospects for this new interdisciplinary offering, but the road to this point in its development may be instructive.

Original interest in launching a course on food policy stemmed from a January short-term experimental course on world hunger in 1977. The teaching team in that course happened almost by accident. (In fact, one member of the team was added at the last minute because of a personnel change in one of the departments involved.) But the interdisciplinary experience on a topic of both current interest and painful complexity was an exciting one for those participating. Indeed, our decision to seek QUILL support, and our efforts since then, are themselves products of the kind of stimulation that interdisciplinary teaching makes possible.

With momentum provided in part by QUILL funds, our next step was to convince the faculty at large that such a venture was worthwhile, perhaps as a permanent feature of the curriculum. Although only limited university resources could be committed in this area (no major sequence program was contemplated), a new course on American agriculture promised to make an important contribution to the social science curriculum and to broader university goals as well. The course we envisioned embraced three main elements: a nutritional analysis of human needs for food; an economic analysis of the supply and demand for food products; and an analysis of the major policy issues concerning America's responsibilities to its farmers, consumers, and the hungry world. We argued that these central problems of the course should be seen holistically; hence the need to build an interdisciplinary team able to bring special knowledge to bear in a discussion of policy alternatives and value choices. Through these latter emphases the course addressed some of the needs recently identified by the faculty as overarching goals for the freshman year, in particular in the areas of problem-oriented instruction and normative analysis.

As the consideration of the course proceeded, some faculty raised questions regarding the appropriateness of such a course meeting a general education distribution requirement in the social sciences. These faculty held the view that interdisciplinary courses are inevitably "mushy" and thus weaken the traditionally discipline-based requirements. This, I think, has not been the case at IWU in the past, but such a view reflects a sentiment that is certainly shared on other campuses as well. In the face of this sort of objection, our argument was that general education credit in the social sciences was appropriate because of the policy-orientation of the course, supported by the distinctive, yet complementary, contributions by the participating disciplines of biology, economics, and history. The aim of the course was thus to increase understanding of a complex process in American society: the production and distribution of food and the policy issues this process raises. This seemed to us to be an ideal subject for social scientific analysis. Our arguments convinced the faculty to support the introduction of the course. Subsequently, a faculty-based academic advising system has enrolled fifty students in the first offering this spring.

Successful staffing of an interdisciplinary course that crosses not only three disciplines but also three major administrative divisions within the university was the next challenge. We felt it was important to recruit strong teachers to the team. This task was complicated by the limited availability of crucial faculty who were, in any case, under heavy student-load pressures already (especially in biology and economics). These problems have been overcome for now, but they will surely recur in future offerings of the course. We hope that the commitment of interested faculty, the value of the teaching experience, and the response of our students will sustain us.

Finally, I come to the role of QUILL funding in this venture. Basically, QUILL funds made it possible to buy faculty time and experience—time to develop their own competence and experience through visits to ongoing programs on other campuses. But outside funding did more than that. At the time the QUILL grant was awarded, IWU was in the third year of a major grant from a private foundation. Much curricular innovation had taken place during the previous two years. The QUILL grant, however, made it possible for a few faculty to take action at a time when the administrators of the larger grant were turning their attention more to "mission statements" for the university at large. Thus the timing of the grant was of special importance. A small grant cannot, of course, sustain our efforts financially or provide campus legitimacy into the indefinite future. In the end, the new course will have to legitimize itself. But during the crucial phases of planning and early implementation, the QUILL grant was indispensable.

Topical Integration of Humanities and Career Education

Landon C. Kirchner

All of us, I would imagine, have heard the complaint that it takes a hundred years for a new idea to gain acceptance in education, and some of us have no doubt read J.B. Hefferlin's often cited simile that "changing the curriculum. . . is like moving a graveyard," which is by no means a small undertaking. Bringing about change in education is commonly regarded as being on the order of a Herculean task, though hopefully not to be compared with cleaning the Aegean Stables.

Yet educators persist in proposing and implementing innovative programs. Curriculum committees are beseiged with new course proposals which are transdisciplinary, interdisciplinary, cross-disciplinary and non-disciplinary. Funding sources are similarly inundated with requests for funds to support a myriad of innovative and novel programs.

This contradiction between attitude and behavior suggests that either innovators are promising a good deal more than they are delivering with their curricular innovations; i.e., the realities of curricular reform are much harsher than innovators recognize, or there is a degree of chicanery involved with innovation proposal, which is to suggest there is some deliberate illusion in our innovative efforts.

The position I wish to recommend is that the realities of curricular change are indeed harsh and there is certainly both "hucksterism" and self-aggrandizement associated with innovation, nevertheless we ought to encourage innovative efforts for reasons other than their potential to produce significant curricular change.

First and foremost we need to recognize that the curriculum of a college is not limited to its course offerings, but rather consists of the total college environment. The climate created by the processes, activities, and attitudes of the college community is every bit as instructive as the courses taught or studied. Therefore, innovation—or the attempt to introduce something new—is as much a part of the curriculum as anything else, as is, of course, non-innovation. A willingness to try the new com-

Landon C. Kirchner is Director of Humanities and Social Science at Johnson County Community College, Overland Park, KS 66210.

municates more about a college than its official catalog.

With this in mind, perhaps we ought not to be disturbed when an innovative program doesn't last. Just maybe there are other advantages to an institution than the permanent addition to the curriculum of women' studies, international education, American studies, or values in contemporary society. I would suggest that the stimulation for the faculty, the excitement for participating students, and the publicity attendant to the novelty, all have beneficial consequences for institutions which support new programs with relatively short life-spans.

The traditional curriculum survives not because it is immovably entrenched and defended by intransigent vested interests, but because it constitutes a paradigm which still has value for us. Provided, of course, that it is not an issue of allocation of scarce resources, we can accommodate innovation and stability, by recognizing the value of the process of innovation rather than the longevity of its individual efforts.

We should also be aware of the regenerative power of innovation for faculty enthusiasm. I believe it is a well recognized fact that teachers enjoy a course more the first time they teach it, provided, of course, it has not been an unwelcome assignment. This is due not only to the novelty of the approach, but also that it largely constitutes a learning experience. Teaching new courses puts us in the happy position of being explorers along with our students.

Surely one of the most productive staff development activities is the opportunity to teach new programs, and this is especially so when such programs are non-traditional, causing the faculty participants to stretch their intellectual capacities a bit. This is in effect an important ingredient in institutional renewal. Colleges that receive and encourage innovation are alive and those that don't resemble elephant burial grounds, inhabited by ponderous intellectual pachyderms waiting around to die.

I would be remiss at this juncture if I did not note that I believe there is considerable institutional value in "reinventing the wheel." The logicians in the audience can no doubt recite this section with me, since it is a patently obvious inference that if the process of innovation is more important than the product, then the novelty of the proposal is not a crucial consideration. Indeed, where reinvention of the wheel means doing over what some other institution has already done, we receive the added value of our predecessor's experience. On the other hand if we should attempt to develop programs without consulting the literature or the experience of others in order to preserve the pristine character of our novelty, this is simply foolish and constitutes a waste of resources.

Certainly funding agencies will continue to evaluate proposals on the basis of their originality and their seminal potential. Still institutional support should be predicated upon the appropriateness of the suggested innovation for that college, and if this means relative novelty then so be it. Copying what someone else has successfully developed is not particularly foreign to education. To my knowledge there is no copyright on curricula.

A caution on this procedure is in order, however. Importing programs from other colleges is a risky business and not a very promising technique for encouraging innovation if done too rigidly. The primary ingredient in successful curricular innovation is enthusiastic faculty, and faculty wax much more enthusiastic over their own materials than those received from external sources. We have had a difficult time making TV courses work for precisely this reason. The faculty have not had a hand in developing the material and consequently don't see it is all that usable for instructional purposes.

This brings me to my final general point, which is that while people are the most important feature in innovative program creation and implementation, good management often makes the difference in success or failure. There are clearly stages or steps to be covered in developing and executing innovation, and lack of attention to them, or getting things out of order, can condemn a program to failure.

There is a good body of literature existent on creating change and academic reform, and I would not presume to improve on or contribute to it. I wish simply to note that innovation has three steps; origination, solicitation, and legitimization, which are crucial.

Unlike Karl Popper's position that it doesn't matter where scientific hypotheses come from, it certainly does matter where ideas for innovation come from, or at least where they must appear to come from. Successful innovation requires grass roots commitment and cannot be imposed from above. The creative administrator with a plan for innovation had better find a way to excite her/his faculty about it or coach someone into coming up with her/his idea.

Once an idea has someone's commitment it becomes necessary to solicit the support of others who must either participate, agree not to oppose, support with resources, or approve the proposal. Careful management of this stage is the true test of administrative ability. To assume that a worthy proposal will be well received on its own merit is the height of naivete. I believe my colleagues Shirley Leckie and John Heyl will have more to say on this issue.

Finally the legitimization stage involves the implementation and publication of the program. The College may choose to develop brochures on the program, or write it up in professional journals, or release a news item, etc., but one of the most effective vehicles for institutional legitimization is receipt of funding. To receive a grant means that the program is legitimate enough to be worthy of someone else's attention, and such funding carries enormous value in promoting the program within the college. Certainly this was the case at JCCC with our QUILL grant, and I will say more about it after we hear from Ms. Leckie and Dr. Heyl.

* * *

One of our approaches to innovation in liberal learning grew out of the traditional guest lecturing activities common to all colleges and out of our unique problems as a community college.

Faculty in the humanities and social sciences at Johnson County Community College have often been asked by their colleagues in other areas to give lectures for them on a variety of subjects. These tended to be random occurrences based more upon personal contact than anything else, and no attempt had been made to formalize these relationships or make them permanent parts of the courses.

However, this existing precedent helped us to solve a problem which has been developing since our college became more comprehensive in its offerings. Like many of other community colleges, Johnson County had been experiencing a rapid growth in occupational programming, and the lack of general education courses in the rigidly prescriptive curricula of these programs constituted a serious concern of all of us.

After consideration of a variety of approaches to addressing this problem we decided that the favorable reception of our lectures suggested that exposure of occupational program students to liberal learning might be accomplished in this manner.

To facilitate the origination stage we did two major things. We established a college seminar series which drew faculty from all areas of the college, and offered the opportunity to discuss social, educational, and professional issues. We also publicized the willingness of some faculty to give guest lecturers and listed things that had been on-going.

These two activities had the desired effect of placing any suggested proposal for integration of humanities in occupational courses in the context of existing practices which had faculty initiative, and they created liaisons between humanities faculty and occupational program faculty. Indeed, by far the more favorable comments on the seminar series were from the people in the career areas who expressed how enjoyable it was to have the chance to discuss these issues. The esteem for humanities education was clearly increased by virtue of the seminar series.

The solicitation stage was facilitated by the funding of a consultant grant from NEH. Dr. William Alexander of the University of Michigan visited our campus on three occasions and met with every instructor in the occupational programs and the humanities. By design his approach was low-key and non-directive. He assessed the institutional readiness for an integrative project and he sought to identify areas where faculty felt such modules would be helpful. He did not rule out any possible way the humanities and occupational curricula might be combined.

As a result of Dr. Alexander's work two humanities instructors Dr. Lois Nettleship and Dr. Scott Yeargain proposed the development of history and philosophy modules to be integrated into regular course offerings in the areas of law enforcement, nursing, and business. They had established cooperative liaisons with faculty in these areas and were responding to specific requests for presentations.

To legitimize their proposals the college granted two sections of released-time to Dr. Nettleship and a one semester sabbatical leave to Dr. Yeargain. An important step in our legitimization stage was the awarding of the QUILL grant for integrating humanities modules in occupational programs. Through QUILL funds we were able to bring consultants to the campus to video tape presentations and to speak to classes and faculty in humanities and career areas. We were able to fund travel to special conferences for our released faculty, and most importantly, we were able to publicize their efforts through announcement of receipt of the grant. QUILL became synonymous at Johnson County with integration of humanities and occupational education.

We are currently in the assessment and modification stage of our overall effort, as we are taking a look at how we might have improved upon some of the modules and how we might broaden our efforts to reach other career programs. We have learned a good deal from these efforts, and we expect this to be one of our continuing focuses in years to come.

Still, even if we decided to not develop another module, I would have to regard the effort as worthwhile due to the impact it has had upon faculty and students. Keeping our institutions alive requires just these sorts of things.

Appendix II

Quality in Liberal Learning
(How to Improve It)

QUILL Assessment Conference

Washington, D.C., March 3-4, 1981

A. Liberal Learning in Continuing Education

Liberal Learning and Individual Educational Planning: Approach to Adult Education

William H. Maehl, Jr.

The QUILL project undertaken by the College of Liberal Studies addressed the problem of how to renew a nontraditional program which had operated so long that it had become a tradition in itself.

The College of Liberal Studies is a unit of the University of Oklahoma charged to offer baccalaureate and masters degrees in liberal education to adult students by nontraditional procedures. The College was founded when the Bachelor of Liberal Studies program was launched in 1961. The BLS was one of the earliest special degree programs for adults, and it paved the way for many of the adult-oriented innovations in higher education that have occurred during the last two decades. The Master of Liberal Studies program was established in 1968. The programs offer interdisciplinary study in humanities, natural sciences, and social sciences for persons who seek broad liberal educational development rather than career oriented study. Their curricula strive for coherence and integration through a thematic organization of study which emphasizes the in-

---

William H. Maehl, Jr., is dean of the College of Liberal Studies at the University of Oklahoma, Norman, OK 73069.

terrelatedness of knowledge. The programs have always sought to avoid the fragmentation of the credit hour system and short, self-contained courses. Instead they proceed by study of large blocks of content and outcome is measured by major comprehensive examinations. Instructional procedures are flexible and adapted to individual students in terms of time and place.

In tackling the problem of curriculum renovation the College shared the current concern among educators to redefine the "core curriculum," although from a somewhat different perspective. We had never moved in the direction of the formlessness of curriculum that many other colleges accepted during the 1960s. Our study programs remained largely prescribed sequences embodying a classic concept of the liberal arts derived from the medieval university and more recently reflected in the College of the University of Chicago during the Hutchins period. We have suffered, however, from overdependence upon disparate studies in specific disciplines which lacked the depth and integration that we sought. In addition the program has not offered enough scope for students to pursue their individual interests. The latter problem was particularly acute, since, as Professor Malcolm Knowles has taught us, adult students feel a strong desire to play a major role in the design of their own programs of study.

The faculty of the College were strongly committed to both objectives of revision of core study and individualization. Further, they saw them as mutually supportive of each other. They believed that individualization could best be carried out within the context of a plan of liberal education that increased learners' awareness of intellectual possibilities and required the integration of specific interests within a general perspective. By providing direction in the early phases of the program, the faculty hoped to lead students to the point where they could take charge of and assume responsibility for major segments of their own educational development. At the same time the faculty sought to help students see greater significance in their individually focussed study effort and to assist them to attain a more coherent and satisfying world view. The goals became the creation of a holistic adult study program that would integrate interdisciplinary core studies in liberal education with individual educational planning.

While the will of the faculty for renovation was present, the practices and views of nearly twenty years about procedures, content and materials were very strongly entrenched. A major problem was to provide the necessary catalysts to bring about change. The QUILL grant was vital to accomplishing that.

With the resources to make modest payments to a few faculty, we were able to appoint six coordinators. Three took leadership in developing new definitions of the core study in humanities, the natural sciences and the social sciences. Another three, while maintaining liaison with the core study coordinators, considered ways to introduce individualized study components into each of the three areas. Both sets of coordinators consulted widely with their faculty colleagues and elicited many suggestions from them, but each coordinator had a personal responsibility for developing a proposal that represented his or her best judgment. Thus we avoided the banality of many committee recommendations while preserving wide participation in the process.

Simultaneously with the studies of the coordinators, we tried to expand our own experience and to benefit from external counsel and advice. Selected faculty made trips to observe other programs that seemed to offer models that would be useful. These included the External Programs Office of the University of Kentucky, Birmingham Southern College and New College of the University of Alabama, and Empire State College. In addition, the QUILL grant enabled us to bring two consultants, Dr. Harold L. Hodgkinson and Dr. Malcolm Knowles, to the campus to meet with faculty and to advise us on the problems that we confronted. Fortunately, we had an additional bonus in that we were awarded a National Endowment for Humanities Consultant Grant that allowed us to use a special consultant in the humanities, Dr. Jacqueline Mattfeld of Barnard College.

Throughout these activities, which extended over several months, the coordinators maintained liaison with the College administration and with the College Faculty through weekly meetings of its Executive Committee.

The core study coordinators were charged to develop conceptual or thematic orientations for each area along with suggestions for text material on which study was to be based. In due course, all three reported with very stimulating proposals. Social Sciences concentrated on the themes of Cultural Differences and Social Conflict. Natural Sciences selected the Environment. Humanities took a different approach by proposing a "core within the core" that developed certain common themes and problems within all the humanities, followed by a number of options among thematic modules from which the student could select.

When the core study proposals were ready the QUILL grant permitted a substantial group of the college faculty to hold a weekend retreat at a state lodge to review and refine the proposals. The retreat was highly successful and resulted in finished proposals that then were submitted to the faculty for approval and implementation.

In parallel, the individual study coordinators recommended that an optional or elective element be allowed in each of our three broad areas of study. They recommended procedures by which students might design unique components reflecting their individual interests. In effect, the way was opened for students and their faculty to form contract agreements establishing the objectives of study, the activities to be undertaken, the form in which the student was to present evidence of achievement and the means by which achievement was to be evaluated.

We believed that this combination of more coherently designed core study accompanied by individual study contracts needed a test before we implemented it fully.

To do so, we undertook a pilot experiment by inviting a group of students to try the new pattern and then to reassemble two months later for evaluation of it. By all indications, the changes were well received by students who tried them and we decided to proceed with the new pattern.

Implementation entailed extensive follow-up work. Since much of our study procedure involves independent study at a distance, it was necessary to prepare totally new study guides orienting students to the materials. Our examination and student feedback procedures had to be overhauled completely in accord with the new plan of study. Also, it was necessary to carry out extensive faculty orientation to the new study content as well as to the novel procedure of developing learning contracts with students. These processes were greatly facilitated by a staff member with considerable skill in curriculum design and faculty development, and the tasks were accomplished within a minimum period of time.

The plan has now been in operation for about eighteen months and seems to be working extremely well. Both faculty and students report satisfaction with the content of the study and with the individualized procedures. Our development process was one in which there was a broad sense of participation, but leadership was focused enough to maintain coherence. Certain administrative adjustments have been necessary to accommodate the new procedures, but staff have been interested in the program and fully cooperative. We believe the effort has given new life to a distinguished and older program for adults, and it has preserved commitments to integration, quality and individuality that are at the heart of liberal education.

A Core Program in the Liberal Arts
for Continuing Education Students

Bernard Mausner

May I begin by describing the "natural history" of the continuing education student at our college in our newly-instituted evening program in business administration. She (more often than he) is between 25 and 45 years of age, has had a year or so of work at a postsecondary institution, usually a community college, and is working at a clerical or first-level supervisory position in industry. The need for a college degree is based on a desire for emancipation from routine repetitive work; the degree represents a ticket of admission to the upper levels of the managerial-professional hierarchy. And so the student comes to our college for the courses in accounting, computer science, finance or management which will furnish that ticket. The goal, in essence, is not education but training.

But the student has wandered into a strange kind of institution called a liberal arts college, one dedicated to education. Our faculty designs curricula which include a fair representation of courses outside the technical fields in which the students will work. The students take these, more or less willingly, especially if the instrumental character of the courses is clear ("writing for careers", "statistics"). In addition, we feel the need for breadth. And so we try to sort out the varied choices for a program in general education—distribution requirements (the Chinese restaurant menu curriculum, four humanities, two lab sciences etc.) vs. core courses vs. credits for "life experiences".

We use the approach of requiring distribution of courses in humanities, social sciences and natural sciences for our regular day-session undergraduates. For many reasons this did not seem attractive for the new evening session program in business administration which we have been initiating during the past two years. Firstly, the number of students was relatively small and so the day-session's range of possible courses was not practicable. Thus the number of choices would be limited. Secondly, many of the courses we could offer would be

---

Bernard Mausner is chairman of the Department of Psychology at Beaver College, Glenside, PA 19038.

somewhat remote from the lives of adult students; we assumed that we could not ask these to suspend disbelief in quite the same way we did the regular undergraduates. Thirdly, we weren't really pleased with the distribution requirements in our regular college and so were ready for experimentation.

Credit for "life experiences" *is* offered by our college. But as a general rule it is not a good substitute for formal course work in the liberal arts. In general, our students have read relatively little, have not acquired a framework of ideas to be used in sorting out their experiences. My own personal reaction is that, except for unusual people, life experience is not a valid basis for exemption from general education. And so the decision was taken, casually and somewhat on the run, to plan a series of core courses, one in each of the three major areas of liberal learning— humanities, natural science, social science. Fortunately the AAC/QUILL program gave us the funds to support some free time for two instructors and some modest start-up costs for two of these three courses. The remainder of this paper is devoted to a brief description of our experiences in this activity.

The goals of liberal learning: One general goal emerged from our discussions. We felt that students should learn to select and store information in an orderly way that permitted retrieval. This information would be useful for the solution of problems, but it would also provide the "prepared mind" which permitted informed response to new experiences. The key is the notion of orderly storage, the conceptual schemes which permit orderly storage function as a kind core for the growth of knowledge and understanding. The metaphor which comes to mind is the crystal in a solution which provides a center for the growth of a gem.

If the goal is the development of a framework of ideas, constructs, and concepts, then no group of narrow areas of subject matter or theoretical schemas is crucial; none of the traditional disciplines is unreplaceable. What is essential is that the student be prepared to enter new areas of knowledge with strategies for ordering experiences.

The new courses: Three courses were proposed as a core in general studies. These covered the traditional areas, humanities, natural science and social science. Since the QUILL grant was not sufficient to support development of all three courses we decided to focus on the first two of these areas, in view of the fact that most students in business administration were exposed to many aspects of social science as part of their professional training. Committees were set up to guide the development of each of the two new courses; these consisted of the project director, the instructor whose time was released, and representatives of each of the major disciplines represented in the courses. The courses were designed during the spring of 1979 and were given first during the academic year 1979-80. At that point the evening college enrolled approximately 200 students for at least one course. However, many were not matriculated as degree students and others had been exempted from the requirement of core courses because of prior work. About ten students enrolled for each of the two core courses. Word of mouth proved a valuable resource; both courses were offered to substantially increased enrollment in 1980-81.

The course in humanities: The specific goal of this course was to enable students to obtain enlarged esthetic experiences and to relate these to the concerns of their lives. The arts were to be represented as they were imbedded in the cultural matrix of the society in which they were developed as well as in the society in which the student lived. In the end, the student, we hoped, would emerge with a cognitive and emotional structure for responding to works of art.

To accomplish this goal Dr. Gerald Belcher and the committee which worked with him drafted a course which included several components. The course began with an analysis of abstract painting from the twentieth century in order to illustrate the role of the humanities in society. This was done in part by beginning with children's art, including some of the works of art created by the children of the students in the group. Children's art was compared to the work of German expressionists such as Klee and Kandinsky. Following this segment the relation of values and art was explored through an analysis of painting and poetry. The social function of art was then analyzed in a study of architecture.

The remainder of the course was devoted to an intensive analysis of the works of art of a single year, chosen because of its importance as a period of transition in both art and society. This was the year 1905. An historical framework was presented, including a discussion of major trends in ideas, the contrast of rationalism and irrationalism in the work of Freud and Einstein. Next some of the important painting of the period was studied, the post-impressionist school in France (the Fauves) and the group known as Die Bruecke in Germany. The conflict of artist and conventional society was illustrated through the discussion of the artist as Bohemian. Literature of the time was exemplified by short works of Gide, Mann and Dreiser published during the year. Lastly, the new prairie school of architecture was presented through the work of Frank Lloyd Wright.

The final meeting of the course was devoted to a discussion of the role of the arts today, especially as they touched the lives of the students. Active participation by the students was the rule; at least one brief paper was written each week and a number of essay examinations were required during the course of the term.

The student's reactions to the course were uniformly favorable. Without exception, they gave positive responses to questions on attitude surveys concerning the interestingness of the course, the relevance to their lives, the effectiveness in awakening interest in continuing contact with the humanities. And, as I indicated above, the word of mouth reports were so good that the enrollment in the course more than the doubled during the following year.

The course in natural science: We had a model for the course in an interdisciplinary course in science developed at the college under a grant from the National Science Foundation, which has been offered for the past decade. Fortunately one of the instructors in that course Dr. Ronald Rowe was available to develop the new course. It had to be different; for one thing the new course was to be aimed at working adults. For another it had to be offered without a laboratory.

The key to the course was the concept of a system. This was first developed in general terms. It was then exemplified through an analysis of several specific ecosystems. Basic concepts of matter and energy were then introduced, as always through the concept of system. Finally, a variety of living systems ranging from complex molecules through cells to organisms were described.

The focus then shifted to the earth as a closed system—the now familiar concept of "spaceship earth." Interrelations of man and environment were illustrated through the study of the use of energy and the dilemmas faced by our society because of the approaching exhaustion of fossil fuels were analyzed. Next the group analyzed population as a system, studying population dynamics, the factors which affected growth and stability of population levels. Lastly, the study of pollution of various kinds and its relation to health was used to illustrate the approach of analysis of systems in the study of health and illness. The course ended with several specific problems of interest to both the instructor and the students— brain function and the problems of research with recombinent DNA.

As with the course in humanities, the students expressed enthusiasm, both formally on attitude questionnaires, and informally in discussion with the staff and among peers. This course was also substantially enrolled the second time it was offered. We are hoping that the course in social science will be offered during 1981-82, although no external support for its development has been available.

As a final comment, I should like to quote the last paragraph of our report to AAC on the QUILL project. It represents a summary of our feelings about the core program.

"In conclusion, the program has demonstrated that it is possible to project central ideas in both science and the humanities to mature students through interdisciplinary courses. These courses were not watered down surveys; they dealt in some depth and with considerable rigor with the key ideas that were presented. Of course, these activities are not intended as substitutes for systematic work in the traditional disciplines. If anything, the background they offer should make the students better equipped to handle first courses in chemistry or literature. But, if they are terminal courses, the students who had them should be better citizens, more capable of making decisions in their work, and should lead enriched lives."

Liberal Arts for Health Professionals: Strengthening the Liberal Learning Component of Continuing Education

Thomas G. Travis

Established in 1974, the Division of General Studies within St. Joseph's College offers a highly individualized degree option to persons living in the New York metropolitan area. While possessing the capacity to meet the needs of a diverse professional population, the program is more fully developed to serve those engaged in the health professions; of the 1,200 students currently working toward the B.S. degree in General Studies, the majority are R.N.s. Adding to their uniqueness as aspirants to the baccalaureate is the fact that they are predominately Black, female, middle aged, and foreign born. Thus, St. Joseph's Division of General Studies is making a significant contribution to the improvement of the area's medical delivery system while, at the same time, serving an adult population heretofore left out of the educational mainstream.

Although there are no specific course requirements or majors for the B.S. in General Studies, students are required to take 60 of the 128 credits needed for their degree from the liberal arts. Students may elect to complete a module of courses for which certificates are awarded. At the present time, two modules are in place—Community Health and Health Administration.

The bottom line of the problem to be addressed by our QUILL project was that the emphasis of adult continuing education was typically skewed toward the professional component of students' programs, depriving these students of the essential skills and understandings long associated with the liberal arts. While many factors contribute to this situation, the most prevalent was that students viewed liberal arts as an irrelevant frill—less appropriate than professional courses for the attainment of success in their chosen field.

This trend is ironic in that increasing evidence is surfacing to indicate that, even in highly technical areas, successful job performance is linked to such generic liberal arts skills as problem solving and critical thinking.

Thomas G. Travis is director of the Division of General Studies at St. Joseph's College, Brooklyn, NY 11205.

Pioneering work has been done in this area by David McClelland and his associates at the Institute for Competence Assessment. In collaboration with McClelland, the FIPSE-funded Competency-based Undergraduate Education (CUE) Center undertook two investigations to determine correlates of superior job performance in the corporate sector and found critical thinking and problem solving capabilities to be important factors. More directly applicable to the health care field, a current NIE-funded study at St. Charles Hospital in Toledo is confirming the work of the CUE Center, indicating that the difference between average and superior nurses is in part explained by the presence or absence of these liberal arts skills.

Overall objectives of the QUILL project at St. Joseph's include the following:

1. Develop, teach, and evaluate a course that specifically addresses the acquisition of generic problem solving skills and their application to the health care field.

2. Develop, teach, and evaluate a course that specifically addresses the acquisition of generic critical thinking skills and their application to the health care field.

3. Develop, teach, and evaluate a course that links the liberal arts with the field of Community Health.

4. Develop, teach, and evaluate a course that links the liberal arts with the field of Health Administration.

5. Create for each course listed above a workbook to ensure that multiple sections of these essentially interdisciplinary courses can be taught by a diverse adjunct faculty without loss of continuity.

6. Integrate the above-listed courses into a recommended sequence with courses already being developed within the Division that address the academic skills of communication and computation.

7. Through the successful completion of the first six objectives, instill in students an appreciation for and understanding of the liberal arts so that each student will be more willing and better able to work with an advisor to create an individualized program that is a balanced combination of professional and liberal arts courses.

In order to meet these objectives, four curriculum development teams composed of two adjunct faculty each worked with the Project Director and the Coordinator for Curriculum Development to create four courses: 1) Problem Solving for Health Professionals; 2) Critical Thinking for Health Professionals; 3) Community Health and General Studies; and 4) Health Administration and General Studies.

As a first step for this project, the director and the coordinator of curriculum development (later designated coordinator of faculty) convened the curriculum development teams composed of one member with a liberal arts orientation and the other from the health field. These teams were brought together as a group twice during the spring of that same academic year, one time to listen to the remarks of Dr. M. Neil Browne, past director of Bowling Green's critical thinking program, and the other time to hear Ms. Wendy Soubel, who was involved in the NIE-funded St. Charles Project, who discussed the general skills of critical thinking (Browne) and problem solving (Soubel). In addition to these individuals, Arthur Whimbey, Resident Scholar in the Center for Academic Skills of CCNY, spoke to various faculty members about his experience in problem solving. For the remainder of the spring, these teams worked to prepare their courses for the summer session, meeting together on their own with varying degrees of frequency.

That summer, two sections of each course were taught at the main campus in Brooklyn. With regard to the degree of uniformity between sections, some of the team course outlines were similar while others were not. At the conclusion of the semester, students in each course completed an evaluation questionnaire.

Toward the end of the summer, it was necessary to train a few additional faculty members to teach the courses in the fall. This was done through one-on-one training sessions between the experienced instructors and those just joining the project.

The fall semester saw an overall increase in sections of the courses as follows: Problem Solving, four sections; Critical Thinking, three sections; Community Health and the Liberal Arts, two sections; and Health Administration and the Liberal Arts, one section. These sections were offered at both the main campus and the Suffolk campus in Patchogue.

On December 10, 1980, Dr. David Sweet, President of Rhode Island College, came to the Brooklyn campus as a QUILL representative. While at St. Joseph's, he met with the director and the coordinator of faculty, visited a QUILL course in process, and participated in a working meeting of the QUILL faculty. At that meeting, the group discussed faculty evaluation methods, training of faculty for the spring semester, and the preparation of the final report.

The number of new sections for that spring increased dramatically, the result of the registration of new majors in Community Health and Health Administration—both of which had the QUILL courses as their core curriculum.

The entire faculty was invited to attend three training sessions, two in Brooklyn and one on the Patchogue campus. The sessions were approximately three hours in length, during which the QUILL faculty explained the nature of their courses. This was followed by a concentrated immersion in the specific courses the new faculty members desired to teach. The total number of sections eventually offered that semester was as follows:

Problem Solving, twelve; Critical Thinking, thirteen; Community Health and the Liberal Arts, five; and Health Administration and the Liberal Arts, six. As was the case the preceding semester, these courses were offered at the main and branch campuses, plus at off-campus extension sites.

On February 29, 1980, the QUILL faculty, both veterans and new recruits, were invited to a wrap-up and evaluation session. At this time, in lieu of a questionnaire, the faculty, through open-ended verbal responses, evaluated the overall project.

The primary objectives of the project—developing, teaching, and evaluating the courses—were, as indicated above, accomplished as planned, although not without surprises—some pleasant, some not.

With regard to developing the courses, the consultants were excellent. They inspired in the project participants great enthusiasm for the venture. Most helped, of course, were the instructors teaching Problem Solving and Critical Thinking. Those faculty linking Community Health and Health Administration with the Liberal Arts were less well served, a failing of initial planning.

Probably the single most pivotal factor in the whole project design centered on the faculty teams. For the most part, the concept worked admirably. Health professionals and liberal arts people truly pooled their resources, especially so in the Community Health/Health Administration and the Liberal Arts courses.

In the Problem Solving and Critical Thinking courses, however, there was a tendency toward divergence. With Critical Thinking, for example, the health professional had a tendency to steer the course toward current health issues while the full time philosophy person could not resist a short stop in Plato's Cave. In this instance, a third faculty member from English—also full time—developed an outline that found the originally intended middle ground.

A word more about this. The proposal was the concept of one person. It was therefore up to that person (the director) to see that everyone was pulling in the intended direction. This approach to institutional change is as open to questions about appropriateness as it is to effectiveness. Given this staggering initial handicap, the success of the overall project is even more surprising.

Another important factor in the planning and development stage was the heavy reliance on adjunct faculty. This proved a case of the double-edged sword. The most pleasant aspect of the faculty's work was their enthusiasm for the project. Once they bought into the initial premise of the courses, there was little obstructionism over issues so significant to members of entrenched departments. The adjuncts had little problem with standing one foot in each department, their heads aloft in inter-disciplinary ambiguity.

On the other hand, because of their part time status, it was an administrative nightmare getting the teams together on a regular basis. Some teams took this burden up willingly and met weekly. Others, due to conflicts in schedules and problems of distance, hardly saw each other at all. The degree of unity between outlines was directly correlated to this.

A factor related to the interdisciplinary nature of this effort described above was the large problem of providing written materials to the students. Particularly in the liberal arts courses, readings were selected from diverse sources. Obviously students could not be expected to buy books from so wide a reading list. But efforts to provide photocopied materials ran amuck of copyright laws. When courses of this nature are put together this quickly and then proliferate into multiple sections the following semester, the problem of providing reading materials becomes awesome—particularly if uniformity between courses is the goal.

The solution to this problem had two parts. First, students purchased inexpensive paperbacks (totaling up to $15 or $20) while the college bought multiple copies of the hardcover works. Second, because of this, the college was further motivated to see that the QUILL liberal arts courses were only offered at one of the principal campuses, where the library resources would be readily available. Eventually, it is hoped that the original faculty teams or their heirs can prepare their own anthologies for publication.

Another objective of the original proposal was to create workbooks to foster replicability of courses, both at St. Joseph's and elsewhere. As was the case with the faculty's ability to link the courses in their outlines, there was considerable diversity in final products. While the nature, contents, and length of the workbooks were outlined with great specificity, the return products were the results of individual efforts—diverse with regard to both form and quality. Fortunately, for each course at least one workbook met with the minimal standard of replicability. It is anticipated that selected outlines will be added to each workbook to add depth and foster development of materials for future instructors.

Also stated as an original objective of the proposal was the integration of these courses into a recommended sequence that would tie in with the academic skills of communication and computation. While more will be said later of the sequencing, it is worthy of note that, at least with regard to communication skills, the division made great advances. A writing committee was formed, with several QUILL faculty participants, to improve students' writing skills. A new course was added, a diagnostic mechanism developed, and the new curriculum was piloted and found highly successful. This, coupled with Critical Thinking and Problem Solving courses, will serve as a cornerstone of the division's next developmental effort, for which outside funding is being sought.

The success of the project in involving student enrollment in traditional liberal arts courses was minimal. The reason for this is that most of the students are health professionals transferring in with large amounts of credit that, in most cases, satisfies portions of the college's liberal arts requirements. Compounding this avoidance of traditional liberal arts courses is the fact that when students select their course work, they look for courses that satisfy both a professional and liberal arts requirement (e.g. Principals of Counseling). Thus, it is difficult to gauge by enrollments alone the degree to which the project instilled an interest in the liberal arts. A better indicator might be the student evaluations outlined herein.

In addition to these more immediate objectives and outlines, the division anticipated that the QUILL project would have a far-reaching impact on its academic program. This was one instance, at least, where we underestimated our potential success. Specifically, simultaneously with the QUILL project, the college was designing its curriculum for new majors, one in Community Health and one in Health Administration. Because of the quality and significance of the experimental courses, the decision was made to make them the centerpiece of the new curriculum. Thus the QUILL courses came to form the core of the new curriculum. While these things are always difficult to ascertain, it is the feeling of the administration that the core curriculum played a large part in the State Education Department's endorsement of the programs.

But success was not without its price. Immediately following registration of the new programs, there was a measurable shift in enrollment from other courses to those developed through QUILL funds. The result with regard to preparation of faculty was frightening. It will be remembered that between fall and spring, 1979-80, the number of QUILL sections jumped from ten to thirty-six. To meet this demand for new instructors and materials, the division had only one month's preparation time. We were forced, therefore, to train faculty in greater numbers and in less time than was optimal. There were snags and problems to be sure, but in almost every case, the training effort succeeded.

This, too, had results serendipitous. Because of quirks in our faculty schedules, it was necessary to orient almost the entire faculty. And because adjunct faculty are desirous of being able to teach as many courses as possible, they attended in great numbers and with keen interest. The payoff was apparent. The pedagogy of generic skill development has been internalized by the majority of the faculty. Not only are they able to teach the course, but they are taking that knowledge and applying it in their other courses.

B. Crossing Disciplines for Liberal Learning

What Often Appears To Result From Interdisciplinary Courses But Rarely Does. . .

G. H. Hinkle

The title and, at times, the tone of these reflections may strike some as bordering on the cavalier, if not the cynical. Insofar as that is the case, I begin them with a word or two about the context in which Professor W.D. Narramore and myself developed the idea for our experiment, were encouraged by Austin College to solicit Project QUILL's support of it, and eventually carried it out.

Whatever else can or should be said for Austin College, it holds something of a record, both in years of effort and in singlemindedness of purpose, as an undergraduate liberal arts institution dedicated to innovation. Consequently, the newness of what we proposed was distinctive in design, but not in spirit, on our campus. We, therefore, entered into and emerged from our interdisciplinary venture with both the self-confidence and the learned scepticism of "seasoned veterans" of team-teaching, interdepartmental exchanges, and the like. In other words, we were no less buttressed by the success we and our colleagues had had in that regard than we were chastened by a number of prior failures on our and their records. We expected problems and were neither undone nor surprised that our expectations were realized, confirming our "worldly wise" outlooks to, as I've suggested, a hard-headed degree.

In a similar vein, but with more confidence than proved to be advisable and with less scepticism than proved to be necessary, we set those expectations aside respecting the untried model we adopted. In fact, we utilized it as a matter of outright advocacy, compounding the situation for ourselves by our decision not only to use the model's scheme for aesthetic inquiry as the focus for the content of the experimental course, but also as the framework for its overall, day-to-day structure. As a result, we could not help but fall short of our own investment of thought and energy, since either or both the content and the conduct of the ex-

---

G. H. Hinkle is professor of philosophy at Austin College, Sherman, TX 75090.

periment stood or fell on the merits of the selfsame theoretical base. Again, we tended by the close of the venture to not know ourselves whether to laugh or to cry over it, whether to be cavalier or cynical.

So much for introspection. I would turn your attention next to the main features of what we attempted. I mean by "main features" those aspects of our experiment which worked or didn't work for us; and I will try to report both the positive and the negative data with special concern for the larger issues our successes and our failures raise regarding interdisciplinary courses in general.

The first of those features was the division of labor we decided upon with regard to lecturing and group discussion leadership. In fairness, but not necessarily in wisdom, we gave precisely equal time to our professorial roles in the classroom and to our separate disciplines. Our model lent itself to such an exacting division, since its theoretical point-of-departure was the two-fold argument (1) that philosophic inquiry into an art without knowledge of, or exposure to, the craft and draftsmen that art represented wrongly objectifies the otherwise subjective essense of artistic endeavor, and (2) that participation in creative undertakings, apart from some systematic reflection on them, wrongly reduces all aesthetic experience to personal consciousness.

The problem with this approach, like the model's contention, was likewise twofold. With an ideal mix of twenty-seven students neither tilted in the direction of theatre majors or in the direction of philosophy majors, we found ourselves—each in turn—lecturing on and discussing our separate fields in the company of a half-comprehending enrollment. Moreover, art—even when half understood—is generally more accessible than is philosophy; and in short order the precise equality of emphasis we presented devolved into a most imprecise, but no less emphatic, student imbalance of sentiment and interest. Need I note which of our disciplines won the students' "straw-vote" of confidence?

This state of affairs raises a fundamental question of consequence to most all interdisciplinary courses: namely, does not the widespread attempt to balance emphases among the academic fields involved in such experiments belie the simply, if oft-unacknowledged, truth that certain modes of intellectual inquiry are more difficult to grasp than others? What service do we render our own chosen fields or our students, when in the name of compromise, colleagiality, Christian kindness, or whatever, we operate an interdisciplinary course as if that were not the case? Put another way, there is nothing intrinsic to any combination of disciplines which guarantees "mutual enhancement" as a result. Rather, although they surely can be treated in concert, each of them nonetheless must be treated to the extent its own models and methodologies demand.

The second feature of our experiment, also dictated by the model to which we were attached with a passion, was the division of the course itself into precise halves structurally: that is, into a half-term devoted to the study of sources and a half-term devoted to classwide involvement, on stage or backstage, in a fully-mounted theatrical production.

Here the problem we confronted, as well as the issue it brings to mind, are less cut-and dried: for, to put it even halfway mildly, our production was a "smash-hit." Our two distinguished outside evaluators, our faculty colleagues, the townspeople of Sherman, our students and their peers, and the local newspaper's self-appointed drama critic all agreed it was among the three or four best plays staged at Austin College in a number of years. Professor Narramore and I blush to agree.

How could this be, and what does it signify, granted the rather uneven results of our efforts during the first half of our venture? In the first place, learning-by-doing commands the attention and elicits the enthusiasm of a random mix of undergraduates to a far greater extent than does regular coursework, even if team-taught and experimental in nature. Indeed, this is true whether or not, as in the case of our arguments for our model, that obvious fact is underwritten by dutifully profound theorizing. Secondly, it suggests that the two of us failed to see that absolutized halving of the course was neither called for by the model nor even in accord with its insistence on integrating the two dimensions of learning it proposed. Finally and most importantly, our error in understanding and judgment speaks to the larger question of the integration of varied intellectual perspectives and learning styles respecting any subject by students in an interdisciplinary offering. Too many times, we fear, others like ourselves arrive as a teaching team at a sophisticated level of such integration by virtue of our having had stimulating exchanges during the planning of such a course, only to "hand over the results" of those exchanges to students with no provision for their having to struggle through to that level of sophistication themselves. In our case at least our evaluation data makes clear that the two halves of the course never came together in more than three or four students' heads. To the contrary, most were enraptured by the play production and embarrassingly forgetful of "what we did before rehearsals started."

The third and last feature of more than parochial value is linked to the first in a somewhat perverse fashion. While, as I noted earlier, the relative accessibility of theatre gave it an edge over aesthetics throughout the first half of the course, in the final "wrap-up" days of the experiment it became apparent that neither discipline had fared especially well. With a number of our students convinced that "anyone can put on a show" and a number of others prepared to inform the world that "no one can understand philosophy," Professor Narramore and I came out about where we went in: he the exponent of what has been called the "ragtag conglomerate" among the arts and I the apologist for what has been called the "step child" of philosophic reflection.

Tempted as I am to set the record straight on behalf of our two be-knighted fields at this point, I instead will pose, as before, a broader question. It is the question of simplistic reductionism wherein several intellectually respectable, carefully articulated, and competently taught individual academic subjects somehow seek out, and sink to, a common denominator of discourse and of comprehension in an interdisciplinary offering which would shame both the professors and the students engaged in them in separate courses appropriate to their own best models and methodologies.

In the few minutes that remain I want to point up two correctives Professor Narramore and I have in mind, as we anticipate repeating our experiment in the next academic year, and then to return briefly to the title I have given to these reflections.

Regarding those correctives, our next version of the course will not merely rehearse major schools of philosophy of art, followed by a review of several theories of drama, but rather will integrate in specific and repeated ways the aesthetic views we cover with illustrative criticism techniques, concepts, and sources from the world of theatre. In addition, we will choose a particular dramatic genre in a particular historical context (e.g. expressionism of the 1930s or absurdism of the 1950s) as both the special focus for study throughout the first half of the course and the representative form of drama to be staged in the latter half of the course. We believe, on the other hand, that this will accommodate the difficulties of philosophy and at the same time make the accessibility of theatre serve its own and philosophy's end; and, on the other hand, we believe that this will better inform and integrate the students' production experience in terms of their lecture-discussion experience.

As for my cavalier or, if you please, cynical title, I place my own emphasis on the phrases of least certainty therein: "appears to result" and "rarely does." The former phrase is intended to caution against the beguiling nature of interdisciplinary undertakings. To borrow a term from my own teen years which is coming back into vogue, there's something "real neat" about getting together with ones' colleagues and a mixed group of undergraduates and letting the intellectual chips fall where they may; and, since most professors and most students are a shade romantic and more than usually affable, the fact that they both "got along" and "got through" an interdisciplinary course is itself taken too readily to constitute a major accomplishment. The latter phrase, "rarely does," is intended to confront the sobering probability that certain features of most all interdisciplinary courses are inadequately designed and ineffectively implemented, meaning among other things that there is not, and should never be, an excuse for conducting them without a view to their constant improvement.

Having, then, heard me out, you may be of a mind with a character in the play Professor Narramore and I staged some fifteen months ago at Austin College. Upon hearing a very unconvincing account of a tragic turn of events in his little Appalachian village, he says to the one giving the account:

That don't make a hellava lot of sense—not when you try to cipher-out what's took place in this town the last three-four weeks.

Should that be your feelings about my reflections at this point, I know of nothing else to say in response other than what that other character in our production said:

No, it don't. But, when you try to cipher-out them kind of things, what *does* makes sense? You always got so much to say . . . you tell me!

The Capacity of the Human Mind: An Interdisciplinary Approach

Thomas Pauly

The interdisciplinary mind course at Jacksonville University was designed to provide both the faculty and students with an opportunity to explore the fascinating topic of the working and structure of the human mind. At our small, private, undergraduate liberal arts and teaching oriented institution, there is too little serious intellectual dialogue among faculty from diverse disciplines. And, while students are required to take a variety of courses in different areas of study, they have few opportunities in their junior and senior years to connect and interrelate the many separate disciplines they have studied. In moving from one subject to another a student often becomes increasingly fragmented. The prospect of including the students in a dialogue involving faculty with distinct specializations was exciting. Seldom does a student in a class hear two faculty members engage in dialogue, disagree, or argue. A course, offering this variety of instructors and materials and probing the intriguing and marvelous capacities of the human mind, would differ substantially from any other course available and properly strike the student as an exciting intellectual adventure into an amazing territory.

So, a philosopher who has studied a little physics, a mathematician who has studied some philosophy and recently become our computer scientist, an organic chemist who is a voracious reader of literature, politics, philosophy and religion, and a psychologist came together full of enthusiasm and hope. Each is an experienced, dedicated, quality teacher, very concerned about intellectual rigor but also very aware of student difficulties and problems. Each was teaching a full load of courses, active in other campus activities and committee work, and planning this course as an uncompensated extra. Our spirits were quite significally raised when the good news of the QUILL award reached us: we were proud of our idea and work thus far, grateful for the support and assistance provided us, and humbled by the quality of the other recipients and number of applications for QUILL awards.

Thomas Pauly is associate professor of philosophy at Jacksonville University, Jacksonville, FL 32211.

Our course was to be a study of the human mind from the standpoints of philosophy, computer science, psychology, and neurophysiology. Neurophysiology has made remarkable advances in recent years. How does the physical scientist approach the nervous system and brain? What methodologies are used? What are the fundamental concepts used in this discipline to understand human consciousness? Is thought a very complex bio-chemical process which is as predictable as a test tube reaction? Is there such a thing as mind, or is this term simply an outworn euphemism for brain? The study of artificial intelligence has also been very exciting in the last few decades. What have the efforts of computer scientists to build machines which solve problems, perceive the external world, speak a language, and simulate humans in a variety of ways revealed about the working and structure of the human mind? How do specialists in artificial intelligence approach and conceive of the mind? Can computers or robots really think, feel, or outsmart humans? And what difference does it make? For the last century psychology has been the science of humans. So what has this well-established separate discipline shown about the nature and functioning of human consciousness? What methodologies do psychologists use? What basic concepts of the mind emerge from or are assumed in research in psychology? Lastly, for thousands of years philosophers have and still do both speculate about and rationally analyze the activities of the human mind. What distinguishes the approach of the philosopher? What have and do philosophers conceive of the mind?

With such exciting, profound, far-reaching, open-ended questions swirling about our own minds, we met to hammer out a workable program. The organic chemist did extensive research to learn about the nervous system, brain, neurons, and the information processing that goes on within organisms, since these areas are not covered in courses he teaches. He also prepared numerous slides to illustrate, often in beautiful color, the processes of our nervous system, and located an outstanding film presenting recent brain research techniques and instruments. Finding a text to cover the material intelligibly and interestingly for nonscience majors was almost an insurmountable problem. The lure of the September 1979 single-topic issue of *Scientific American* devoted to the brain proved irresistible, though students, even with lots of good, helpful assistance, found it very, very rough.

The computer scientist, quite capable of teaching students various programming languages, computer uses and the workings of this amazing machine, had to bone up on what more philosophically oriented students of artificial intelligence have asserted regarding the relationship between human intelligence and machine or artificial intelligence. Again, finding a text to present in a clear fashion what has been achieved in the areas of computer problem-solving, perception, language use and robots was a difficult task. She settled on Bertram Raphael's *The Thinking Computer: Mind Inside Matter,* which proved to be a good text, though too long to cover in its entirety. In addition she made good use of *Computer Power and Human Reason: From Judgement to Calculation,* a book by Joseph Weizenbaum, an authority in artificial intelligence who devised a program simulating a psychologist probing a client's problem and who became quite disturbed by people seeing his work as actually substituting for a human psychologist, and who consequently wanted to distinguish clearly between human judgement and logical calculation. Our computer scientist was also blessed with an excellent Nova film entitled "Minds and Machines" which examines the basic issues of her portion of the course.

The psychologist invited to work with us considered talking about the origin and early history of psychology as a distinct scientific and academic discipline, discussing Wundt and Freud, the various reactions to their psychological methods, and more recent approaches to and views of the human mind. He decided to distinguish the methods of the scientific psychologist from that of the philosopher and then focus on visual perception, elementary types of learning, and our higher mental processes, thinking, problem solving, decision making, and creativity. Students were asked to purchase R. L. Gregory's *Eye and Brain: The Psychology of Seeing* and to read various chapters of Munn's *Introduction to Psychology* on reserve in the library.

As the philosopher I wanted the students to appreciate and understand the dualistic view of the human being, found classically in Plato and Descartes and still argued by a number of twentieth century thinkers. The opposed view, according to which each human being is a unified whole, and the various criticisms of dualism also had to be presented. Because both behaviorism and the identity theory are so closely allied to the advances in the sciences, these philosophical positions had to be examined. Since most of us first learned about the nature of humans from our Judeo-Christian religion, I was eager to invite a knowledgeable, professional, religious person to present the biblical view of the soul. I wanted to include Buddhist and Hindu thought somehow, in view of the interest in oriental thought the last 15 years. And I flirted with inviting a local, competent, psychic to talk both about various unusual psychic capacities, their implications and the underlying view of the human mind. These last two hopes were never realized. Feeling comfortable with no particular text, I chose Antony Flew's anthology *Body, Mind, and Death* which would have been satisfactory had I been more selective and less ambitious in my reading assignments.

We decided that the first section of the course should be the philosophical approach. Here students should be presented the various different common sense meanings of the term "mind" (e.g., the conservative mind, Joe has a quick mind, mind your own business), the fundamental views of the human mind in our Judeo-Christian Western tradition, noting the moral, political, and social ramifications of these views, and lastly some contemporary philosophical analysis of the mind. The stage would then be set for the psychological approach, which, in emulating the astounding advances made in the physical sciences, emerged from the philosophical approach and addressed the human scientifically. The more abstract and technical approach of neurophysiology would come next, followed by the perspective of the computer scientist.

At the end of each section the instructor would prepare and then grade a test covering that section. The student's grades were determined primarily by these tests, though two short papers, which I will describe later in this paper, and class discussion also influenced the grades. Concerned that students would be confused by having to face four different teachers and tests, we vowed to be as clear as possible about what each expected of students and to hand out study questions and outlines.

Fearful that students would perceive each of our sections as a self-contained mini-course, and anxious to build into the very structure of the course as much continuity as possible, we considered having me take a class before each of the other sections to draw connections and relationships. This we rejected because we wanted all four of us to bear responsibility for integrating the various topics. Each would be present for all classes, and feel free to make comments and ask questions but always tactfully, so as not to intimidate or discourage students from speaking up. Two class periods were set aside at the end of the term to review, summarize, identify key issues, positions and problems and point out relationships and connections. And we decided that students would at the beginning and end of the course write a short (2 page) paper entitled "Human Nature, Science and Computers: A Personal View" incorporating their own thoughts about what is unique about humans, whether any part or aspect of the human survives death, whether human experience and behavior can be adequately understood using the scientific method or in terms of electro-chemical interactions, and whether some activities of the human mind cannot be reproduced by computers.

Thirty-four sophomores, juniors, and seniors enrolled for the course which met for seventy-five minutes twice a week for fifteen weeks. Twelve were majoring in the social sciences, and fourteen in mathematics, biology, or the physical sciences. Eight had high grade point averages, four had low ones. A humanities professor attended class regularly and occasionally an engineering professor dropped in.

Our successes were numerous and gratifying. Though comments, observations, and questions came mainly from a core of bright students, most students appeared interested and enthusiastic about our different, innovative, intellectual adventure. We presented our material in an orderly, clear, interesting manner, making good use of excellent slides and outstanding films as well as helpful study questions and outlines, all of which were appreciated by the students. Students were able to note various intriguing connections and relationships among these four distinct disciplines, and profound differences. Many science students had their first exposure to philosophical reflection and analysis, while many humanities students had their first exposure to neurobiology and computer science.

The quality of the dialogue, and the atmosphere in which the dialogue took place were invigorating and refreshing. The free, open, honest, and sometimes critical remarks faculty members made to other faculty members as well as the exchanges between faculty and students on issues which divide intelligent people made this course a unique one for most of the students. Four or five students stated this. Two students cited "an atmosphere of academic freedom and equality" as the best part of the course.

The organic chemist and mathematician found their considerable research in preparation for this course to be an exciting, beneficial broadening of their own professional perspectives. Each of us learned a great deal about the other three disciplines, thereby, widening our points of view, and each valued the dialogue with the others.

Our shortcomings were also numerous and disappointing. A majority of students did perceive four self-contained mini-courses, and while they found the variety interesting, most of their effort and energy was concentrated on mastering the particular subject matters presented, with little focus on interrelationships. This was in part because this course satisfied one of the university's general distribution requirements, and consequently many students were taking what they regarded as a required course. The course is really suited for upper class, brighter, highly motivated honors students.

The philosophical anthology and *Scientific American* on the brain were much too difficult. The anthology could be used, but the individual assignments would have to be shorter, more carefully made, and accompanied by introductory remarks so the student can grasp the significance of the selection. More emphasis must be placed on contemporary philosophical approaches to the mind.

The *Scientific American* articles are just too technical and detailed. Largely because our organic chemist did so much stimulating and exciting research into just how the nervous system operates and information processing occurs, this was given too much attention. Too little time was devoted to a discussion of what notable neurobiologists think ultimately about the mind and its relationship to the brain, a discussion paralleling to some extent philosophical discussions.

The psychology section should have included more discussion of the diverse methodologies (Freudian, behaviorist, phenomenological, humanistic) within that discipline. Such disagreements in approach stem from different basic commitments about the nature of the human being, and are rather philosophical.

While interrelationships were noted, parallels drawn, and dialogue occurred, it didn't take each of us long to get into the more technical, specialized, detailed areas of our disciplines. Students struggling with the latter understandably had trouble focusing on the former. Clearly they need to see what these commitments and methodologies entail in practice; they need to see how the professional operates. An inherent problem with interdisciplinary courses is deciding just how much time to devote to displaying the ways the specialists work and how much to clarifying and critically reflecting on the basic commitments and methodologies.

As we prepared for this course, we were too soft on one another. Each was too individually responsible for his or her own discipline's approach to the human mind. Because each was so grateful for the other's participation in this venture, and each so respected the other's competence in his or her own professional discipline, we were hesitant to criticize and make judgements about what the others should or should not do. Clearly, I am the most blameworthy. Our habit of mind somewhat reflected our institution's past lack of support for interdisciplinary courses: someone always had to freely devote his or her services, receiving no direct compensation for the work done. The course was taught on top of one's normal load. With our new administration, this will change.

On the whole we were pleased with what took place but recognize that more work will have to be done regarding texts and the coordination of the topics covered, whether the course be taught for honors students, as we expect to do next year, or the course be taught for the general student. Let me again express our appreciation to George Hazzard and Project QUILL for the encouraging support we've received.

The Anatomy of Knowing—Liberal Education in the Multiversity

Robert E. Shoenberg

In *The Reforming of General Education,* Daniel Bell asserts that the central purpose of the college is "to teach modes of conceptualization, explanation, and verification of knowledge." Bell makes clear that the distinctive mission of undergraduate education is not instruction in some particular bodies of knowledge. It is, rather, development in students of the skills by which they can analyze, abstract from, organize and communicate their experience. To put it more simply, the business of a college education is teaching and learning how to understand.

My story is about a group of faculty members who took this idea seriously and tried to convey it to an average group of brand new freshman students at a very large public university. To undertake such a task may strike you as extraordinarily naive and quixotic. I must confess that in retrospect it strikes me so, too. It also turned out to be a most valuable experience for many reasons, some foreseen and some serendipitous.

Our initial motivation in undertaking this project was the perception that many undergraduates have very little notion of what colleges and universities are about. Most of the students have some idea of why they have come to college, but in many respects those ideas are not congruent with the university's mode of operation. In particular, many students never get beyond a simplistic idea or two of what liberal education means, why there is a general education requirement, or why faculty—even in subjects like business or engineering—are always being so theoretical. We have students who leave us still innocent of all notions of intellectuality.

For our QUILL project, we chose to address this problem through a new kind of orientation course, which we called "The Anatomy of Knowing." The subtitle of the course, "The University and Its Curriculum" provides a better clue to its subject matter and intentions. We wanted to bring students, at the very beginning of their undergraduate

Robert E. Shoenberg is dean for undergraduate studies at the University of Maryland, College Park, MD 20742.

careers, to an understanding of the purposes of a unversity in general and of an undergraduate program in particular, and to show how these purposes are reflected in the curriculum. The subject matter of our course was the kinds of knowledge with which universities deal and the modes of discourse in which the university carries on its intellectual business.

The course met in discussion sections of between 13 and 23 students. There were six sections, four of them taught by a single instructor, two of them by a pair. We all used the same syllabus, but each instructor taught all the material to his or her own class. Since this format meant that each of us was dealing with unfamiliar ideas most of the time, we met as a staff almost weekly throughout the semester to share ideas and expertise. The course was an exercise in mutual education for us.

The course content was divided into seven sections. The first dealt with the general idea of "knowing" and examined such issues as the different ways in which the verb "to know" is used, the kinds of knowledge the students already had and how they came to have it and a week or so of formal logic to give students a sense of its power.

We then went on to talk in the second section about universities: their history, their kinds, their purposes. Naturally, we used the University of Maryland, College Park as a particular example.

The core of the course was the next three sections, three weeks each on the sciences, the social sciences, and the arts and humanities. Except for the section on the social sciences, we did not talk about particular disciplines but rather about the different modes of conceptualization and discourse that characterize each of these sets of subject matters. In simplified form, our basic question was: "What is scientific about the sciences; What is humanistic about the humanities?" And, at every opportunity, we added the question, "What does it mean to you?" We tried to get students to see how various formal systems of thought helped them to understand their own experience in ways that might influence their behavior, or had, in fact, radically affected the ways in which large numbers of people thought and behaved. For example, the class on the "scientific revolution" of the seventeenth century focused on the radical shift in what people regarded as acceptable validation of claims to knowledge brought about by people like Galileo, Descartes and Newton. Thus students got some sense that there was a time when the world did not accept the methodology of empirical science, whose modes of analysis have so permeated our own world that we are scarcely conscious of them.

In the sixth section of the course, we began to draw the "moral." If I had to state that moral in a sentence, it would go something like this: "Only by understanding the world in multiple sets of terms can one become a fully autonomous person and make responsible decisions." Raising consciousness of the fact that that is so and teaching some strategies

212

for developing that autonomy is, as I see it, the goal of liberal education. We tried to make that point both in the abstract and in terms of a specific case, the decision to develop and then use the atomic bomb. This paradigm case of the need for multiple approaches to a problem constituted the seventh and last part of the course.

Believe it or not, this outline of the intellectual strategy of the course is not a rationalization after the fact. We did understand from the beginning where we wanted to take the students. I wish I could tell you that most of them followed us there, but that would be claiming not only more than I have a good way of knowing, but, sadly, more than I believe to be true.

The reasons why, in retrospect, it appears we fell short of our goals say a good deal about the current state of education in the United States, at both the secondary and higher education levels. I would like to dwell on those reasons at some length.

Since, like most large universities, we teach freshmen mostly in large lecture courses or in discussion groups presided over by graduate teaching assistants, most of our group, all but one of whom were full and associate professors, had not taught freshmen face to face for quite a while. We had forgotten two things. The first of these has always been true. Beginning college students have trouble dealing with questions that don't have right answers. With too few exceptions, teaching in the public schools emphasizes facts, lists, pat definitions, simplified explanations. The kind of testing to which students are predominantly subjected elicits short answer responses that are either right or wrong. Only occasionally are students asked for responses which require complex explanation or a weighing of competing alternatives.

It has been the role of the college to wean its freshmen away from dualistic thinking, from reducing the world to black and white. I recall a mild joke that was current during my undergraduate years. A young man came home for his first vacation after having gone away to college. As he walked in the door, his doting mother, having missed her boy terribly, threw her arms around him crying "Jimmy, how are you?" To which her by now well trained son responded, "Relative to what?"

We realized that this kind of training was our task, too; but we were not prepared for the resistance we encountered. We were not helped by the fact that very little of what was going on in the students' other courses reinforced the intellectual attitudes we were trying to inculcate. To put it another way, big universities aren't much in the liberal education business. At its best, liberal education has been the business of the entire curriculum. In the best undergraduate programs, the teaching of "modes of conceptualization, explanation, and the verification of knowledge" goes on in every course, whether part of the general curriculum or the major. But in recent years, as even the liberal arts disciplines have become increasingly vocationalized, the emphasis has shifted to fact, technique and methodology. The entire burden of liberal education has been transferred to the general education program and become synonymous with it. And when most general education courses are first courses in a vocationalized discipline, the rare course that tries to assert the first principles of liberal education will seem anomalous, baffling and unfairly demanding to most students.

This is a problem that large universities have created for themselves. However, the second problem of which we failed to take prior account ought to be dealt with before students come to us. We found that students were quite capable of understanding the content of reading assignments when the writing was at an appropriate level of cognitive complexity. But we were quite unprepared for the difficulty they had in applying, connecting or drawing conclusions from the ideas they encountered. In a course like "The Anatomy of Knowing," the readings are for the most part illustrative of general principles. In other words, the subject matter of the reading is not the subject matter of the course. When we made a point of this idea at the beginning of the course, the students didn't know what we meant. When a few weeks into the course they began to understand, they didn't know what to do about it and didn't like it.

I remember trying to teach George Orwell's "Shooting an Elephant." The essay recounts an experience of Orwell's as a British colonial officer in Burma. The nub of the incident is his being forced by the expectations of a mob of Burmese to do something foolish in order to maintain his image. At the class meeting in which we discussed this essay, my pedagogical creativity was operating about as well as it ever has. I was at my Socratic best. But no matter what handsprings I turned, I could not get that class to see that they had all been in Orwell's position at one time or another, forced to do something against their better judgment in order to save face. My students could not, even with a lot of prompting, see the essential significance of the incident and connect their own circumstances to those of another time and place.

By the end of the semester, the students had begun to see that mastering content is only the beginning of understanding. But it still seemed to us as instructors that they should have come to college with this awareness, that we should have been able to take it for granted.

However, all was not frustration. The students were responsive as often as not and they were always tolerant of our gropings and mistakes. And mistakes there were, for none of us had tried to teach a course like this before, one in which we did not have the support of our scholarly expertise. I hasten to add that we intended it this way. There is no better way to promote faculty interaction across disciplines than to put instructors in a situation in which they have to rely on each other for survival. In respect to that interdisciplinary interaction the project was a roaring success. We found a surprising number of faculty members hungry for the opportunity to deal with the kinds of large intellectual issues the course addressed. Many more than the eight would have participated had their circumstances permitted, and, indeed, almost as many more did join in a semester-long preparatory seminar during the spring of 1979.

The meetings of the course faculty were enlivened by the excitement of good talk and new intellectual discoveries. Whatever happened to the students, teachers got an education which has served to make them far more versatile instructors.

Most importantly of all, we found the nerve to venture out from the protection of our scholarly expertise to grapple with intellectual issues that transcend our disciplines. We operated, not as experts, but as habitually thoughtful and intellectually trained men and women, trying to show students how to approach a serious piece of writing intelligently. We tried to show students that the life of the mind is worth pursuing, that there is pleasure and profit in ideas, and that ideas do matter. For many of our students, "The Anatomy of Knowing" will be the only course in which they get such a message.

Not so their successors. While a change in our general education requirements leaves no place in the freshman year for a course like ours, those same new requirements specify two such courses for every student in the junior or senior year. The offering of "The Anatomy of Knowing" made a significant contribution to effecting this change. A lot of people knew the course was being offered, were intrigued by it, and impressed with the fact that undergraduate courses could be conceptualized in such terms. At least partly as a result of these perceptions, the campus came to understand the importance to the undergraduate curriculum of courses that force students to think complexly about intellectual issues and their practical significance. So "The Anatomy of Knowing" has led the way to what we hope will be a serious effort at renewing the spirit of undergraduate education. In the multiversity, that is a rather remarkable undertaking.

C. Liberal Learning and Career Education

Why It's Difficult To Get Faculty To
Teach Kant and Careers

Muriel Dance

The School of New Resources is committed to the Liberal Arts, those arts necessary for intelligent living in a free society, as the most suitable vehicle for the education of adults. Our program enables adults, most of whom are full-time working people, to enter or return to the academic world for a Bachelor of Arts degree. We recognize the special needs and strengths of adult learners, who differ from younger counterparts in many ways; one is the sense of urgency they have about career opportunities. New Resources has articulated a three-fold educational process to address this difference.

1) Students learn to recognize their life and work experience as the basis for learning and developing a plan of study—their curriculum.

2) With a seminar setting, students learn to conceptualize, understand, and interpret their experiences in the light of academic disciplines and theories.

3) Students learn to transform traditional liberal arts into arts that relate to a better and more fully human life—their career.

We felt our program fell short of achieving the third stage, so we developed a project, funded by QUILL, to help realize this ideal.

The purpose of the project was to develop a form of career education which was both appropriate for adults pursuing a B.A. degree and rooted in the liberal arts. We defined our task as assisting selected faculty to clarify the integral connection between learning and career skills and, more specifically, between a given academic discipline and the skills and attitudes which are required for successful careers in those fields. Specifically we worked with faculty 1) to identify skills necessary for competency within their disciplines and to pinpoint the relevance of these skills to work settings; 2) to develop a plan to use the independent project, part

---

Muriel Dance is director of curriculum at the School of New Resources, College of New Rochelle, New Rochelle, NY 10801.

of every seminar, for gathering information about professionals who are working in careers related to disciplines studied in the course.

We chose seven faculty members who had expressed concern about the needs of their adult students for more help with career planning. In addition, some of these faculty had left academia; thus they knew the benefits of a liberal arts education. Given faculty interest and background, the surprise in the project was the difficulty these faculty experienced in making connections between their liberal arts courses and careers (both their own careers and the possible careers of their students). I would like to explore four tentative answers to the question of what hinders faculty, who have a great deal of experience in making connections, from making these particular connections easily.

One unexpected hindrance was the faculty fear that they and their students were experimental subjects engaged in something not quite academically acceptable, the outcomes of which were unknown. One explanation for this particular fear might be that faculty lack self consciousness about the skills developed by their academic training. Graduate schools do not teach students to think about their disciplines as preparation for other careers besides teaching. Thus, even if faculty move out of academics they often attribute the move to external factors—the declining opportunities in teaching, or knowing someone who just happened to be able to get them a job—instead of attributing it to a self-conscious assessment of the skills developed by their graduate work. The least successful faculty member in the project, as measured by a post-test of her students' understanding of the concept of transferable skill, had just completed a Ph.D. While teaching the class, she was facing up to her own difficulty of translating graduate education into something besides college teaching, and so she had very little feel for teaching her students to make this translation.

A second answer to the question of why faculty have trouble making connections between liberal learning and careers is that their own love of their subject, their sense that they have an important body of knowledge to communicate to students, makes them reluctant to entertain the question either for themselves or for students. The relationship of learning to careers seems tangential and interfers with the coverage of their subject. When pressed by students who want to know why they should read Plato, faculty might cover over their "embarrassment" at not knowing more about these connections by simply insisting on the intrinsic interest of Plato's imagined world.

Adults themselves communicate to faculty a complicated attitude about careers. While they may be back in college to prepare for career changes, they still experience college as a place protected from the pressures and difficulties of working life. Thus, adults at times may validate faculty perceptions that it is more important to understand, for instance, the precise distinction between psychoses and psychoneuroses than the question of how does an interest in abnormal psychology translate into a career. The faculty member in the project who taught the abnormal psychology course had full-time academic appointments subsequent to completing his Ph.D. He said that his students complained he was pushing them into "jobs" rather than helping them master a body of knowledge.

And finally, traditional educators in the liberal arts have always assumed the value of students' mastering a discipline without knowing exactly what it prepared them for. These educators believe that to learn for the sake of discipline and pleasure alone necessitates a kind of risk—hard studying with no sure reward, no sure career; that unless students can run this risk, they can neither gain the full benefit of a liberal arts education nor hope to obtain a satisfying career, since such careers require the skill of disciplined risk-taking.

These initial resistances of faculty to the project were in part overcome when they were able to build on subject matter strengths they already had. The sociology instructor was able to use C. W. Mill's *White Collar* to connect the sociology of work with the concerns of his students to improve their skills and change careers. The instructor of logic and critical thinking saw that he could teach the concept of logical fallacy by getting students to test their ideas about work and careers in order to expose their misassumptions and illogical conclusions.

The integration of career and liberal arts worked best when faculty could infuse a sense of the skills students were developing into the classroom discussion and entertain questions when they came up about the application of these skills outside the classroom. Not so surprising perhaps is the fact that our most successful instructors in the project had worked for many years outside academia. Faculty discovered anew the need to individualize the extent to which they encouraged students to pursue a career-related question through projects or papers. Even a sensitive approach to careers is not always of interest to every student in the class. For adults who are ready, opportunities to ask themselves what knowledge and skills they were developing and to find out what careers people entered when they had similar skills and interest were welcome and stimulating.

Our project showed also that faculty who have themselves made career changes and who have the benefit of career education do make an impact on adult learners' ability to think about careers. I'd like to close with one example of such an impact:

A student who was an ex-bartender, enrolled in logic and critical thinking because he saw its connection to a hoped-for law career. He had only the vaguest notions about the daily life of law, although he was excited about how logical fallacies could become part of court room drama. He was asked to test his ideas to see if they were free from deductive errors. He had assumed, for example, that by studying hard and applying at the end of his undergraduate work, he would be able to get into law school. His teacher had him interview a number of lawyers to gather observations to test his hypothesis. He found out that the lawyers with whom he spoke believed that working in the field was necessary in addition to hard study to enter law school. He induced from these interviews, that working in law, in addition to hard study, would not only increase his changes of getting into law school, but would also help him understand the career to which he aspired, which is, as he was beginning to induce, not just the uncovering of fallacies of lawyers and witnesses in the courtroom. This student learned about induction and deduction, the uses of the syllogism and the danger of false premises from this teacher's ability to integrate careers and liberal arts. With his ideas "world tested" he was better able to continue his schooling in a meaningful way.

Furman University's "Humanists in the Working World" Program

Judith T. Gatlin

For a traditional liberal arts college like Furman University the idea of applying for a Project QUILL grant to create a program for linking liberal learning with career education was somewhat questionable. The very term "career education" raised faculty eyebrows, for our institutional commitment is to liberal education. But in the fall of 1978 we developed the idea of having six professors work for six weeks in non-academic internships and the decision was made to apply for two grants to support this summer program: one from the National Endowment for the Humanities to cover stipends and travel, the other from AAC to fund an orientation program and a follow-up convocation for the university community. In November we were informed that we had our Project QUILL grant, and we began serious planning.

The objectives of the program were to help faculty understand the relationship between their academic disciplines and jobs their students might have, to increase their awareness of the value of internships and experiential education, and to emphasize the value of liberal arts majors to businesses and the community. Planning began with the selection of faculty members who would be open to a new experience and who would represent Furman well in a non-academic internship. The project director talked with interested professors and attempted to identify possible placements. Some didn't work out: a Japanese historian finally decided against an internship with the South Carolina Economic Development Board; a philosopher of ethics felt that he would not make a great enough contribution working for a federal appeals court judge. By mid-winter four internships had been tentatively confirmed, depending on funding from NEH, and two others were being discussed. At the same time John Royston Coleman agreed to speak at our orientation luncheon for interns and a workshop for the entire faculty.

During the first week of April we were informed that NEH had funded our faculty internship program and final plans were confirmed. Dr.

Judith T. Gatlin is director of career programs at Furman University, Greenville, SC 29613.

220

Coleman spoke to faculty with great effectiveness and the program was launched. During the summer the project director and a photographer visited each intern to check on progress and to record the faculty's experiences on slides. In September six enthusiastic professors returned to campus, and shared with their colleagues experiences as an assistant circuit court solicitor (a political scientist), as a television commercial maker (the chairman of modern foreign languages), as a public relations writer (an English professor specializing in 18th century drama), a museum employee (an art historian), a researcher (an historian), and a radio script writer (a French professor). For each it was a renewing and revitalizing experience.

In October a day-long "Humanists in the Working World" program was held for the entire student body. At a convocation professors were introduced through a slide show assembled by the Spanish professor who had worked at a local television station. Then each faculty member discussed his experience and emphasized what he had learned about the relevance of a liberal arts major to a job. Alumni in eight departments were invited back to the campus to discuss their own careers, first with faculty in their departments, then with students in afternoon seminars. Four months later a dissemination conference on the program was held for some 37 representatives of 29 liberal arts colleges.

We learned a great deal from this brief summer program. First, never to refer to the "working world" when we meant "non-academic." Faculty members were not pleased with the suggestion that they didn't work. Second, that two grants can be worked together to present a really first rate program. However, the project director needs nerves of steel when one grant is delayed for as long as NEH's was. Third, that the enthusiasm of a few can affect the attitudes of many. Eighteen additional faculty members indicated interest in an internship after hearing of their colleagues' experiences; student internships, too, were viewed in a new light. Fourth, that a university's image can be greatly enhanced through a program which makes a real effort to serve the community. Local newspaper and television coverage of the program was extraordinary; a carefully edited publication reporting on the program spread the word to a really substantial number of colleges and universities throughout the country.

This first Project QUILL grant afforded Furman the opportunity to try out an idea that other institutions had been considering; our success has encouraged others to experiment also. We were fortunate in having the support of the administration, the trust of the faculty members, the cooperation with business and non-profit organizations, and the funds to provide faculty stipends. We are grateful to the foundations which supported Project QUILL and to the staff at AAC who became friends during the program.

Liberal Learning for "Job-Minded" Undergraduates

Darrell Reeck

I shall begin these reflections with a vignette. A teacher is standing at the front of a college classroom filled with juniors and seniors. This course, entitled "Professional Ethics for a Technological Era," is beginning its eighth hour of meeting and the professor is preparing to classify the types of ethics to which the students have been previously exposed. He is writing on the blackboard, deriving two important terms— deontology and teleology—from their Greek roots. From the rear of the room a student is heard, intervening to make a mild protest:

> When are we going to get down to something *interesting* in this course—something practical, related to business? I thought this was a *business* course. But it's been more like a *philosophy* course so far!

The speaker represents one clearly discernable type of student likely to enroll in courses aimed at fusing liberal and career education. Since their time perspective is limited to a near horizon and their primary interest lies in acquiring job skills, an appropriate designation for students of this type would be the "job-minded." If my limited experience is generalizable to other universities, our culture has just now delivered to us a college population with an unusually high percentage of job-minded students. They present quite different teaching challenges than the more reflective sort of student, whose longer time perspective and greater interest in cultural significance makes him more eager for the traditional concerns of liberal education.

Reflective students are quite aware of the differences between themselves and their job-minded peers. For instance, a physical therapy major

Darrell Reeck is chairman of the Department of Religion at the University of Puget Sound, Tacoma, WA 98416.

More detailed information about the program discussed in this paper is to be found in Darrell Reeck and Jill A. Sharrard, "The Professional Ethics Course," *Bioethics Quarterly* II(2), Summer, 1980, pp. 112-117. A book growing out of the course will be published in 1982 by Augsburg Publishing House: *Ethics for the Professions: A Christian Perspective*, by Darrell Reeck.

222

who understood the mentality of the job-minded type, while not sharing it, explained:

> Some of the physical therapy students enrolled think that this course is a waste of time. They feel they've already had their humanities in earlier years, and what they want now is to learn the skills needed to do as well as possible technically in their first positions.

We who are committed to the goal that every college graduate should be able to think logically and independently, communicate effectively, and develop a personal philosophy of life and values face a monumental challenge in teaching the job-minded.

At the University of Puget Sound, an independent institution in the Pacific Northwest enrolling about three thousand undergraduates, we have a laboratory for experiments in liberal education with both the job-minded and students of a more reflective sort. Our educational areas include four undergraduate professional schools as well as the usual arts and sciences. About as many students major in the professional disciplines as in the arts and sciences. The university is intentionally structured so as to avoid heightening the distinctions between professional programs and the liberal arts.

In this setting two colleagues and I have been working to build a two-course sequential program entitled "Professional Ethics for a Technological Era" with the aid of a QUILL grant. Approximately one hundred fifty students will be involved in the program this year. The program begins with a fall term course "Professional Ethics," in which the philosophical and religious background of the ethical tradition is presented first before moving on to more specific professional applications. The Winterim (January) course, "Public Policy: Conflict and Compromise," explores a single case in depth. Due to its growing popularity, we have begun to repeat the fall term course for a new group of students in the spring term.

In the following I'll focus my observations on how teachers committed to liberal education might effectively approach the job-minded student.

First, the natural allies of the teachers are the students whose interests go beyond the limitations of acquiring entry-level skills. In every class are many like the one who pulled me aside to say, "This course is really interesting to me. There's a little ambiguity to the material. It's refreshing! It's such a change from accounting, where there's no room for ambiguity at all!" Proponents of liberal learning can be certain that intellectual curiosity is still alive in a substantial percentage of our students in the professional disciplines. They will cooperate with us in infusing professional education with liberal learning, especially through their questions and comments. Thus, one effective way to promote liberal learning among the job-minded is to let its members have a chance to hear their more imaginative peers speak of their concerns and interests. This we have provided for by developing a lecture-discussion classroom style and also by dividing the large class into small groups for intensive discussions.

In our program we have found it effective, in the second place, to provide role models who are committed to reflective thought and humane values. Teaching responsibilities in the fall term course in the skills of ethical decision-making are shared by a professor of business administration, Dr. Robert Waldo; a chemist with a specialty in clinical biochemistry, Dr. Jeffrey Bland; and myself, an ethicist. Students regularly comment on the strength brought to the course by a business professor making links between ethical principles and business organization, a biochemist analyzing actual cases encountered in his consulting, and a social ethicist reflecting on professional problems. Team teaching as a way of providing role models has been fruitful in inducing liberal learning.

In addition, our courses have been enormously enriched by presentations made by practicing professionals—at least four each term—from the health sciences and business administration. For instance, a physical therapist who owns a private practice and also represents the state P.T. association to the legislature has spoken on various issues of moral concern to her field. The Business Conduct Committee of the Weyerhaeuser Company has presented a session to our class each term. For many of our students the role-modelling element of our program has been perhaps the most important factor in stimulating their interest in liberal learning. In psychological terms, a transfer occurs through which some job-minded students become more open to reflective thought.

One other element of our program with demonstrated merit is the use of case studies. The job-minded student quoted above came after class to mend fences with the teacher. When invited to make a positive suggestion, he said, "Why don't you give a case every session?" In fact, that is our intent and we have discovered cases to be effective in stimulating student interest and discussion. The case approach, however, has its limitations. If one never leads the student beyond the level of particular cases, has liberal learning truly been served? Not in a full sense, since the student will not necessarily have thought synthetically, nor have been exposed to the slightest bit of intellectual heritage. The case method mainly provides a useful starting-point for luring students into liberal learning.

An additional teaching strategy that has crystallized as an imperative could be called the "double frame of reference." The frame of reference of job-minded undergraduates, as already mentioned, is initially limited to the first employment position and the time horizon is two or three years in the future. The teachers, in contrast, want to imagine themselves as educating future senior management and policy-making professional leaders. As teachers we have had to learn that the concerns of the job-minded, though more immediate and less consequential than those of senior professionals, are legitimate and should be addressed. But we also remain committed to cultivating the breadth of knowledge and reflective ability needed in senior positions. As a consequence, we now attempt to relate each major topic to both the more immediate concerns of many of our students as well as to policy-making.

Finally, to be convinced of the value of liberal learning, the job-minded students must have institutionally secure teachers. The teachers must have, as we have at U.P.S., the backing of a committed administration. The president, the dean and school directors must be willing to support the relatively higher costs of team-teaching and the principle of infusing liberal learning into professional education. The professors must have evaluators who are willing to make allowances when the unavoidable problems involved in this kind of teaching are reflected in student evaluations that are lower than usual. The academic teaching team must be able to count on practicing professionals to take time out from work to appear before the class. Without these fundamental elements of institutional support, the struggle to achieve both effective teaching of the job-minded and professional survival is likely to be lost.

This is risky and difficult teaching. Even with the appropriate educational means and circumstances such as those described, success in convincing the job-minded of the value of liberal learning is impossible to guarantee. The teacher who takes on such an educational mission is dealing with pedagogical problems no less difficult than those described by philosophers Jean Piaget, Alfred North Whitehead, and others who explored the difficulties in helping young learners to move from the stage in which primary concern is focused on technical mastery to that in which interest is invested in general knowledge. Such teachers must be persuasive and vigorous in defending a reflective approach to professional education.

The attempt to infuse liberal learning into professional education does provide greatly rewarding moments. Some of the closest bonds we have developed with students have been with the reflective members of our classes who respond spontaneously and warmly to the humane course perspectives. However, perhaps even greater rewards come from signals of success with the job-minded group, many of whom have also responded warmly to liberal learning, but sometimes only after they have gone into that land of promise, the first position. My colleague, Bob Waldo, reports his experiences of business graduates a year or two into their first positions who say something like this: "I never understood what you were talking about when I was in that ethics course, but now I see what you were trying to do." Sometimes the success comes more quickly, as when, on the final day of class, the job-minded student quoted earlier paused on the way out of the room to say, "And by the way, I *did* appreciate your course. . . after all!"

Such indications of the emergence of liberally educated professionals suggest that our educational goals have been effectively served.

D. Business/Industry and Liberal Learning

The Liberal Arts Major in Bell System Management

Robert E. Beck

The potential and progress of Liberal Arts majors in management has never been much of an issue in the Bell System. In fact, it took a special study to bring together the information presented here. It is not because the Bell System lacks research interests or capabilities that the data were previously unavailable; in fact, our professional staff probably does more research in human resources than any other company in the country. The reason for omitting research on college major is that we never thought it made that much difference in selecting future managers.

Diversity of academic preparation has been characteristic of Bell System managers for a long time. Among the top 10 executives at AT&T, four are electrical engineers, two have degrees in business, and two in the social sciences. In addition, one has a Ph.D. in physical chemistry and one never attended college! Engineers traditionally have been well represented since the Bell System is a highly technical company, spurred by many innovations in the Bell Laboratories. But the company is also people-intensive. With nearly one million employees, it is important to be well endowed with managerial skills as well as technical skills.

At the present time our operating companies employ more than 6,000 college graduates a year. Of these more than 1/3 are liberal arts graduates, including those with humanities, social science, math and scientific backgrounds. In addition, a wide variety of engineers and business majors as well as specialists such as computer programmers are also important as college recruits. There recently has been an upturn in the number of business majors hired, since we are attempting to increase our direct sales staff to meet the challenges of deregulation and competition.

New college graduates are typically hired into the first of seven levels of management in a Bell System operating company. The hope is that all of them will show enough promise to rise at least to the third level, which is the entry into middle management. Some, of course, will go much

---

Mr. Beck is assistant vice president for human resources of the American Telephone and Telegraph Company.

higher and eventually become the top executives of the corporation.

To answer the question of how different college majors compare in managerial potential and progress, a pool of long-standing research data was tapped by the Basic Human Resources Research group at AT&T. This group has been doing longitudinal studies of managers for the last 25 years. These studies are confidential, with no information reaching managers or supervisors to affect the careers of the individuals involved. The research is quite comprehensive, with a great variety of information and numerous follow-up points.

The first of these studies, the Management Progress Study (MPS), was begun in 1956. A total of 422 managers were selected from six different operating telephone companies to participate in the study. Of these, 274 were college graduates when employed. Reflecting the typical such hire in the late 1950s, all were white males. The participants were considered part of a general management pool who were expected to have a good chance to reach middle management in the years to come. These men are still being studied in middle age and mid-career, and present plans are to follow them into retirement.

In 1977 a new project, the Management Continuity Study (MCS), was begun. This study was designed to parallel the Management Progress Study as closely as possible to examine differences and similarities between the new generation of college recruits and the last. To date, 204 college graduates from 13 operating companies have undergone the first phase of MCS. One half of these participants are females and one third are minorities, reflecting the race/sex mix of college graduate hires in the late 1970s.

The major method used to study the participants in both studies was the management assessment center. Originally developed at AT&T as a technique for studying the lives and careers of the participants in the Management Progress Study, it soon showed promise as a method for selecting managers for advancement. Its validity for that purpose was established by MPS when it became clear that the assessment staff had been able to identify with remarkable accuracy which participants would receive later promotions. As noted earlier, advancement was not influenced by the confidential research data. Assessment centers are now used company-wide on an operational basis to determine potential for advancement to positions from the first to the fifth levels. Over 250,000 people have been assessed in the Bell System to date, and the method has spread to hundreds of other companies, both nationally and internationally.

The assessment center method consists of several important elements. First are the dimensions, or statements defining the behaviors and characteristics being measured. These are developed by job analyses of the positions for which the assessments are conducted. Examples of dimensions might be Organizing and Planning Ability or Leadership Skills.

A second essential element of an assessment center is a set of exercises. Both individual and group techniques are used and they include at least one simulation. Some typical individual exercises are interviews, questionnaires of motivations, personality, or attitudes, and aptitude tests. Group exercises may be business games or leaderless group discussions. A popular simulation is the In-Basket, in which candidates are faced with a fictional manager's letter, memos, telephone calls, and so forth and must decide how best to dispose of the various items.

Performance in the exercises is observed and evaluated by multiple assessors, the third essential ingredient in the method. The assessors receive up to three weeks of intensive, standardized training in how to conduct and evaluate performance in the exercises and write reports on what they have observed. The group of assessors come together for final integration sessions in which all the information on each candidate is read aloud and the assessors pool their judgments to rate the dimensions. Although managers are trained to be assessors in operational centers, the research assessment centers developed for MPS and MCS use a professional staff of psychologists, both AT&T's and outside academicians. Two of these outside assessors have served on the studies for 25 years!

Research with the Management Progress Study and other assessment centers has shown that there are several basic characteristics identified by assessment that relate to later advancement into management. A primary characteristic is administrative skills, consisting of the dimensions Planning and Organizing and Decision Making. Interpersonal Skills are equally important; these include such things as face-to-face leadership, oral communications skills, and making a forceful and likeable personal impact. Intellectual ability is also critical, and research has shown that both verbal and quantitative skills relate to success in an organiztion like the Bell System. Finally, motivation for advancement is a strong determinant of later progress; those who want to succeed are much more likely to do so.

With these characteristics in mind, it is possible to explore the data from the basic research studies and relate them to college major. First to be considered are the current crop of college graduates from the Management Continuity Study. Table 1 shows the distribution of the MCS sample by college major. As can be seen in the first two columns, 44% of them are liberal arts majors, distributed about equally between humanities/social science and math/science. The participants in the longitudinal studies were to represent general management hires, so technical specialists such as computer programmers were generally not included.

The right hand columns of Table 1 indicate those within each major who had master's degrees. For the total sample, 28 percent had master's degrees, but these degree holders were not distributed equally across the various majors. Liberal arts majors were much more likely to have a master's degree (39 percent), especially when compared to the engineers (8 percent). Since whether or not a candidate had a master's degree did make a difference in the quality of that candidate, this would introduce a bias in the data on college majors if it were not taken into account.

Illustrations of the impact of the master's degree in the MCS data are shown in Tables 2 and 3. Both tables show differences in average ratings of assessment center dimensions between those with a bachelor's degree and those with a master's degree. The dimension ratings are made on a five-point scale, where "5" is always high. The asterisks in the tables show where average scores are different at a statistically significant level according to t-tests between the two groups.

Two categories of dimensions are shown on Table 2, administrative skills and interpersonal skills. Those with masters degrees scored higher on the dimensions noted with asterisks, and the group differences just missed statistical significance on those without an asterisk. The largest differences were in the interpersonal areas of Leadership Skills and Perception of Threshold Social Cues, or social sensitivity. Interpersonal dimensions showing somewhat less significant results were Forcefulness,

TABLE 1

MANAGEMENT CONTINUITY STUDY UNDERGRADUATE MAJOR AND EDUCATIONAL LEVEL

	Total		Master's	
	N	%	N	%
Liberal Arts	90	44%	35	39%
Humanities	16	8%	9	56%
Social Science	30	15%	11	37%
Math	33	16%	10	30%
Science	11	5%	5	46%
Engineering	26	13%	2	8%
Business	76	37%	16	21%
Other	11	6%	3	27%
Total	203	100%	56	28%

Behavior Flexibility, which indicates ability to modify behavior to achieve a goal, and Social Objectivity, which means freedom from prejudices. On administrative skills, those with more education made more appropriate and timely decisions on exercises like the In-Basket and were more creative in their approaches to management problems.

The master's degree was not as clearly an indication of superiority in the areas shown in Table 3, intellectual ability and managerial motivation. Although the better educated had broader interests, they were not more intellectually capable. Those with master's degrees scored no higher than those with bachelor's degrees on mental ability tests, nor were various examples of their writing skills any more impressive.

In two areas of motivation, having a master's degree had little impact. One of these is reflected in the dimension Primacy of Work, meaning the extent to which work is one of the most important things in life. Neither were there significant differences on Inner Work Standards, defined as having one's own high standards for work, regardless of external requirements. Where the master's graduates did show heightened motivation was toward extrinsic rewards. The better educated recruits were more interested in both advancement and money. Perhaps this is a major reason they went on for a master's degree in the first place.

TABLE 2
IMPACT OF MASTER'S DEGREE - I

Assessment Dimensions:	Average Rating 1 = low, 5 = high		
	Bachelor's		Master's
Administrative Skills			
Organizing And Planning	2.8		3.1
Decision Making	2.5	*	2.9
Creativity	2.0	*	2.4
Interpersonal Skills			
Leadership Skills	2.6	**	3.1
Oral Communication Skills	2.9		3.2
Behavior Flexibility	2.7	*	3.0
Forcefulness	2.6	*	3.1
Social Objectivity	2.9	*	3.2
Perception of Threshold Social Cues	2.9	**	3.3
N	147		56

*Group differences significant at p<.05   **p<.005

In summary, those with master's degrees showed superior performance on administrative and interpersonal skills and had higher motivation to advance in the company. However, they were not more intellectually capable than those with bachelor's degrees. The impact of the additional degree prevailed regardless of undergraduate major or whether the master's was an M.A., an M.S., or an M.B.A.

Because of the differences related to the master's degree, it is necessary to separate the influence of level of education from analyses of the impact of college major. In the four tables of MCS data that follow, this has been accomplished by analysis of covariance techniques, and the scores presented have been adjusted for level of education. These charts compare four groups by major, the first two comprising liberal arts: humanities/social science, math/science, engineering, and business. Those categorized as "other", which included education majors and a few specialized degrees, have been excluded, so the total sample size in these comparisons is 192.

Table 4 contrasts the four major groups on administrative skills. For all three dimensions, Organizing and Planning, Decision Making, and Creativity in solving management problems, the group differences were statistically significant. A comparison of the average assessment ratings shows that the non-technical majors (humanities/social science and business) were superior in administrative skills to the technical majors

TABLE 3
IMPACT OF MASTER'S DEGREE - II

Assessment Dimensions:	Average Rating 1 = low, 5 = high		
	Bachelor's		Master's
Intellectual Ability			
Range of Interests	2.8	**	3.2
General Mental Ability	3.1		3.0
Written Communication Skills	3.1		3.0
Managerial Motivation			
Primacy of Work	3.0		3.1
Inner work Standards	3.2		3.3
Need for Advancement	2.9	**	3.6
Financial Motivation	2.9	**	3.5
N	147		56

**Group differences significant at p<.005

(math/science and engineering).

The differences in interpersonal skills by major were even more pronounced, as shown in Table 5. On all three dimensions, Leadership Skills, Oral Comunication Skills, and Forcefulness of Personal Impact, the humanities/social science majors were clearly ahead. Weakest were the engineers and math/science majors. Evidence from a sample of exercises to support the dimension ratings are also shown in Table 5. The scores for the group exercise ratings use five-point scales with "5" a high score; two assessors concurred on these ratings within one point. Oral presentation was based on a five-to-ten-minute talk given by each assessee on an assigned topic. In the competitive discussion that followed the oral presentations, assessees in groups of six had to compete for funds for their assigned cause. Assessor ratings on these group exercises indicated the humanities/social science majors turned in the best performance. They also had the best leadership skills in a group discussion (not shown in the table) that was free from assigned competitive roles and simply left resolution of the problem to the group members.

Some reasons why the humanities/social science majors were more apt to turn in a better performance in interpersonal tasks were illustrated in personality questionnaires. Three personality questionnaires were administered in MCS: the California Psychological Inventory (CPI), the Guilford-Zimmerman (G-Z) and the Edwards Personal Preference Schedule (EPPS). The humanities/social science majors described themselves as more socially dominant on several of these scales, such as the CPI Dominance and G-Z Ascendance scales shown in Table 5. In addition, there were significant group differences with the humanities/social science majors the high scorers on the EPPS Dominance scale, measuring liking to assume leadership roles, the CPI's Social Presence scale, measuring a manipulative type of sociability, and the CPI's Self Acceptance scale, measuring sense of personal worth.

In contrast, the engineers and science/math majors tended to score lowest on the social dominance scales. The engineers described themselves as a conservative group who did not want to stand out in a crowd. They scored lowest on the EPPS Exhibition scale (liking to attract attention), lowest on Change (enjoying doing new and different things), and highest on Endurance (liking to persist at a job). On the CPI they scored highest on measures of conservative conformity, such as Socialization (having internalized social values), Self-Control (showing restraint of impulsivity and irrationality), and Communality (conventionality). Thus the humanities and social science majors had self-concepts which promoted standing out from the crowd as leaders, while the engineers were more apt to define themselves as consistent background workers.

Table 6 shows the differences among the college major groups with respect to intellectual ability. Here it is important to attend to what is not

TABLE 4
ADMINISTRATIVE SKILLS

AVERAGE RATING
(1 = low, 5 = high)

| Assessment Dimensions | Liberal Arts | | Engineering | Business |
	Humanities/ Social Science	Math/ Science		
*Organizing And Planning	2.9	2.7	2.4	3.1
*Decision Making	2.8	2.3	2.3	2.9
*Creativity	2.5	1.9	1.8	2.3
N	46	44	26	76

*Group differences statistically significant at p<.05
  Adjusted for level of education

TABLE 5
INTERPERSONAL SKILLS

Average Score
(1 = low, 5 = high)

| | Liberal Arts | | Engineering | Business |
	Humanities/ Social Science	Math/ Science		
ASSESSMENT DIMENSIONS				
**Leadership Skills	3.1	2.3	2.4	2.7
**Oral Communication Skills	3.4	2.9	2.5	2.9
**Forcefulness	3.2	2.3	2.3	2.8
GROUP EXERCISE RATINGS				
*Oral Presentation	3.4	2.9	2.7	3.1
*Competitive Discussion	3.3	2.6	2.7	3.1
PERSONALITY QUESTIONNAIRES[a]				
**Dominance (CPI)	56%ile	34%ile	38%ile	50%ile
**Ascendance (G-Z)	78%ile	48%ile	55%ile	67%ile

[a]Bell System College Graduate Norms, 1978
*Group differences statistically significant at p<.05, **p<.005.
  Adjusted for level of education

significant as well as what is. Noticeably *not* significantly different among the majors were verbal skills. The non-technical majors did no better than technical when it came to performance on a verbal ability test (from the School and College Ability Test or SCAT) or on ratings of written communications skills. The greatest difference in intellectual ability occurred in quantitative skills. The math/science majors and engineers were clearly superior to the others, but the humanities/social science majors scored particularly low, at the 17th percentile. For managerial positions requiring quantitative analyses, this must be considered a particular disadvantage. The humanities/social science majors and engineers did have somewhat broader interests than the other two groups. Scores on the General Information Test of a range of knowledge reflected this trend, although the group differences were not statistically significant.

When managerial motivation was considered, differences by major appeared only for certain kinds of motivation. There was no impact of college major for Primacy of Work, Inner Work Standards, or Financial Motivation (see Table 7). Rather, the motivational differences by major were concentrated in the need for advancement. On ratings of the dimensions the humanities/social science and business majors were equally

TABLE 6

INTELLECTUAL ABILITY

Average Score
(1 = low, 5 =high)

| | Liberal Arts | | | |
	Humanities/ Social Science	Math/ Science	Engineering	Business
ASSESSMENT DIMENSIONS				
*Range of Interests	3.2	2.7	3.1	2.8
General Mental Ability	3.0	3.2	3.2	3.0
Written Communication Skills	3.2	3.3	3.0	2.9
ABILITY TESTS				
General Information Test[a]	63%ile	54%ile	61%ile	52%ile
SCAT-Verbal[b]	60%ile	47%ile	47%ile	48%ile
**SCAT-Quantitative[b]	17%ile	50%ile	56%ile	35%ile
N	46	44	26	76

[a]Bell System College Graduate Norms, 1978, N=589; [b]1958, N=585

*Group differences statistically significant at p<.05, **p<.005.
  Adjusted for level of education

235

TABLE 7
MANAGERIAL MOTIVATION

Average Score
(1 = low, 5 = high)

| | Liberal Arts | | | |
	Humanities/ Social Science	Math/ Science	Engineering	Business
ASSESSMENT DIMENSIONS				
Primacy of Work	3.0	2.9	2.8	3.3
Inner Work Standards	3.1	3.2	3.2	3.3
* Need for Advancement	3.3	2.8	2.8	3.3
* Ability to Delay Gratification	3.2	3.7	3.6	3.2
Financial Motivation	3.1	3.0	2.8	3.3
PAPER/PENCIL TESTS OF MOTIVES				
Advancement (Questionnaire)[a]	49%ile	44%ile	38%ile	60%ile
Money (Questionnaire)[a]	46%ile	54%ile	50%ile	62%ile
**Achievement/Advancement (Projective Ratings)[b]	3.0	2.8	3.1	3.5

[a]MCS - Norms

[b]5 - Point Rating Scale

*Group difference significant at p<.05, **p<.005.
 Adjusted for level of education

high on Need for Advancement and equally low on Ability to Delay Gratification of a Promotion, while the technical majors scored in the opposite direction.

A questionnaire measure of need for advancement pointed to the business majors as being highest in these interests, although the group difference with the analysis of covariance was not quite statistically significant (p .06). Group differences on projective measures of need for achievement and advancement were significant, however, with the business majors clearly the highest scorers. These projectives ratings were made on a five-point scale and based on responses to two incomplete sentences tests and six stories written to Thematic Apperception Test pictures. These exercises attempt to reveal underlying motivations that are less subject to the various distortions that can affect questionnaires. By these measures, the business majors seemed most anxious to get ahead, although the assessor ratings of dimensions assigned equally high advancement motivation to the humanities/social science majors.

The MCS results have shown the present relationships between college major and managerial potential. A consideration of the Management

236

Progress Study results can indicate the relative stability of these findings and also point to relationships of college major with later progress in the Bell System. Table 8 shows the distribution of college recruits of more than 20 years ago who were MPS participants. Of the total sample of 274 college graduates, 38 percent were liberal arts majors, only slightly fewer than in MCS. However, their distribution among the technical and non-technical majors was heavily weighted to the humanities and social science majors. In fact, it was not possible to perform reliable analyses with the math and science majors since there were so few of them (18).

Table 9 gives a summary of the original assessment center findings with the MPS participants by college major groups. Results are presented by each major category that relates to managerial success. In the table an H stands for high scorers among the groups by major and an L for low scorers. Results for corresponding dimensions and tests showed statistically significant differences among the groups using analysis of variance techniques. Since almost none of the MPS participants had a Master's degree, this effect did not have to be controlled.

The humanities/social science majors turned in the best overall performance. They were high scorers on all but one category, but there they revealed the same weakness shown in the MCS results: quantitative skills. Their scores on the SCAT Quantitative scale was only at the 23rd percentile of the same Bell System norms shown previously (Table 6).

The engineers had a pattern of strengths and weaknesses directly opposite to those of the humanities/social science majors. They were the highest scorers on quantitative ability but weak on all the other managerial skills. Thus both the humanities/social science majors and the engineers have shown a consistent pattern of strengths and weaknesses that held over a 20 year period of time in the two longitudinal studies.

The business majors in MPS did not perform quite as well as those of MCS. Although again they showed strengths in interpersonal skills and motivation to advance in management, their intellectual ability was not up to that of the more recent business majors. This may be due to higher standards in business schools today.

On overall ratings of potential for middle management, made by the assessors after reaching consensus on the ratings of the dimensions, there were highly significant group differences. Nearly half (46 percent) of the humanities/social science majors were considered to have potential for middle management, compared to only 31 percent of the business majors and 26 percent of the engineers.

College major was also examined for the Management Progress Study in relation to various criteria for management success. These results are presented in Table 10. The first line of the table shows the number of years to achieve an initial promotion into the second level of management. The group difference was highly significant, with the engineers taking about 1-1/2 years longer to be promoted than the humanities/social science and business majors. By the end of eight years, the average management level of the humanities/social science majors was highest, with the engineers still trailing well behind. By year 20, the same trends were evident, but the differences were no longer statistically significant. In terms of average management level achieved, the engineers made the greatest gains between years 8 and 20, so that the humanities/social majors were only slightly ahead at the end of this time.

TABLE 8
MANAGEMENT PROGRESS STUDY UNDERGRADUATE MAJOR

	N	%
Liberal Arts	105	38%
Humanities	27	10%
Social Science	60	22%
Math	4	1%
Science	14	5%
Engineering	68	25%
Business	96	35%
Other	5	2%
Total	274	100%

TABLE 9
MPS ASSESSMENT RESULTS AND COLLEGE MAJOR
HIGH (H) AND LOW (L) SCORERS

	Humanities/ Social Science	Engineering	Business
Administrative Skills	H	L	
Interpersonal Skills	H	L	H
Intellectual Ability			
Verbal	H	L	L
Quantitative	L	H	L
Advancement Motivation	H	L	H
Have Middle Management Potential	46%	26%	31%
N	87	68	96

TABLE 10
PROGRESS IN MANAGEMENT
BY MAJOR

AVERAGE

	Humanities/ Social Science	Engineering	Business
**Years To Reach 2nd Level	4.0	5.4	3.9
N	57	47	68
**Level At 8 Years	2.6	2.2	2.4
N	48	46	60
Level At 20 Years	3.4	3.2	3.2
N	43	40	47
% 4th Level or Higher, Year. 20	43%	23%	32%
N	43	40	47

**Group differences statistically significant at p<.005

Another way to view the 20 year data is to consider the proportion of men who had achieved at least the fourth level, a midway point in the management hierarchy and usually considered a sign of considerable success. Among humanities/social science majors 43 percent had achieved at least the fourth level, compared to only 32 percent of the business majors and 23 percent of the engineers. This group difference is not quite statistically significant. Thus in the long run, the early advantages of the humanities/social science majors were somewhat but not completely overcome.

To recapitulate the findings on liberal arts majors, the humanities/social science majors showed especially strong interpersonal skills and were similar to business majors in administrative skills and motivation for advancement. Their greatest weakness was in quantitative skills. The relative quality of their other managerial skills was reflected in their progress in the Bell System, especially during the early years. The math/science majors were similar to the engineers in their strengths and weaknesses. They had strong quantitative skills but were weak in administrative and interpersonal skills and had rather low motivation for advancement.

One overall conclusion from these data is that there is no need for liberal arts majors to lack confidence in approaching business careers. The humanities and social science majors in particular continue to make a strong showing in managerial skills and have experienced considerable business success. We hope and expect this to continue.

Liberal Learning As Preparation For Business Careers

Thomas R. Horton

As I understand it, the theme of this Panel is "Liberal Learning as Preparation for Business Careers." I believe that the emphasis is clearly on the right word: *career*. The term *career* implies one's life work, the path one takes—at times straight, at other times winding, circling back, perhaps branching into several paths, over a substantial passage of time. There is another meaning of the word when it is used as an intransitive verb; *career* means to go at top speed, especially in a headlong manner. It is my plan to talk about the noun rather than the verb.

It is, I think, difficult to say anything very fresh or new about the liberal arts and careers, as anything one can say has probably been said many times. In addition, there is a certain hazard (no relation to George) in a corporate executive's agreeing to appear before educators to talk about the importance of the liberal arts. The usual riposte is the assertion that although corporations *talk* about the importance of history, literature, language, the arts—they *hire* accountants and engineers. To this I say, there are indeed engineering and accounting tasks to be done and a consequent need for qualified people to do them. Moreover, if corporations were to take the reverse stance and to hire *only* liberal arts graduates, then establish training programs to teach engineering, accounting, finance, computer science, etc., would not the corporations then be accused of taking unto themselves a task which belongs to the university? So we have the usual dilemma, wrapped in an enigma, presented once more by a panel devoted to that same old riddle: how does a humanist, a generalist, survive in a pragmatic, specialized world?

Part of the answer to the riddle, of course, is that a broad, liberal education may or may not help one to get his or her *first* job. Chances are that an art history major may experience some rough going in seeking an entry-level position in competition with other job applicants, those who have majored in economics, science or finance. The advantage of the humanities is clearly not at the entry-point. Rather, the benefit is one which

Mr. Horton is director of university relations for the International Business Machines Corporation.

slowly accrues over time, over the course of one's career. As a person experiences and develops his or her career in a large corporation, it may even be true that the occupational courses taken, the courses specifically pointed toward accounting, for example, or engineering, are of the greatest value early in one's career. My own educational background includes graduate study in mathematics. Yet I would be hard pressed to think of any time in the past quarter century that I have been called upon to use anything resembling advanced mathematics in my everyday work. Far more important has been an understanding of human motivation, some comprehension of the way groups of people behave and the rest of the body of knowledge and skills which has been gradually accumulated by learning on the job—in other words, by observations, by analysis and synthesis, by the exercise of the curious mind—through the use of mental skills that college catalogs of liberal arts institutions claim to develop and, indeed, probably do.

A pastiche of quotations from such catalogs claims that those who will be given degrees, as they "enter into the company of educated men and women" will be "those who think critically about what they know, those who are able to consider fairly the attitudes of others, those who are willing to contemplate questions which the ignorant consider unworthy of contemplation, those of refined culture, etc. etc." Indeed, what one catalog describes as the "essential habits of the educated man—curiosity, rigorous observation, tolerant understanding, and enlightened judgment"— these qualities sound very much the same as those one would desire in an executive in a business corporation or chief executive officer of a college or university. Common to all who hold executive responsibilities is the authority which one has over others and the need one has to inform, to persuade, to reward them, and, at times, to judge their actions. J. Douglas Brown claims in *The Human Nature of Organization* that no one without a keen sense of tragedy should have authority over others, and he recommends Shakespeare as mentor.

One's values are informed by great literature, as one's inner self can be nourished by poetry and music. Life *does* imitate art. What long-running legal trial of today reminds one of the case of Jardyce vs. Jardyce from Dickens' *Bleak House,* the trial which had gone on for so many years, across generations, that there was no one alive who could remember the principles or substantive merits of either side of the case? How better can one attain some sense of perspective, some feeling for the value of one's own endeavors in the context of a wider world, some appreciation of the fact that values do collide, life does have shades of gray (but not all of it is gray!)—Is there any better way to obtain understanding and to develop wisdom than through the study of writers and thinkers of the past? Yet some troubling questions arise. One wonders whether some proponents of the liberal arts or the humanities are not guilty of boasting, rather gleefully, of their ignorance of other fields. A lack of knowledge of the sciences is hardly the mark of a liberally educated person. Each weekly newsmagazine seems to bring reports of more technical progress in genetic engineering; international struggles for superiority in the design and fabrication of submicron silicon structures are reported; new theories in behavioral science are put forth. Against this background, is it a virtue to be educated *only* in the humanities? Can one be liberally educated without a liberal exposure to the sciences, or at least a moderate one? Yet a recent study by the National Science Foundation reported that fewer than ten percent of all high school students take as much as one year of physics or chemistry.

Some who deplore the alleged mismatch between business and the liberal arts even seem somehow proud of the nonutilitarian nature of their studies. I think this is rather odd and also a bit unfair. In any contest of the lack of utility of one's education, I would put my graduate work in number theory up against the studies of any scholar of the humanities. What could be more useless, in the extreme, than a dissertation on the topic of the equivalence of quadratic forms? The best such thesis on this topic is of less utility than a good poem or a mediocre song. So let us not exaggerate the impracticality of the liberal arts, especially since at their center are such subjects as language, including the English language.

Some time ago a leading business school polled a sample of its successful graduates to determine which of their college and university studies were considered most important and which of their current skills most contributory to their success. Oral communication was listed as the most frequent response, written communication the next. We all know that good communication comes from hard work and that stylish, elegant writing stems partly from the *reading* of good literature and letters. This is not the stuff that is taught in business schools. As business becomes more globally interdependent upon the economics, laws and customs of other nations—and it has certainly been speeding in this direction for the last many years—a knowledge of *place*—(once called geography) and of *custom* (which comes through a study of history) becomes essential.

One could go on, citing example after example of the ways in which the subjects of the humanities, the liberal arts impinge upon the needs of businesspeople. The successful businessman or businesswoman today is not a Babbitt. Babbitt simply won't hack it. As evidence that the business executive finds the humanities of interest, I should point out that one of the educational experiences most desired by our senior executives is the executive program of the Aspen Institute of Humanistic Study. I attended this a few years ago, rubbed shoulders with other business people, foundation executives, college professors, etc. Supported by our employers, we reflected upon *The Federalist Papers.* We thought about Jane Adams' advice to her husband, not to forget the ladies. We pondered the meaning of the kiss in *The Grand Inquisitor*—hardly the daily grist of a business executive, yet full of human meaning, as is all great literature. Of course, neither Dostoyevsky nor John Adams can be of any great help to us in such activities as cost accounting or budget preparation, but then again neither would an accounting course be of particular help to the business executive who is confronted with the task of composing a graceful letter to the widow of a deceased employee or preparing a presentation to his board of directors on public responsibility, or any other task which intimately involves the human condition.

Last month Judd Alexander, a senior vice president of the American Can Company, wrote in *The Wall Street Journal* about his discovery that a number of the senior officers of his corporation came from a background of the liberal arts. He stated that "obviously there is no single 'best background' for business," and he reported that his company has set up a small recruiting program for high-achieving, liberal arts graduates. This is encouraging, but I doubt that it signals a general trend. I do not foresee any great change in the way in which corporate recruiters go about doing their job, when there are indeed still accounting and engineering to be done, and a need for liberal arts graduates who have coupled some professional training with their humanities and science. I suspect that it is the senior corporate executive, rather than the junior recruiter, who would testify with more conviction about the value of the liberal arts to his career. If this be true, a program of visiting senior executives to campus might help to convince students and faculty of the practicality of a broad education. Yet that same senior executive would probably stress the need for a student majoring in the humanities to try to make his or her education more marketable by the infusion of at least a few courses on economics or possibly computer science. Clearly, this is not an either/or matter—what is probably needed is a balanced combination of the intensely practical with the ineffably profound; a rigorous pursuit of each may serve to inform the other. Institutions of higher education now offer a great variety of such combinations, and approaches vary widely according to the type of institution. For example, Pace University's Graduate School of Business offers an excellent course in management which uses as reading assignments some of the great novels and plays of literature. Mount Holyoke College provides a program of study of the administration of complex organizations, complete with internship possibilities, all embedded in a liberal arts institution. Sweet Briar College offers a career counseling program which deeply involves its faculty. Worcester Polytechnic Institute and Babson College have found ways to strengthen the liberal arts components of their engineering and business curricula, respectively. You who are participants in the QUILL project could list many other examples, I am sure.

One needs to seek ways to help students visualize how their college-acquired knowledge can be helpful in a variety of settings, including business. Recently I came across a rather interesting tabulation which one small, liberal arts college had produced for its students, a listing of what its alumni do for a living, arranged by category of academic major. It was quite enlightening to see the range of occupations of those who had majored in English, history, or mathematics, for example. This seemed to be certainly an inexpensive, yet quite useful tool, just one way to help liberal arts majors visualize possible career futures for themselves. Career counseling, of course, is central to any discussion of this matter, and today there are many well developed such programs, particularly for women. Catalyst and other organizations have put fresh thought and enormous energies into such programs, in the conviction that women particularly need such guidance. I agree, but so do men, and I suspect that there is much to learn from these programs which is broadly applicable both to men and women.

These, then, are some of my thoughts, the thoughts of a mathematics major who did not take courses while in college to prepare for a business career, the thoughts of a business executive who still wishes that he were more liberally educated in the humanities and sciences.

The Interdependence of the Professional and Humanist Worlds

Ralph Z. Sorenson

Let me at the outset declare my colors. Even though I head up an educational institution that is committed to management education, I am a believer in liberal education. I believe in it, first, because I think that liberally educated professionals are much more effective in doing their jobs, and second, because I think a liberal education, in and of itself, makes life much more interesting, rich and full. Moreover, I think I have some company from among the top ranks of executives in this country. One doesn't have to look too far for pronouncements by senior managers about the need for broad and liberal education among professionals generally and for management leadership in particular. For example, David Rockefeller wrote about executive qualities for *The Wall Street Journal* recently, and said the following: "The chief executive in the year 2000 will have to be more broadly gauged to deal with the delicate and divergent internal and external forces of the day. In addition to being a 'generalist' in the very best sense of the word—with a feel for history, politics, literature, current events and the arts—he will have to be sensitive to public opinion and respectful of the public franchise over which he presides."

Or again, recently Irving Shapiro, who just retired as chairman of Du-Pont, said, "If I were choosing a chief executive, I would not be overly concerned with his education or specific background. I would ask if he relates to the larger world or if he only knows how to produce widgets but can not do anything else."

In agreeing with this point of view, Howard Johnson remarked on the occasion of his inauguration as president of M.I.T. in 1966, "The future will demand of M.I.T. a great deal more than that it simply bridge the supposed schism between two cultures where the not so well rounded scientist can be as ignorant of Shakespeare as the humanist is of the sec-

---

Dr. Sorenson is former president of Babson College, and is currently president of the Barry-Wright Corporation. His remarks are based on a paper delivered at the American Council on Education 1980 Annual Meeting in San Francisco, CA.

ond law of thermodynamics. We shall have to provide true generalists capable of dealing with the great problems cutting across every area of our lives."

So there does seem to be recognition at the top among senior managers of the importance of liberally educated professionals. The problem, however, is that the people in organizations and companies who are actually doing the hiring of young people—recruiting officers plus some line and staff officers—typically place a much higher value on what they perceive to be practical and professional skills, such as accounting, finance, marketing, engineering, computer science, than on an individual's grasp of history, politics, philosophy, literature, science, or the ability to think critically.

Frequently, students themselves with an eye toward starting salaries and what they perceive to be the practical realities of "getting a job" tend to give short shift to the humanities and to liberal arts. All too often, they consider these as medicine to be taken like castor oil, only under duress. I think that this attitude is reinforced by starting salary differentials commanded by, say, accounting graduates as opposed to students of the humanities and liberal arts. Recently, *The Wall Street Journal* reported that the average liberal arts undergraduate who joined the work force last June was able to command a starting salary of $12,900. This compares with starting salaries for people with accounting degrees of $15,500, computer science—$18,700, people with electrical engineering backgrounds—$20,300. Those are major differentials and students are just being practical when they take such factors into consideration as they design their curricula.

Now it seems to me that the situation is not helped by various professional associations such as the American Assembly of Collegiate Schools of Business (AACSB) which is the accrediting body for business schools. The AACSB, in its accrediting standards, seems to have adopted the attitude that the liberal arts should be taken almost exclusively in the first two years of college with the final two years reserved almost exclusively for business subjects. This attitude has led to a dichotomous view of society—the practical professional world versus the world of the humanities and the liberal arts.

I, personally, disagree with this view. Instead, I believe that there is a common thread which runs through both of the foregoing worlds. What is that thread? Is it the ability to think critically and independently, the ability to identify and define problems, the ability to marshal and analyze evidence, the ability to reach independent conclusions, the ability to formulate solutions or recommendations and the ability to implement these solutions and recommendations? These abilities are commonly referred to as the scientific method. An additional, vital thread that runs through the worlds of both the professional and the humanist is the ability to articulate one's ideas and thoughts in a clear and persuasive fashion, both orally and in writing. And finally, perhaps most important of all, is the ability needed by both professionals and humanists to inject flair, humor, compassion, good values, and zest into all that one does.

All of these things are important and they are important regardless of what one does with one's life. Certainly they are important in the field of business and management. To give you some examples, it seems to me that a knowledge of the liberal arts and humanities is critical if we are to create satisfying work environments for our employees; for this purpose an understanding of psychology and sociology is essential. Building constructive relationships between business and government requires basic exposure to political science and some sense of the historical evolution of the interface between the private and public sectors. Decisions concerning the design of new products, new factories or new buildings ideally should be made with a keen eye for aesthetics as well as function. Involvement in multi-national business today clearly makes knowledge of foreign languages, geopolitics and cross-cultural relationships very desirable. And certainly those who are making decisions concerning the sponsorship of TV programs and the design of advertising campaigns should be able to appreciate the difference between good art and bad art, good literature and bad literature.

In some ways, it seems that our big problem may lie in the term "liberal arts" itself. It is a term which is at best fuzzy and at worst misleading and misunderstood. Some people ascribe to it political overtones: the liberal leftist arts as opposed to the more conservative rightist professionalism. These are the kinds of people who refer to pointy-head intellectuals. Some people equate liberal education with non-useful education, as opposed to professional or useful education.

And those in the other camp, in the "liberal arts camp," tend to speak pejoratively and patronizingly of narrow vocationalism as opposed to the only true education, which in their view is rooted in the liberal arts and humanities. Recently in a press release put out by the Commission on the Humanities, the following statement was included: "While the Commission recognizes the problem of liberal arts graduates in the job market, it nonetheless considers vocationalism a dangerous trend."

As long as we have people who believe that vocationalism is a dangerous trend, there is going to be a natural tendency to lash out against it, to fight it, and to end up with a "two-world" mentality. I once heard David Riesman from Harvard say that the mere fact that the liberal arts are called liberal arts is no guarantee that these arts, whatever they may be, will be taught in a liberal fashion. Nor is there any guarantee that the humanities will be taught in a humane fashion. By the same token, he suggested that there is no reason why vocational or professional skills cannot be taught in a liberating, humane way rather than in a confining, inhumane way. Or put another way, those teaching the liberal arts are not immune from narrow-mindedness just as those teaching vocational or professional skills are not by definition excluded from the fraternity of liberal thinkers.

Through these opposing sets of prejudices we have managed to get ourselves into a tremendous jam where, it seems to me, we are in two armed camps. I think by way of prescription and recommendation the first thing we have to do is to break down this armed camp mentality. We need to destroy the notion that the liberal arts and the professions are at war with one another. Those in the liberal arts must get away from the idea that vocationalism is dangerous. Narrow vocationalism, yes, but vocationalism in and of itself, no. Those in the professions and business by contrast must shed the mentality which says that the liberal arts are a waste of time. What we really are all seeking is liberally educated professionals, people who are skilled businessmen, engineers, doctors, lawyers and at the same time are full, richly compassionate human beings. The two are integrally entwined. Consequently, we need in our colleges and universities a greater willingness to interweave curricula so that even in undergraduate programs at liberal arts colleges we recognize that the concerns for careers and the concerns for one's future vocation are very real and legitimate concerns. We must try increasingly in those institutions to provide opportunities for students to get a feel for or exposure to different kinds of career paths, even though the major emphasis at the undergraduate level may be on the liberal arts and humanities. In turn, in colleges such as Babson, which are primarily oriented toward management or professional education, we need to provide exposure for our students to subjects such as history and political science, literature and languages, either through cross-registration with other institutions, or through interdisciplinary programs on our own campuses.

Chief executive officers in the world of business must make sure that in their organizations the people actually doing the hiring are people who will look for liberally educated professionals rather than narrow specialists with skills that have a very short half life. These same chief executive officers have to, it seems to me, in the future serve more vividly as role models. They need to speak out in an articulate fashion about the importance of the liberal arts.

For all of us, it is my belief that what is important is to realize that education isn't something that takes place when we are young and ends with a college diploma or even a graduate degree. Rather, education is a continuing adventure throughout one's life. In the course of that adventure there are two integral halves to the whole. One half has to do with technical, professionally oriented skills and the other half has to do with the liberal arts and the humanities and all of the subjects that create a full, rich culture and enable us at the same time to be better professionals.

E. The Relevance of Liberal Learning to the Professions

Liberal and Pre-Professional (Premedical) Education

Carleton B. Chapman

The key question in considering the relevance of liberal learning to the professions has nothing directly to do with what are or ought to be the requirements for admission to medical or law or engineering schools. The key, and very pressing, question is: Do we really believe that liberal education is an ideal worth pursuing? Or are we merely paying it lip service? And if we actually believe the ideal is vital and urgent, as it seems fashionable to claim, what shape should liberal education in the late twentieth century take? Adequate answer to the question is urgent. And in this connection, I believe a very solid case can be made for the proposition that if prebaccaluareate education can be made truly liberal and appropriately general, the problem of professional requirements, including those so uncritically prescribed by the medical schools for well over half a century, simply and utterly vanish.

Our current dilemma is usually blamed on the medical schools which is not altogether wrong. It is, however, an oversimplication; and, more important, it serves as an excuse for some faculty groups that are more concerned with protecting disciplinary or departmental interests than with liberal or general education by any valid definition.

Liberal Education as a Concept

The notion that there is a definable body of learning that all educated citizens should share is part of the heritage of the West from Rome and, less directly from Greece. Plato's ideas about education are, in the present connection, more confusing than relevant,[1] but several Roman authors dealt with the concept of liberal, or common or general, learning much more convincingly. The earliest of them described liberal or

---

Dr. Chapman is professor and chairman, Department of The History of Medicine, Albert Einstein College of Medicine, Yeshiva University, Bronx, New York. He has also served as president of the Commonwealth Fund.

general education in terms of recognized categories of learning in the first century B.C., as a prerequisite for the study of architecture. This was Vitruvius, who noted that

> . . . all studies have a common bond of union and intercourse with one another . . . for a liberal education forms . . . a single body made up of all these members.

The architect, he said

> . . . should be a man of letter, a skilled draftsman, a mathematician, familiar with historical studies, a diligent student of philosophy acquainted with music, not ignorant of medicine, learned in . . . (the law), familiar with astronomy and astronomical calculation.[2]

Cicero (106-43 B.C.) about the same time had much the same thing to say but the chief goal, and indeed the justification, was less narrowly preprofessional than it was in Vitruvius' account. Cicero was describing the training of the orator who, in the Roman scheme of things, was the man of politics who might also on occasion serve as advocate in court proceedings and who was expected to serve the state in or outside Rome as a full—or part-time career.[3] To Cicero, the properly trained orator ought to be conversant with ". . . the whole of the contents of the life of mankind," which, to him, was synonymous with liberal education; and in this connection he approvingly quoted Hippias' definition of the liberal education of a gentleman.[4]

It was, however, Quintillian (born 35 A.D.) who, in the first century A.D., forged the concept that liberal education (including "inquiry into the causes of natural phenomena") is an indispensable requirement for those who view public service, or politics, as a moral obligation and a profession in its own right. Quintillian's focus was on the Roman who ". . . can really play his part as a citizen and is capable of meeting the demands both of public and private business, the man who can guide a state by his counsel, give it a firm basis by his legislation, and purge its vices by his decisions as a judge . . . ."[5]

A little later Plutarch (born circa 47 A.D.) transmitted the same theme in describing (in tedious detail) the ideal education of the free-born Roman from childhood to early adult life. He should not, said Plutarch,

> . . . be allowed to go without some knowledge . . . of every branch . . . of what is called general education, yet these he should learn only incidentally . . . (for perfection in everything is impossible), but philosophy he should know above all else.

He then goes on to urge familiarity with literature and the use of books in order ". . . to study knowledge at its source."[6]

It is tempting to regard these comments in the context of our own time; but this, of course, is not without its hazards. Even so, what comes down across these many centuries is a powerful concept of general education, made up of both the humanities and the sciences as they have been defined and redefined with the passage of time, as something that is of paramount social importance and essential preparation for public life and service to society.

Tracing the concept from the first century A.D. to our own time has commanded the attention of many historians and classicists[7] and it is, to say the least, a complicated and demanding assignment. But through it all, the basic concept has remained remarkably intact. In the early Renaissance and after, there were those who, like Erasmus, thought that Latin and Greek literature contain ". . . almost everything worth learning . . ."[8] But Juan Luis Vives, Erasmus' star pupil, while recognizing the importance of the classics in his system of education, nonetheless emphasized observation and experiment and, perhaps more important, deemphasized Aristotelian natural science as the scholastics had viewed it.[9] If we only apply our minds, said Vives, "we can judge better over the whole round of life and nature than could Aristotle, Plato, or any of the ancients."[10]

All of which emerges ". . . as an essential tributary in the stream that takes us to Locke and Newton"[11] and beyond. The emphasis throughout remains on general education very broadly defined within the context of the times of writing. Some of the giants along the way had their own special quirks: Locke, for example, had a puritanic distrust of poetry which he linked closely to gambling, and Elyot, writing a century before Locke, put the classics ahead of natural science in his plan for education. But neither excluded either classics or natural science and both regarded liberal education as "an important dimension of statecraft."[12]

The notion that natural science, on the one hand, and the liberal arts or the humanities, on the other, are rigidly separate and mutually exclusive was made a household phrase in the English-speaking world after World War II by C.P. Snow, who exploited it in his novels about the two cultures. Appropriately enough, the action in his novels takes place in the Senior Commons rooms of Oxford and Cambridge, both of which placed the classics above all else until the middle of the nineteenth century, carefully ignoring the message of Cicero and Quintillian. They could find no place for natural science, or even history, until the pressures of the times and the example of the bustling University of London forced them, late in the nineteenth century, to come of age.[13]

In this country Yale's *Report on the Courses of Instruction in Yale College* of 1828[14] firmly backed the ideal of liberal education. One of its authors, Jeremiah Day, was ". . . uneasy about the prospects of a nation at the mercy of superficially educated demagogues and uncouth millionaires. Day saw Yale and the rest of the (American) colleges as the "ramparts of a free people."[15] Another of its authors said that "the mere divine, the mere lawyer, or the mere physician has less chance of success than if his early education had been of a more liberal character."[16]

The Yale Report was a pace-setter for a time and was vastly influential through most of the nineteenth century. Rather surprisingly, few American colleges or universities were quite as firmly committed to the classics as were Oxford and Cambridge, although many of them found the ideal liberal arts curriculum difficult or impossible to achieve. But 117 years after the Yale Report was published, Harvard produced a powerful restatement of the same ideal. Harvard's Red Book of 1945 spoke glowingly of a common bond of general learning and defined general education in terms that would have been easily acceptable to Cicero and Quintillian.[17]

A lot happened on the scene of American higher education between the appearance of the Yale Report of 1828 and Harvard's Red Book in 1945 and much of what happened tended to impair the acceptability and respectability of the liberal arts concept. Still, over most of that time it remained a viable concept, and a Bachelor of Arts degree from an American college or university in itself was a commendable academic achievement; by definition it guaranteed some familiarity, at least, with a common body of learning that was not limited to classics or natural science. But by the fourth decade of the twentieth century, curriculum began to fall apart owing, according to Professor Rudolf, to "The rise of science, the death of Greek, the emergence of professions . . . (and) the resounding victory of intellect over piety . . . ."[18]

The Narrowing of Educational Goals

One may quarrel about the specific causes and other dates; but not with Rudolf's characterization of the status of the liberal arts concept since World War Two:

> Breadth, distribution, and general education were the hobby horses of new presidents, ambitious (but ignorant) deans, and well-meaning humanists of the sort who were elected to curriculum committees by colleagues as a gesture of token support for the idea of liberal learning. When the gesture collided with the interests of department and the major field, only occasionally did the general prevail over the special.[19]

One event, however, looms larger than most in helping to create the climate Rudolf describes: That was the pattern for premedical and preclinical education that was laid down in 1910 with the best of intent and the most pious of hopes by Abraham Flexner. The growth within the university structure in the power and size of the department, and the gradual degradation of supra-departmental mechanisms for control of curriculum, were well under way by Flexner's time; but they were factors and tendencies that Flexner, who had never been an active university faculty member, either failed to understand or in someway underestimated. But much more important, Flexner had a very low view of college education in his time. In his words:

A college education is not in these days a very severe or serious discipline. It is compounded in varying proportions of work and play; it scatters whatever effort it requires, so that at no point need the student stand the strain of prolonged intensive (intellectual) exertion.[20]

Then he goes on to say that medical science and practice rests solidly on natural science. In his words:

. . . physiology presupposes anatomy on lines involving antecedent training in biology; it leans just as hard on chemistry and physics. The functional activities of the body propound questions in applied chemistry and applied physics . . . The normal rhythm of physiological function must . . . remain a riddle to students who cannot think and speak in biological, chemical and physical language.[21]

Partly because of all this—the need for preparation in natural science, plus the inadequacy of college education in science—Flexner sought to create a medical school model that was, at least temporarily, scientifically self-sufficient.[22] To be sure, he prescribed the premedical requirements in science as we know them today, using the Hopkins practice as his model:

The John Hopkins requires for entrance (to medical school) a college degree which, whatever else it represents, must include the three fundamental sciences (biology-botany, chemistry, physics), French and German.[23]

But what existed at Hopkins was not the rule for all the nation's colleges and universities. There must be some sort of transitional phase. "The less (the student) brings to the (medical) school, the more the school must do for him."[24] He recognized that the practice in some medical schools of teaching natural science in the first year might be necessary; but ultimately, as other colleges and universities came abreast of Hopkins, he seems to have thought that a new plan for the teaching of science to future doctors would emerge. His ideal was the medical school that was fully integrated academically into the university, that shared the university's academic ideals, that vigorously encouraged intimate communication between its own departments and "the general science work of the institution."[25] And when we read the Flexner Report of 1910 carefully, we find these significant statements:

The college has already taken chemistry wholly out of the medical curriculum; it may be allowed to take biochemistry too . . . (but) the endeavor to improve medical education through iron-clad prescription of curriculum or hours, is a wholly mistaken effort.[26]

Looking back to Flexner's effort seventy years later it is easy to see that some of his premises were wrong. For example, there was no reason even in his own time to assume that to understand gross anatomy one had first to be methodically schooled in biology and botany, or that if one is to comprehend the mechanisms by which infectious agents invade the body one must first be familiar with those natural sciences that Flexner, in his day, considered fundamental. Medicine does indeed have its scientific underpinnings and it is grossly wrong to say, as many still do, that it is more art than science. But the actual scientific knowledge that underlies clinical medicine has never been precisely defined, and our present premedical and preclinical science offerings almost certainly represent a sort of academic overkill, courses being planned as if every student proposes to become chemist, biologist, microbiologist, or pharmacologist: but not a practicing physician. This is not to say that natural scientists should plan their elementary courses solely for students who propose to enter medical school. Far from it, but neither should these elementary courses be planned solely for those who propose to become natural scientists. In these several connections, the Harvard Red Book of 1945 said that elementary courses in the natural sciences (and it could as well have included the *preclinical* sciences) are ". . . professionalized introductory course(s) . . . (that) have not often overcome the narrowness which is an inevitable aspect of academic departmentalization," and it called for ". . . science courses at the introductory level which have general rather than specialistic education as their primary aim." Such courses should, the Report said, ". . . be taught so as to convey some integrative viewpoint, or the development of scientific concepts . . . they should convey some understanding of this . . . evolution of fundamental concepts . . ., the progression from description to analysis and synthesis, and from the qualitative to the quantitative."[27]

It was, in other words, the sequence, not the scientific content, that was wrong: The development of basic concepts, not specific method and quantification, should be the route by which the beginner is led into the vast kingdom of the natural sciences. Then, in later years—but only then—if the intent is to become biologist or chemist or microbiologist, specific method and legitimate considerations of the specialty can be taken up. May it not now be possible to design a conceptually-oriented exposure to the main features of natural science that would require little more than one academic year, that would be intellectually stimulating and challenging, that would be suitable for all students whatever their ultimate goals, that would postpone minute details of method, reduce quantitative aspects to a sensible minimum and ignore archaic definitions of boundaries between disciplines? Students preparing to enter medicine would then have abundant time at the college level to broaden their preprofessional educational experiences; and once in medical school, courses in the so-called basic medical sciences would require relatively little modification to compensate for the change in premedical science requirements. There are those who maintain that there is no such thing as the basic medical sciences, and I am inclined to agree, with only a few reservations. In any event most of them ought, as Flexner himself noted, to be university courses and departments instead of being tightly bottled up in medical schools.

What Flexner thought would be a dynamic process, which would progressively integrate the preclinical sciences into the life of the university, became arrested and remains so to this day. Although he didn't quite spell it out, he obviously thought that the natural scientists and the preclinical scientists, instead of remaining rigidly independent and, indeed, suspicious of each other, would at least integrate their offerings and eliminate overlap and redundancies. But it hasn't happened and Flexner himself was horrified, in later years, at the academic result his well-intentioned survey and report had produced.[28]

Many, and I believe the majority, of students opting for medicine today plod dispiritedly through both the premedical and preclinical sciences in which curriculums have grown, year by year, largely by a process of uncritical accretion.[29] Then finally, with a few exceptions, they enter on their clinical training with bitter sighs of relief and with minds set against bioscience. All that academic detail is behind; now to get on with the real business of medicine.

Back to Liberal Education

In all, we are producing an educational result at enormous prices, in terms of the use of academic resources, that is far from satisfactory: Medical graduates are ordinarily neither liberally educated nor are they expert bioscientists; and the academic structure which Flexner thought was in a state of dynamic evolution has either stalled or is moving at a glacial pace. I hasten to add that even if we could once and for all abolish the premedical science requirements as laid down by Flexner, the movement away from liberal or general education and toward tighter and tighter specialization would still not be checked. The responsibility for this phenomenon is not to be laid solely at the door of the medical school. It is a movement that insidiously influences course planners in many fields, including the natural sciences.

No one seems to be willing to say that the liberal education ideal no longer has validity and that all students seeking to go beyond the secondary educational level should plunge directly into specialty or professional training. Yet that may be what is happening despite the fact that Commissions and Committees all deplore the fact. The most recent is the

Report of Rockefeller Commission on the Humanities, which said, among other things, that

> Liberal education and the humanities, their fates still linked, were (in the 1970s) willed to the periphery of undergraduate learning.[30]

That is the accurate diagnosis; but what is the treatment, assuming that the patient has not already been tacitly written off?

To Conclude

I share the opinion that the patient's life must be saved, and for reasons that are not very far from those used by Jeremiah Day to justify Yale's adoption of a liberal education program in 1828. As for what Lewis Thomas called "the baleful and malign" influence of premedical science requirements on liberal education[31] there are hopeful developments, vis-a-vis the interface between premedical and preclinical education, in certain of our universities that almost certainly will proceed, however slowly, to useful conclusion.[32] And the time will come, I believe, when some, at least, of what are now called departments of basic medical science will become university departments and will, as Flexner hoped, relate meaningfully and effectively to appropriate departments of natural science. One of the results—but by no means the only result—may be that those choosing medicine and the biosciences as careers will finally acquire educations that are truly and generously liberal, plus scientific and professional expertise.

But the rescue of the liberal education ideal cannot be accomplished solely by revision of premedical and medical education. The problem is larger than they; and were I to attempt an attack on the larger problem, I would not turn to the crystal ball for the shape of the future; I would, by preference, turn to the record of past performance in this country. It seems to me that the liberal educational programs of some of our colleges and universities have in the past been remarkably effective, if not altogether ideal. Then, for reasons that are not always clear but that never seem altogether adequate, those programs have been abandoned or modified beyond recognition. Why did it happen this way? And may we not now select what was sound from past experience and, adapting it to present need as appropriate, and build a liberal or general educational program that approaches the ideal? One means to this end is, I believe, to design an elementary course that will confer what President Steven Muller at Hopkins calls bioscientific literacy on all students, including those opting for medicine, as part of a liberal or general education.

The broad charge to faculties and the reality of the dilemma have been eloquently laid out by Bronowski and Mazlish:

> Every thoughtful man who hopes for the creation of a contemporary culture knows that this hinges on one central problem: to find a

257

coherent relation between science and the humanities. In education in particular this problem faces us in two forms. We have to give the future scientist an abiding sense of the value of literature and the arts: and at the same time we have to give those whose preoccupation lies with the liberal arts a glimpse of the methods, the depth, and the inspiration of science. These are living problems . . . focused most sharply in the universities, where the traditional division between science and the humanities cannot be rooted out of the timetable in one generation.[33]

Perhaps not. But it is up to the ancient and honorable academic profession to get on with the job with all possible dispatch.

Notes

¹Mostly in Books II and III of *The Republic*. The aim of Plato's proposed system of education was, however, to produce the philosopher-ruler in a tribal, oligarchic state. The education of the citizen voter in a democratic political setting was not Plato's concern.

²Vitruvius, *De architectura*, Bk. 1, Ch. 1, 3-11. Loeb Classical Library, no. 251, pp. 9-17.

³Cicero, *De oratore*, I. v. 20. Loeb Classical Library, no. 348, p. 17.

⁴Ibid., III. xxxi. 124; III. xxxxii. 127. Hippias' definition required knowledge of mathematics, music, literature and poetry, and the doctrines of natural science, ethics, and political science. Loeb Classical Library, no. 349, pp. 99-101.

⁵Quintillianus, *Institutio oratoria*, Bk. I, 10-16. Loeb Classical Library, no. 124, pp. 11-13.

⁶Plutarch, *Moralia*, I (The Education of Children), 10. Loeb Classical Library, no. 197, pp. 33-37.

⁷For example, see R.R. Bolgar, *The Classical Heritage and its Beneficiaries* (Cambridge: Cambridge University Press, 1954), especially chapters 6, 7, and 9.

⁸Desiderius Erasmus, *De ratione studii* (On the Right Method of Instruction), in *Collected Works of Erasmus* (Toronto: University of Toronto Press, 1978), vol. 24, p. 667.

⁹Juan Luis Vives, *De tradendis disciplinis* (On Education). (Totowa, NJ: Roman and Littlefield, 1971), pp. cii-ccii.

¹⁰Ibid., pp. 8-9. See also Joan Simon, *Education and Society in Tudor England* (Cambridge: Cambridge University Press, 1979), p. 116.

¹¹Bolgar, p. 289.

¹²Kenneth D. Benne, "The Gentlemen: Locke" in *The Educated Man*, pp. 200-204. See also Thomas Elyot. *The boke named the governour* (1531), (London: J.M. Dent and Co., 1907).

¹³In the seventeenth century there was a brilliant cluster of scientists, including William Boyle, Christopher Wren, and John Wilkins, at Oxford; but not until 1850 could students read natural science. Charles E. Mallett, *A History of the University of Oxford* (New York: Barnes and Noble, 1958), vol. 2, pp. 399-402; vol. 3, p. 364.

¹⁴"Original Papers in Relation to a Course of Liberal Education," in *American Journal of Science and Arts*, 151: 297-358.

¹⁵Frederick Rudolph, *Curriculum: A History of the American Undergraduate Course of Study since 1636.* Carnegie Council on Policy Studies in Higher Education. (San Francisco: Jossey-Bass, 1977), p. 71.

¹⁶"Original Papers," p. 331.

¹⁷Harvard University, *General Education in a Free Society* (Cambridge:

Harvard University Press, 1945), p. 40. "General education," states the report, "is . . . that part of a student's whole education which looks first of all to his life as a responsible human being . . . ."

[18]Rudolph, p. 245.

[19]Ibid., p. 253.

[20]"Medical Education in the United States and Canada," in *Bulletin of the Carnegie Foundation* 4 (1910), p. 25.

[21]Ibid., p. 25.

[22]This important and neglected observation is included in *A Program in Medicine and Human Biology* (The Madansky Report), (Baltimore: John Hopkins University, 1971), pp. 37-38.

[23]*Bulletin of the Carnegie Foundation*, p. 28.

[24]Ibid., p. 46.

[25]Ibid., pp. 71-72.

[26]Ibid., pp. 74 and 76.

[27]*General Education in a Free Society*, p. 221.

[28]Abraham Flexner, *Medical Education, A Comparative Study* (New York: Macmillan, 1925), pp. 142-143 and 151. See also his article in *Atlantic Monthly* 112(1913), p. 654.

[29]Alfred North Whitehead calls this process 'educational inertia.' "Schools of learning," he wrote, ". . . (become) overladen with inert ideas. Education with inert ideas is not only useless; it is, above all things, harmful." *The Aims of Education* (New York: Macmillan, 1929), pp. 1-2.

[30]*The Humanities in American Life*. Report of the Commission on the Humanities. (Berkeley: University of California Press, 1980), p. 66.

[31]Lewis Thomas, in the *New England Journal of Medicine*, 298 (1978), p. 1180.

[32]Alfred Gellhorn, *An Outsider's Evaluation of the Interface Program*. Annual Report of the Commonwealth Fund, 1979-1980, pp. 13-20; see also pp. 23-40.

[33]J. Bronowski and Bruce Mazlish, *The Western Intellectual Tradition from Leonardo to Hegel* (New York: Harper and Row, 1975), p. vii.

Appendix III

QUILL II: Liberal Learning for Leadership

Summaries of the first group of awards made in the winter of 1981 under a modified form of the Quality in Liberal Learning Program. Additional competitions will be sponsored as funds become available.

Furman University

Careers and Values: An Interdisciplinary
   Seminar/Forum Program for Future
   Professionals

Development of a pilot program combining a small career honors seminar with a complementary open evening forum program to demonstrate the University's continuing commitment to the humanities and liberal learning in conjunction with the career goals of its students. A sophomore-level honors course, designed by faculty members from economics/business, English and philosophy and representatives from the local business community, will be aimed at those students planning to enter business or industry upon graduation. A complementary series of extra-curricular forums for the college and local community will deal realistically with the practical concerns of a career in the corporate sector.

	Contact:	Judith Gatlin
		Director of Career
		Programs
		Furman University
		Greenville, SC 29613

Linfield College

Economics, Ethics, and the Environment

Development of a team-taught honors seminar by faculty members from the biology, economics, and religious studies departments to deal extensively with the relationships between environment and economics and with the ethical questions inherent therein. In support of the college's dedication to the study of environmental problems, this course will utilize a problem-solving approach to arrive at an integrated model for rational decision-making, with the energy future of the United States as a focal point.

Contact: John Hare
            Assistant Professor of
               Biology
            Linfield College
            McMinnville, OR 97128

Metropolitan State University

Liberal Learning for Working Adults:
   Perspectives from Business and Corporate
   Leadership

Support for a working conference of approximately 30 business leaders, corporate executives, liberal arts faculty, business administration faculty, and adult students to produce written materials that would bring their perspectives on the value of liberal learning into a planning course required of all entering students. Insights of business and corporate leaders will address questions and issues raised by adult students about liberal learning and business careers, uncertainty about the connection between liberal learning and successful employment, as well as skepticism about the practical value of liberal learning for professional roles.

Contact: Thomas B. Jones
            Coordinator of Degree
               Planning
            Metropolitan State
               University
            St. Paul, MN 55101

Oakland University

Development of a Course at Oakland
   University Identifying Skills Acquired in
   Studying Humanities which will be
   Valuable for Future Professionals

Development of a sophomore-level course to identify, examine, and
enhance those skills a student acquires in being educated in the
methodologies of the humanities. As an integral part of the university's
new cooperative education program, this course will assist (1) students
with a particular career in view (especially in the professional schools) to
decide which of the humanities might prove most useful to study, and (2)
students concentrating in the humanities to understand how their education prepares them as future professionals.

> **Contact:**   J. Clark Heston
> Coordinator, Center for
>   Community and Human
>   Development
> Rochester, MI 48063

Suffolk University

Sociology and Urban Problems: Learning
   About and Working in the Urban
   Environment

Modification of sociology curricular offerings through the creation of an
integrating core course required of all career-oriented majors to combine
the focus of "academic" and "applied" preparations in developing informed portraits of the city, its problems and the social organization of
their solution. This core course will provide unprecedented focus, coordination and grounding to the educational experience of career-oriented
students by helping them identify and penetrate the particular problems
and processes with which they will be intimately involved.

> **Contact:**   Steven Spitzer,
>   Associate Professor
> Department of Sociology
> Suffolk University
> Boston, MA 02114

University of Tennessee at Chattanooga and Knoxville

Seminar on the Working Experience

Introduction of a liberal arts dimension to established CETA programs at Knoxville and Chattanooga via a seminar on the working experience. The seminar, which will provide a traditional faculty with knowledge of and experience with the needs of nontraditional students, will draw upon the services of an oral historian, cultural anthopologist, sociologist, philosopher, and improvisational drama company to work with the CETA trainees to examine their backgrounds and prepare them for unsubsidized employment. This project also proposes widespread dissemination of non-traditional liberal education to orient a traditional liberal arts faculty.

Contact: Kitty C. Kirby, Director   Ferdinand Alexi Hilenski
            Adult Educational Services   Assistant to the Dean
            University of Tennessee   College of Liberal Arts
                at Chattanooga   University of Tennessee
            Chattanooga, TN 37402   at Knoxville
                                              Knoxville, TN 37916

Villanova University

Development of a Liberal Arts Core Course
    for Engineering Students

Development of a team-taught multidisciplinary core course for all engineering students, focusing upon technologically sophisticated objects (i.e., an atomic power plan or the Brooklyn Bridge) and the questions and issues in the liberal arts that they generate. This course will serve as the foundation for a revised engineering curriculum designed to present the questions, methods, values, and concerns of the liberal arts as part of the humanistic dimension of engineering, stressing the natural connections between the role of the engineer and issues in the liberal arts that that role generates.

                          Contact: John H. Fielder
                                      Associate Professor
                                      Department of Philosophy
                                      Villanova University
                                      Villanova, PA 19085

William Paterson College

Representations of Humanity in the World
of Work Today: An Honors Course for
Adults with Off-Campus Public Forums

Combination of off-campus public forums with a related course in the evening honors curriculum which will furnish humanistic perspectives on the current character of work in management, health sciences, applied science, and criminal justice. The forums will feature locally prominent speakers and college humanities faculty discussing contemporary concerns, while the course will proceed retrospectively from the current world to historical and philosophical comparisons which illuminate the present. This dual effort is intended to confront pragmatically-oriented adult students with the applicability of the humanities, supplying a basis for integrating subsequent thematic and chronological treatments of Western culture.

Contact: Angelo Juffras
            Professor
            Department of Philosophy
            William Paterson College
            Wayne, NJ 07470

Appendix IV

PHOENIX

Dawn breaks upon Phoenix
Revealing proud concrete forms
Challenging the sky
With peaks and valleys
Reflecting in steeper slopes
Brown jagged mountains
Cloaked in morning mist
Standing stolid witness
On surrounding level earth

Uneven mountains rise
As incongruously
As towers of glass and concrete
Constructed from earth and water
Dwarfing the endless spread
Of tree high buildings
Their roofs forming
A plain upon the plain

Metal birds descend
From purple gray clouds
Like giant eagles
Screeching shrill whistles
Fiercely swooping upon
Unsuspecting prey
One upon another
They come down
To gorge their bellies
With carrion of oil and flesh

Enclosed in a cliff cave
Twenty floors above cement ribbons
Forming patterned rectangles
Reminding me of the impression

Made by a window screen
Pressed against soft earth
I look down
Through space and time

Feeling the presence
Of another soul
Who centuries ago
Looked upon the sunrise
From his mountain perch
I wonder if the sun he saw
Was mine
He lived at a time
When jagged line held forth
As nature's favored form
A delineation replaced by
Perpendicular lines
Prescribing sharp edged cubes

His eagle no longer soars
Nor swoops to catch a rabbit
In its sharp talons
His mountains no longer stand
As unrivaled lords
Shedding their refuge
Through serpentine gorges
Winding endlessly
Seeking level ground

Morning light reveals
Two worlds of equal order
Both governed by their cycles
The rain that bathed Phoenix
Three days running
Washed the settled dust
From those brown slopes
As day and night flush occupants
From these buildings
Into the streets
Connecting concrete ribbons
Running coast to coast

A generous host is nature
For she allows all creatures

The illusion of dominion
Over their individual realms
Blinded by the fire
Of their consuming ambition
Each fails to see
New order taking wing

Composed by QUILL project director Landon Kirchner of Johnson
County Community College during the 1980 Annual Meeting of the
Association of American Colleges.

INDEX

INSTITUTIONS RECEIVING QUILL GRANTS

PROJECT DIRECTORS AND CONTRIBUTORS